MARKAN PUBLIC DEBATE

SOCIETY
OF BIBLICAL
LITERATURE

DISSERTATION SERIES

edited by
Howard C. Kee

Number 48
MARKAN PUBLIC DEBATE
LITERARY TECHNIQUE, CONCENTRIC STRUCTURE,
AND THEOLOGY IN MARK 2:1–3:6
by
Joanna Dewey

Joanna Dewey

MARKAN PUBLIC DEBATE
LITERARY TECHNIQUE, CONCENTRIC STRUCTURE, AND THEOLOGY IN MARK 2:1-3:6

Scholars Press

Distributed by
Scholars Press
101 Salem Street
Chico, California 95926

MARKAN PUBLIC DEBATE
LITERARY TECHNIQUE, CONCENTRIC STRUCTURE, AND THEOLOGY IN MARK 2:1–3:6

Joanna Dewey

Ph.D., 1977
Graduate Theological Union

Advisers:
John L. Boyle
Anitra Bingham Kolenkow
Ernest R. Martinez

Library of Congress Cataloging in Publication Data

Dewey, Joanna, 1936–
  Markan public debate.

  (Dissertation series—Society of Biblical Literature ;
no. 48 ISSN 0145-2770)
  Originally presented as the author's thesis, Graduate
Theological Union, 1977.
  Bibliography: p.
  1. Bible. N.T. Mark II–III, 6—Criticism,
interpretation, etc. 2. Bible. N.T. Mark XI–XII—
Criticism, interpretation, etc. I. Title. II. Series: Society
of Biblical Literature. Dissertation series ; no. 48.
BS2585.2.D43 1979   226'.3'06   79-17443
ISBN 0-89130-337-5
ISBN 0-89130-338-3 pbk.

Printed in the United States of America
1 2 3 4 5
Edwards Brothers, Inc.
Ann Arbor, Michigan 48106

TABLE OF CONTENTS

ABBREVIATIONS AND NOTE ON TRANSLATION

Abbreviations follow those used in the *Journal of
Biblical Literature* (as specified in vol. 95
[June, 1976] pp. 339-346).

Most of the biblical translations are my own.
Quotations from the RSV are so indicated in the
text.

ACKNOWLEDGMENTS

I would like to thank my teachers, my fellow graduate students, and my friends among biblical scholars for the encouragement and assistance they have given me throughout my graduate studies and particularly in the writing of my dissertation.

First of all, I wish to acknowledge my indebtedness to Edward C. Hobbs of the Church Divinity School of the Pacific and the Graduate Theological Union who, in introducing me to New Testament scholarship, communicated to me his fascination with the gospel of Mark, and his conviction that a literary approach to the gospel would elucidate our understanding of it.

Second, I wish to thank my teachers and fellow graduate students at the Graduate Theological Union who introduced me to the approaches of the analysis of literary structure and rhetorical criticism. I am indebted above all to John L. Boyle, S.J. He first introduced me to the work of Catholic scholars on literary structure--including concentric structure in Mark. Further he has been the coordinator of my dissertation project. He has been consistently helpful and supportive in that not-always-to-be-envied role. I should also like to express my appreciation of James Muilenburg and his graduate student, Don Christianson, for the introduction they gave me to the methods and excitement of rhetorical criticism.

For the dissertation itself, I wish to acknowledge my debt to my committee for their helpfulness in providing constructive advice and much needed support. My thanks go to Frederick H. Borsch and Victor R. Gold for their help in the preliminary stages of my writing. My thanks go especially to the final readers of my dissertation, to Ernest R. Martinez, S.J., Anitra Bingham Kolenkow, who was ever available and willing to evaluate sections of the manuscript, and, of course, to John Boyle.

Finally, I wish to thank John E. Huesman, S.J., for his administrative support, John H. Elliott of the University of San Francisco and Norman Perrin of Chicago for their scholarly support and advice, and Albert Henrichs, now at Harvard

University, and Neal Flannagan for their helpful and detailed critiques of my initial presentation of the structure of Mark 2:1-3:6, published in *JBL* 92 (1973).

INTRODUCTION

Rhetorical criticism, so named by James Muilenburg, is a
methodological approach which is increasingly being applied to
biblical writings. It is the study of the literary techniques
and rhetorical structure of a text to see what light such analysis sheds on the interrelationships of the parts of the text
and the meaning of the text as a whole. The rhetorical approach
employs as its material the final text without consideration for
historical questions of what is redaction and what is tradition.
It involves the careful and detailed rhetorical analysis of the
content, form, small structures, and use of word repetition in
a text in order to determine the larger structure and rhetorical
emphases of that text. Through the study of the literary means
of a text, rhetorical analysis seeks a fuller understanding and
appreciation of the text.

Rhetorical criticism, like form and redaction criticism,
can only examine small portions of a narrative at a time. The
following study is a contribution towards the rhetorical analysis
of the gospel of Mark by its rhetorical analysis of the Galilean
controversy section of Mark 2:1-3:6, and its survey of extended
concentric structure or symmetrical rhythm in the gospel of
Mark.

The focus of the study is two-fold: first, the actual
practice and results of rhetorical criticism; and second, a
consideration of the methodology appropriate for the rhetorical
analysis of Mark. The rhetorical analysis consists of a detailed investigation of Mark 2:1-3:6[1] and a much briefer consideration of the rhetorical structure of Mark 1:1-8; 4:1-34,
and 11-12, the Jerusalem ministry with its several public debates. The methodological portion of the study focuses primarily
on the issues of concentric structure, first, the question of
adequate criteria for identifying concentric literary patterns,

---

[1]I first presented my analysis of the overall structure of
Mk 2:1-3:6 in "The Literary Structure of the Controversy Stories
in Mark 2:1-3:6," *JBL* 92 (1973) 394-401.

and second, the question of how recognition of a symmetrical
pattern helps the reader to interpret the text.

Rhetorical analysis, as it is practiced in this study, is
not a branch of redaction criticism, but an independent approach.
However, as contributions to the knowledge of markan redaction,
(1) Mark 2:1-3:6 and 11-12 are investigated to see if the overall literary structure of the public debate sections is markan
or premarkan, and (2) the gospel of Mark is surveyed to see if
the concentric organization of material may be considered a
markan literary technique.

The first two chapters of the study concern preliminary
matters. Chapter One is an introduction to the methodology of
rhetorical criticism, its relationship to other methodological
approaches, and its debt to and dependence upon previous research on the gospel of Mark. Chapter Two is an introduction
to the issues involved in studying Mark 2:1-3:6 and 11-12,
primarily by means of an evaluation of hypotheses for premarkan
controversy collections. It is concluded that a premarkan collection for 2:1-28 is a possibility but not a certainty, and
that no premarkan controversy collection lies behind Mark 11-12.

Chapters Three and Four present the detailed rhetorical
analysis of 2:1-3:6. Chapter Three contains a description of
the literary techniques and rhetorical structure of the five
individual pericopes that make up the Galilean controversy
section. It contains a limited discussion of the implications
of the results of the rhetorical study for the exegesis and
determination of the redaction of the pericopes. Chapter Four
first describes the overall concentric rhetorical pattern of
2:1-3:6, and then explores the significance of both the linear
development and the concentric structure for understanding the
content and meaning of 2:1-3:6.

Chapters Five and Six deal with issues raised by the
rhetorical analysis. Chapter Five focuses on concentric structure in the gospel of Mark: criteria for identifying such
literary patterns, the question of audience recognition of
rhetorical symmetry, and the existence of concentric patterns
elsewhere in the gospel of Mark. On the basis of a brief
rhetorical analysis of the structure of Mark 1:1-8, 4:1-34, and
12:1-40, it is concluded that concentric structure is one of

Mark's literary devices for organizing and structuring his
material. In Chapter Six, it is argued that the rhetorical
structure of 2:1-3:6 is due to Mark's redaction of tradition,
not to his interpolation of a source. Finally, the role of
2:1-3:6 in the narrative and theology of Mark is summarized.
Thus, the study contributes to the development of the
methodology of rhetorical criticism. It also contributes to
markan studies (1) through the identification of extended symmetrical structure as one of Mark's literary devices, (2) through
the determination that Mark 2:1-3:6 is a markan compilation and
not a premarkan source, and (3) through an increased understanding of the theology of 2:1-3:6. Further, it indicates how the
rhetorical approach can assist other methodological approaches
in their respective tasks.

The rhetorical analysis will show that the author of the
gospel of Mark is a writer of considerable narrative skill,
adept at interweaving the elements of his story. It is hoped
that this study will lead the reader to a better literary
appreciation of the gospel of Mark, for the literary or rhetorical critic is engaged in the enterprise of educating or sensi-
tizing the reader to the gospel as a reading experience.

CHAPTER I

RHETORICAL CRITICISM:

ANTECEDENTS AND METHODOLOGY

The term, "literary technique," in the broadest sense may cover everything from minor style characteristics such as an author's fondness for the historic present, through use of rhetorical devices, techniques of anticipation and contrast, to the means of structuring an entire work. Basically, literary techniques are the tools available to any author or story teller to convey what he or she wishes to say. An author may use simple or complex techniques, he may use techniques which are familiar to his audience or ones strange to them, he may use techniques skillfully or awkwardly, intentionally or unconsciously. But he must use techniques--that is, he must relate his content in words, and structure the words in some way--if he is to get his content or message across to his audience at all.

From the point of view of the literary critic or researcher, a study of literary techniques employed in a text is one way of studying a text. It is the study of *how* a narrative is written (or told) or a poem constructed. Such a study may be done for its own sake, the study of style. It may be done for historical or comparative reasons, to trace the development of a literary tradition, to contrast techniques of oral and written composition, or to compare one author with another. Or such a study may be undertaken, as in this dissertation, in order to achieve a better understanding of a text. Literary techniques are isolated and analyzed in order for us to become conscious of their occurrence in a text and to see what and how they contribute to the meaning and/or effectiveness of a text. A study of techniques, then, is one way toward a fuller understanding of a text, and how its creator intended it to be read.

The presupposition of such a study is that the text, in this case the gospel of Mark, may be treated as a legitimate literary entity, even if it does contain layers of tradition and redaction. The final text is considered to have a validity of its own, independent of its prehistory. The text may be

studied in itself. The same presupposition of literary validity
underlies a structuralist approach to a text. Structuralism,
however, attempts to identify the deep structures underlying
the text and its parts, while the focus of this study is on the
surface structure or patterns in all their particularity and
concreteness.

The first step of the study is to describe the occurrence
of literary devices in the text. A review of the literature on
the gospel of Mark suggests that repetition of words and motifs,
and symmetrical techniques, from insertion through intercalation
to extended concentric structures, are devices employed with
great frequency in Mark.[1] This stage of the analysis is basically
descriptive and relatively objective. On the whole, scholars
should be able to agree on whether or not a literary device is
found in a text.

The second step, and where the study goes beyond a description of style, is to interpret how each occurrence of a device
functions in the literary expression of the text. Generally
speaking, a technique may function as an indicator of structure
or as an indicator of rhetorical purpose--emphasis, climax,
contrast, etc.--without indicating structure.[2] Some devices
may always serve a particular function, while others may act in
a variety of ways. A device may serve more than one function.
Structure, as determined by literary devices, functions to
interrelate the parts of the structure to each other. Such an
analysis of narrative function is both art and science. Its
value depends on the sensitivity and acumen of the critic as
well as on the data provided by the text.

The third step is to see what light the literary-rhetorical
understanding of the text may shed on our understanding of the
text's meaning or theology. An awareness of structure, the
interrelationship of parts into a larger whole, and an awareness
of rhetorical stress should lead to a better understanding of
the theological intentions and emphases of a narrative. Further,
rhetorical analysis should serve as a control on exegesis, limiting the possibilities of understanding, excluding some interpretations on the grounds that they conflict with the rhetorical
features of a passage.

The aim or purpose of the study, then, is twofold. On the
literary level, the rhetorical critic strives to educate or
sensitize the reader to the gospel of Mark as a reading (or
aural) experience. On the theological level, the rhetorical
critic seeks to clarify our understanding of a text as a whole
through study of "the indications of how the author wanted us
to read and understand the story,"[3] and, using the approach as
a control on other methodologies, to resolve *some* exegetical
difficulties and theological ambiguities. The rhetorical method,
then, is a valuable *additional* methodology, largely untapped,
for understanding the biblical material.

Relation of the Rhetorical Method
to Redaction Criticism

Today, the dominant methodology for studying the gospel of
Mark is redaction criticism. But the model for this dissertation
is not to be found in such studies on Mark, even as they have
come to employ more of the methodology of general literary
criticism. The aims are different: redaction criticism attempts to understand Mark's theological intentions and the *Sitz
im Leben* of his gospel; it attempts to answer historical questions
raised by the text and by our interest in early Christianity.
Rhetorical or literary criticism does not concern itself directly with historical questions about Mark, his community, or the
traditions he used, but rather views the text as a given and
attempts to illumine its meaning through study of its means of
expression.

The difference in the two methods can be seen clearly in
the way they employ literary techniques. Redaction criticism
has used literary techniques (in particular intercalation and
insertion) as a means of separating markan redaction from tradition,[4] or as a direct index to Mark's theology, a superstructure
deduced from the text.[5] The rhetorical approach to literary
techniques uses them as a tool for achieving a literary understanding of the text. They serve as a guide to determine the
literary structure of a text, and as a means for grasping in
what light a passage is meant to be read.[6]

Thus, no systematic attention is given in this study to
whether or not each particular occurrence of a device is Mark's

original composition, redaction, or reporting of tradition. Nor
is any attempt made to establish literary devices as definitive
criteria for distinguishing redaction from tradition. It is
doubtful that any such exact criteria can be established whereby
literary techniques in isolation from other factors could discriminate between Mark and tradition. Mark unquestionably has
a fondness for certain literary devices. Nonetheless such
devices belong to a pool of techniques generally available to
all narrators--whether of oral or written material. And it can
be as problematic to determine the origin of any specific
instance of a literary device as it is to determine if any given
saying in the gospels contains the *ipsissima verba* of Jesus.
The same problems exist that exist in the use of style as an
indicator of Mark's active redaction of a text: the use of the
historic present and *καί* parataxis are unquestionably markan
stylistic characteristics, yet both are also characteristics
of oral literature. Any individual instance of an historic
present verb, for example, does not provide enough information
to tell us whether the occurrence is due to Mark or his use of
tradition. We can only draw inferences on the basis of
"sufficient" markan stylistic characteristics in a given length
of text[7] *and* of additional information such as vocabulary,
usage, content, place within or connecting pericopes, and
congruence with Mark's thought.

The present work, however, will contain a systematic testing
of the larger concentric structure I shall identify in Mark
2:1-3:6 to see if the structure is to be attributed to Mark or
to his incorporation of a prior collection or source. Such a
test is possible because the section is sufficiently extensive
to provide enough data, both linguistic and theological.[8] It
is necessary because the section of the gospel chosen for detailed study is one in which many scholars hold that Mark has
incorporated a premarkan collection. If the literary pattern
I identify is actually the structure of an earlier collection
which Mark has used unmodified, then no generalizations can be
made from that structure to the composition techniques of the
gospel, or to the theology of Mark. The redactional aspect of
this study, which will show the final structure to be markan,
is a useful contribution to our knowledge of markan compositional

techniques and redaction. It is also a confirmation of the
presupposition of the study--that the text may be treated as
a literary whole.

Also, as a beneficial side effect, the rhetorical analysis
does sometimes shed light on questions of tradition and redaction.
Awareness of how the individual parts fit together into a larger
structure and of the placing of rhetorical emphasis can aid the
reader in determining how things which seem strange in the
gospel of Mark--e.g., the two uses of Son of Man in 2:10,28 or
the acclamation "the coming kingdom of our father David" in
11:10--are to be interpreted. If they are not stressed rhetorically in the narrative, and if they do not bear on themes being
emphasized by the structure, then they probably represent traditions which Mark could assimilate but which were not important
to his own theology or polemic. If, on the other hand, the
strange material is highlighted by the structure or by literary
devices that focus attention on it, then probably the material
may be considered a markan emphasis.[9]

The study of literary structure and rhetorical emphasis
can upon occasion help confirm conclusions reached by form and
redaction criticism: when, for instance, a form-critical study
of an individual pericope, of a premarkan collection, and a
literary study of the structure of a final text reach the same
conclusion about the tradition history of the text, then perhaps
scholars can agree that it is fact (the criterion of multiple
methodologies). Also, occasionally, the approach via literary
techniques and structure which provides a different perspective
upon tradition history questions, will thereby suggest solutions
to some questions that other methodologies have been unable to
answer. So while the present study is not an exercise in
redaction criticism and no attempt is made to address many of
the questions a redaction critic would ask concerning the same
material, this study does make a contribution to markan redaction
criticism.

For the two approaches, rhetorical-literary and redactional-
critical, are complementary. Both seek to understand the meaning
of the gospel, and they can aid each other in the task. The
literary approach builds on source, form and redaction criticism,
that is, on that which is already known. In particular,

rhetorical analysis which ignores the forms of early Christian discourse is liable to produce some rather grotesque results.

Likewise, form or redaction criticism that ignores the rhetorical function of something in Mark's text is building on an unsound base. For example, the reappearance of the Pharisees and Herodians in Mark 12:13 functions as a rhetorical cue to the hearer to recall the controversies of Mark 2:1-3:6 and the Pharisees' and Herodians' decision to plot against Jesus. Therefore, it is exceedingly questionable that the mention of the Herodians in 12:13 is reliable evidence to help answer the historical questions of the extent of a premarkan controversy collection or of Jesus' actual opponents.[10]

Further, the understanding of literary structure is fundamental to good exegesis, for it is the pattern that indicates the relationship of the individual part to the larger units or to the whole. Thus, a literary approach can assist redaction criticism (and control some flights of fancy) by its insistent reminder that the text must be understood first of all on its own terms, as a narrative, and not just as a key to history or theology.

Relation of the Rhetorical Method
to Literary Criticism

If the model for this dissertation is not a redaction-critical study, neither is the model a comprehensive literary analysis. This study focuses on one aspect of literary criticism, that of literary techniques and structures, and studies what it can tell us about other literary aspects such as plot, character and point of view; and then from the literary understanding moves to questions of meaning or theology. The procedure is in a sense arbitrary: one can enter the circle of literary criticism at any point. The means of literary expression are used in order to convey the content and meaning of the text; the content and meaning are expressed through techniques and structures.

The model for this study, then, is one particular branch of literary criticism: the study of literary techniques and structure. In biblical research, the model has been used to advantage especially in the work of two groups of scholars:

in the Old Testament field, the "rhetorical criticism" advocated
and practiced by James Muilenburg and his students,[11] and second,
the unlabeled literary approach practiced in particular by such
Catholic scholars as I. de La Potterie, Albert Vanhoye, J.
Lambrecht, and N. Lohfink, who have been associated with the
Pontifical Biblical Institute in Rome.[12]

James Muilenburg set forth his program in his presidential
address to the Society of Biblical Literature in 1968, "Form
Criticism and Beyond."[13]   He describes the method as follows:

> What I am interested in, above all, is in under-
> standing the nature of Hebrew literary composition,
> in exhibiting the structural patterns that are
> employed for the fashioning of a literary unit,
> whether in poetry or prose, and in discerning the
> many and various devices by which the predications
> are formulated and ordered into a unified whole.
> Such an enterprise I should describe as rhetoric
> and the methodology as rhetorical criticism.[14]

The first aim of his method is to define the limits or scope of
the literary unit.[15]   The second concern is

> ...to recognize the structure of a composition and
> to discern the configuration of its component parts,
> to delineate the warp and woof out of which the
> literary fabric is woven, and to note the various
> rhetorical devices that are employed for marking,
> on the one hand, the sequence and movement of the
> pericope, and on the other, the shifts or breaks
> in the development of the writer's thought.[16]

Muilenburg states the aim of the enterprise as follows:

> And this leads me to formulate a canon which should
> be obvious to us all: a responsible and proper
> articulation of the words in their linguistic pat-
> terns and in their precise formulations will reveal
> to us the texture and fabric of the writer's thought,
> not only what it is that he thinks, but as he thinks
> it.[17]

Muilenburg's call to build upon the generalizations and
classifications of form criticism and go beyond to "the actuality
of the particular text"[18] can apply as well to the New Testament
as to the Old. And in markan studies, as in the Old Testament,
the rhetorical approach to the final text must build upon the
general understanding of forms gained in form-critical research.

The work of Albert Vanhoye on the Epistle to the Hebrews[19]
serves as a good example of the method, purpose and results

typical of the Catholic literary scholarship and as a partial
model for this study.   Vanhoye first identifies the structure
of the letter and its subdivisions through its employment of
literary devices such as inclusios, hook words, key words,
alternation of genre and extensive symmetrical arrangements.[20]
The analysis of the structure of the individual parts of the
letter constitutes the major portion of the work.   The book
concludes with a discussion of the interrelationship of the
major sections, and of the literary structure of the epistle
as the framework or backbone of the thought of the epistle.   The
method, Vanhoye concludes, is justified by its results:

> L'étude de la structure s'est avérée très utile
> pour l'exégèse de l'Épître.   Elle a permis d'en
> saisir le mouvement d'ensemble et de discerner
> l'importance relative des divers développements.
> Elle doit normalement contribuer à la solution
> de bien des difficultés et plus encore à la mise
> en valuer des richesses contenues dans le texte.
>   Elle ne peut, assurément, se substituer aux
> autres recherches, philologiques, historiques,
> théologiques.   Son rôle est seulement de leur
> assurer des bases plus solides.[21]

The aim of this study of the literary techniques and
structure of portions of the gospel of Mark could be stated in
very similar terms: it is useful for exegesis, for understanding the interrelationships of material, for solving some difficulties and exhibiting some of the richness of the text.   The
literary study does not seek to replace either historical or
theological studies of the gospel of Mark; it hopes rather to
provide them with a solid base.

Research on Mark from a literary-rhetorical perspective.
Edward C. Hobbs suggested as early as 1956 that the model for
a commentary explicating the meaning of an evangelist might
well be found "among the interpretations of great literary works
such as Shakespeare's plays, or Sophocles' *Oedipus*, or even the
work of James Joyce."[22]   In 1966, Leander Keck wrote, "it is
clear that much more attention must be paid to the relation
between the structure of Mark's thought and the structure of
his text."[23]   Norman Perrin suggested in 1971 an approach via
the insights of general literary criticism, albeit somewhat
apologetically:

> The Gospel of Mark is after all a literary text,
> and it should therefore be interpreted according
> to the canons of literary criticism.... The
> evangelist Mark may not be an author in the
> conscious and sophisticated sense of a William
> Shakespeare, Henry Fielding, or James Joyce, but
> he is an author, he has written a literary work....24

In 1976, Perrin called unequivocally for a literary-critical approach to Mark.[25]

As yet, however, work on Mark from a literary-rhetorical perspective has been limited. There has always been the occasional scholar who has used a literary approach. James Hardy Ropes' little work on the synoptic gospels first published in 1934 is still well worth reading.[26] Austin Farrer's work certainly should be mentioned.[27] In his study of Mark, he posits elaborate recurring patterns, many of which are symbolic. While his method is too subjective and uncontrolled for his results to be convincing, many of his individual insights are brilliant.

The most work has been done in the attempt to determine the overall structure of the gospel. Notable recent attempts have been made by R. Pesch,[28] N. Perrin,[29] I. de La Potterie,[30] E. Schweizer,[31] and E. Trocmé.[32] There is considerable but by no means absolute agreement among them as to the major divisions of Mark. There is sometimes less agreement on the method of determining major breaks in Mark, which vary from stichometric counting (Pesch), through observations of literary devices, to strict theological schemes and combinations of the above. Since the overall structure of Mark's gospel is outside the scope of this study, the details of the debate need not be considered.

Two points, however, are worth noting. The fact that critics have used both literary and theological criteria reflects the close relationship between literary means and content; they cannot exist without each other. Second, the difficulty of scholars in reaching agreement about certain major breaks may not be the result of different methods or different levels of skill among the scholars. It may instead be due to our attempt to superimpose upon the gospel of Mark a single more rigid structure than the gospel possesses. Patterns and structures may overlap; sections may be transitional; major sections may not all be of about the same length; there may be no major structural break in Mark 6.

Productive research has also begun to be carried out on the rhetorical structure of individual sections of the gospel. Such work has centered on the middle portion of the gospel, with its threefold repetition of the pattern of passion prediction, misunderstanding of the disciples, teaching on discipleship,[33] and on sections of the gospel over which interpretation is most divided--for example, Mark 13.[34] Occasional articles have appeared on other sections of the gospel. Many sections of the gospel, however, have yet to be studied in detail from the point of view of structure or rhetoric.

Practically no work has been done in the area of Mark's literary expression as an indication of how Mark intended the gospel to be read. An exception is Vanhoye's excellent short pamphlet, *Structure and Theology of the Accounts of the Passion in the Synoptic Gospels*.[35] He states his intention as follows:

> We propose to examine the literary composition of
> the accounts of the three Synoptics in order to
> discern the principal orientation of each of them.
> A study of this type offers to be of obvious doc-
> trinal and pastoral interest, for it ought to help
> us place ourselves more faithfully in the perspec-
> tives of the inspired authors.[36]

This is a statement very close in meaning if not style to Muilenburg's statement of purpose.[37]

Vanhoye briefly surveys the narrative progression of the passion accounts. He does not try to unravel the many narrative difficulties of the text. Rather he sees lack of explanation as characteristic of Mark's style, and what information is given is often "less to explain the facts than to underline the paradoxical and shocking features of the scene."[38] For example, the fact that according to Mark the false witnesses do not agree, does not raise for Vanhoye the logical problem of how could prearranged testimony fail to agree. Rather, the point of the designation of the witnesses as "false" heightens the contrast and paradox. *Even* employing false witnesses, no "legitimate" grounds can be found against Jesus.[39]

Selection of Material for Analysis

Ideally a literary-rhetorical analysis of the gospel of Mark would cover the entire gospel. For only when we have detailed analyses of the literary techniques and structures of all

the individual parts of the gospel will we truly be in a position
to grasp Mark's overall structure. Only then will we be able to
see the varieties of literary techniques that are employed and
the different ways they function.

Such an undertaking, with all its detailed analysis of the
text, is obviously beyond the scope of one dissertation. Detailed study of literary techniques and structure must be limited
to selected portions of the gospel so that the investigation is
reduced to manageable proportions. The rhetorical method with
its focus on literary structure indicates that a block of contiguous material should be selected, rather than a series of
isolated texts chosen on the basis of form or content. Since
this study attempts to test the usefulness of a method which
moves from literary techniques to structure, and only then from
the literary understanding to theology, it seems preferable to
select a section which is not a center of controversy for determining Mark's theology. The method may well prove most valuable
as an aid in interpreting controversial sections such as Mark 13.
However, the rhetorical approach should first be tested on
material whose meaning appears fairly self-evident.

The public debate material in Mark appears suitable for
study. The term "public debate," as used in this study, is a
description of content, open public debate between Jesus and
those who are not disciples, usually opponents. The designation
of the material as Galilean or Jerusalem refers only to its
location in Mark's geographical outline, and does not imply anything about the provenance of the material.

The Galilean public debate section, Mark 2:1-3:6, is an
appropriate text for detailed analysis. It consists of five
pericopes, the healing of the paralytic, the eating with tax
collectors and sinners, the question about fasting, the plucking
of grain on the sabbath, and the healing of the withered hand
on the sabbath. The text is of suitable length and it is not
a major focus of debate in markan scholarship.

Further, while 2:1-3:6 consists primarily of public controversy material--what Martin Albertz calls *Streitgespräche*, or
Bultmann, in his larger system of classification, controversy
apophthegms--it also includes materials which are not, form-
critically speaking, controversy apophthegms. Mark 2:1-12, the

healing of the paralytic, has generally been considered a mixed
form containing a miracle story and a controversy apophthegm.
Mark 2:13 is one of the ten passages identified by K.L. Schmidt
as markan *Sammelberichte*.[40] Mark 2:14, the call of Levi, is a
biographical apophthegm. The controversy over fasting in 2:18-
20 has appended sayings in vv. 21-22. The incident of plucking
grain on the sabbath contains two different dominical answers,
one in vv. 25-26, and another in vv. 27-28. The text of 2:1-3:6
has an obvious topical and form-critical unity, yet it presents
a sufficient variety of material for analysis.

Moreover, as a test of the value of a rhetorical approach,
the Galilean controversy section has much to recommend itself.
It has been argued, and many scholars have agreed, that Mark has
incorporated a pre-existing controversy collection. The theory
has been put forward in order to explain apparent difficulties
in the material, the atypical use of the title, Son of Man, and
the too early mentions of Jesus' death in the bridegroom allusion in 2:20, and of the plot against Jesus in 3:6.[41]

Yet, the literary-rhetorical approach assumes that the text
can be understood on its own terms, without recourse to external
solutions. The extent to which this study can resolve or dissolve the problems that led earlier scholars to hypothesize a
premarkan collection, and can understand those issues within the
markan framework, to that extent the approach is justified.
That something can be understood in the markan framework does
not exclude the possibility that Mark is also using a source or
earlier tradition. It does, however, invalidate some of the
arguments for a source.

The Jerusalem public debate section in Mark 11-12 is a
suitable text for comparison with 2:1-3:6. Like 2:1-3:6, it
consists primarily of public debate material: the question on
authority, the questions on tribute, the resurrection, and the
great commandment, and the question about David's son (11:27-33;
12:13-37). It is the second major block of such material in
the gospel.[42] As scholars have proposed a premarkan source to
explain difficulties in 2:1-3:6, so also scholars have proposed
external solutions to explain difficulties in Mark 11-12. The
public debate material in Mark 11-12 presents a challenge to
the rhetorical critic to see if the material can be explained
in terms of the markan literary framework.

In addition, the Jerusalem section poses a different problem
from 2:1-3:6 in terms of determining structure. Mark 2:1-3:6
clearly constitutes a coherent literary unit within Mark's gospel. The entire section is dominated by the theme of the
Pharisees' hostility to the acts of Jesus or his disciples,
culminating in their decision to plot to destroy Jesus (3:6).
Further, the section is sharply set off from its surrounding
context, which displays Jesus' popularity with the crowd. The
public debate material in Mark 11-12 is not an obvious rhetorical unit. The parable of the wicked tenants (12:1-12) inter-
rupts the sequence of debates. Moreover, the debate on the
first commandment is a school debate containing no hint of conflict (12:28-34); and the saying about David's son is not in
response to any question of opponents (12:35-37). Further, the
debate material is followed by the warning against the scribes
and the story of the widow's mite (12:38-44), before a new
section of the gospel begins in Mark 13. Finally, one cannot
discuss the material in 11:27-12:37 without also discussing the
temple cleansing in Mark 11:15-18. Although not a controversy
in form, it clearly resulted in controversy.

Thus, unlike 2:1-3:6, the first task of a rhetorical critic
in regard to the public debate material in Mark 11-12 is to
establish the limits of rhetorical units larger than the pericope. The entire pattern of the Jerusalem public ministry must
first be surveyed to determine if there are any rhetorical sub-
structures in the Jerusalem section, to see how the public debates fit in, and to see if an analysis of rhetorical structure
will provide clues about the function of the public debate
material in the Jerusalem ministry.

The major portion of the following study is devoted to Mark
2:1-3:6 as a test case for the rhetorical method. Mark 11-12
will be studied much more briefly, to indicate how the rhetorical method may help clarify its structure and the role of the
public debate material within it.

Building on Previous Research

As has been noted, relatively little work from a literary-
rhetorical perspective has been done on Mark, and virtually none
has been done on the public debate material. That does not mean

that this study begins with a clean slate. It is grounded in and builds on the results of research on Mark using other methodologies. The efforts of source critics have provided us with the basic picture of Mark's style. The form critics have provided us with the description of the "typical" controversy story form from which we can see how the actual forms occurring in the text of Mark deviate. The redaction critics have added to our knowledge of Mark's style and literary techniques, by their use of them as indices to Mark's redactional activity and theological concerns. All three groups of critics, but particularly the redaction critics with their interest in markan composition and structure, have added to our knowledge of how Mark created (or compiled) his gospel.

The work of these scholars will be briefly surveyed, as it is relevant to the following study under the topics of style, literary techniques, Mark's composition of the gospel, and form. But first the presuppositions about the gospel of Mark which underlie a literary-rhetorical approach will be enumerated. For they are presuppositions that have emerged and been confirmed by the work of source, form, and redaction critics.

Presuppositions

The methodological approach of rhetorical criticism is based on three suppositions about the gospel of Mark which are generally or increasingly accepted by markan scholars today:

First, Mark is a compiler. He uses, interprets and orders into a connected narrative already existing traditions which consisted largely of isolated stories and sayings.

Second, contra Bultmann, Mark is in fact master of his material. He is an author in his own right, using and developing his materials to present his own point of view or theology, even if we as scholars do not agree on what that is. This supposition is an important one, for it means that all of the text of Mark may be used to interpret Mark's theology. (Where we can ascertain how Mark has modified or developed tradition, we have clues as to how Mark's theology differs from other theological understandings of the time. This can sharpen our grasp of Mark's purpose, but not necessarily of his theology. For his theology cannot be restricted to areas of disagreement with others.)

Finally, the gospel of Mark, however inelegant its Greek,
and however far it falls short of classical literary standards,
is a literary composition, and the study of it as such provides
us with an additional methodology for understanding this gospel.

Style

The basic picture of Mark's style emerges from the work of
the early commentators, such as Swete and Lagrange, and above
all from the quantitative compilation of Hawkins' *Horae Synopticae*.[43] The gospel, although one-third shorter than either
Matthew or Luke, tends to be wordy in the material it does relate, containing vivid but inessential details, and is frequently
pleonastic. The style is simple, with preference for the connective καί and the use of the historic present, and occasionally
crude or harsh.

This basic picture of Mark's style has remained largely
intact, with details added by later scholars. C.H. Turner, in
his excellent series of articles in the *Journal of Theological
Studies*, 1924-1928, has described Mark's use of the impersonal
plural in place of the passive voice, his use of auxiliary and
quasi-auxiliary verbs with a participle for the imperfect, and
the characteristic use of ἄρχομαι plus an infinitive. Turner
further describes as a markan characteristic fondness for parenthetical construction. In his list of markan parentheses, he
includes examples varying in size from Mark's aside to the
reader in 7:2 (τοῦτ' ἔστιν ἀνίπτοις) to the Old Testament citation in Mark 1:2-3 as a parenthetical interposition into 1:1-4,
to the intercalation of the Beelzebub controversy (3:22-30) into
Mark 3:20-35.[44]

Max Zerwick, in his *Untersuchungen zum Markus-Stil*, confirms Mark's fondness for parentheses, while suggesting it might
be helpful to distinguish between true parentheses and larger
insertions.[45] Zerwick also studies Mark's use of καί and δέ,
his use of tenses and of word order. He points out the frequency of chiastic word order and what he calls chiastic rhythm
in phrases, noting that they could have been found in the tradition or be due to Mark.[46]

Frans Neirynck has documented exhaustively Mark's fondness
for pleonasms, redundancies, and repetitions, classifying them
according to thirty different categories.[47]

K.L. Schmidt observed that in contrast to the overall vividness of the gospel, there are passages which are colorless and
devoid of particulars.[48] These he calls *Sammelberichte*, and
believes them to be markan compositions. Josef Schmid has
emphasized that Mark is by no means always wordy. Such to us
theologically important events as the call of the disciples or
the institution of the last supper are presented concisely, even
sketchily, in contrast to the wealth of detail in reporting such
incidents as the miracles in Mark 5:1-43 or the death of John
the Baptist in Mark 6:14-29.[49]

Though our knowledge of the details of Mark's style has
grown since Hawkins' day, the general picture remains much the
same. This is easily seen by reading Hawkins and then reading
Vincent Taylor's excellent summary of Mark's style in his commentary[50] or reading Ernst Haenchen's description in his.[51]

Literary Techniques

The line between style and literary technique is an in-
distinct one. The repetitiousness so thoroughly listed by
Neirynck in many instances may be precisely a stylistic fondness for repetition. But when Neirynck concludes that "progressive double-step expression" is a general characteristic of
Mark's manner of writing and editing,[52] he is making an assertion
about Mark's literary technique or method of composition.

So also Mark's fondness for parentheses may vary from a
stylistic quirk to a literary device to interrelate extended
blocks of material. While C.H. Turner and Zerwick were describing these as aspects of stylistic preference, Ernst von
Dobschütz was studying them as literary devices.[53] He described
two techniques: first, true "sandwiching" or intercalation such
as is found in Mark 5:21-43 and 14:1-11, which functions both
to create an illusion of time or distance and to heighten the
tension for the hearer. The second technique is to point to a
second story at the beginning of the first in order to bring
them into some inner connection, e.g., 3:20-35, 14:54-72. What
the actual inner connection is, varies according to the example:
in Mark 3:20-35, it is to emphasize the contrast between the
friendliness of the relatives and the hostility of the scribes;[54]
in 14:54-72, it is a device to indicate the simultaneity of
Peter's denial and Jesus' trial.

Dobschütz' interest in literary devices as a way of understanding Mark's literary expression was unusual for his time.
Commentators have always mentioned in passing the markan "sandwiches" or intercalations but they have viewed them mainly as
an elementary technique to indicate passage of time. Werner G.
Kümmel lists only three devices as characteristic of Mark:
1) intercalation or sandwiching; 2) preparation of the reader
in advance (e.g., mentioning the boat in 3:9 to prepare for
4:1); and 3) the addition of summary reports (*Sammelberichte*).[55]
Literary techniques become a real focus of attention only
with the rise of redaction criticism. For they offer a possible
avenue for the redaction critic to ascertain Mark's editorial
activity and/or his theological concerns. The literary devices
most mentioned have been circular or symmetrical ones: the
long-familiar "sandwiches" or intercalations, insertions, and
framing techniques.

Intercalations. The following passages are generally considered intercalations: Mark 3:20-35; 5:21-43; 6:7-32; 11:12-
26; 14:1-11. Sometimes 14:12-25 and 54-72 are also included.
Robert Stein is conservative in his estimate of the usefulness
of the intercalations for determining Mark's theological concerns. For if "both incidents took place at the same time or
were located in the same place," or if they deal with a similar
theme, the intertwining may be irrelevant for markan thought.
Only if it can be demonstrated that one pericope helps to interpret the other are sandwiches of theological interest.[56] Stein
fails to see (or agree) that the device of intercalating episodes by definition brings them into some literary relationship
with each other. It is the job of the rhetorical critic to
determine in each instance what the function of the intercalation
is--to indicate passage of time, to retard the action in order
to heighten dramatic tension, for emphasis, contrast--and then
to see how that helps to understand the meaning (theology) of
the text.
     Other redaction critics have not been as cautious as Stein.
T.A. Burkill, for example, sees Mark using them as a literary
means either to stress a parallel or make a contrast.[57] John R.
Donahue has perhaps tried to carry the direct theological significance of intercalations the farthest. He affirms that "there

is a dialectical relationship between the inserted material and
its framework whereby the stories serve to interpret each
other."[58] He then goes on to try to establish a systematic
theological pattern that applies to all the intercalations.[59]
Donahue concludes that "sections leading to the suffering and
death of Jesus are framed by discipleship material," and therefore, "Mark uses the technique of intercalation to underscore
two major themes of his gospel, the way of suffering of Jesus,
and the necessity of the disciple to follow Jesus on this way."[60]
That these are major themes in Mark is undeniable. But Donahue
appears to force the interpretation of passages in order to make
the intercalations fit his theological pattern. For example,
in 3:20-35, the inner story does describe the scribes' hostility
to Jesus' healings, but Jesus triumphantly answers his opponents
and the incident contains no hint of the coming suffering.

More basically, Donahue's use of literary techniques as a
direct indicator of theology ignores the reality of the gospel
as narrative. Intercalation is primarily a literary device and
should be studied first in rhetorical terms, to see how the
intercalation affects the progression of the narrative. Only
when its literary function is understood, can one correctly
interpret how an intercalation may add to our understanding of
Mark's theology. Further, intercalations may function differently from each other.[61]

Insertions. Stein and Donahue, among other redaction
critics, have called attention to "insertion" as a markan literary technique. Insertions might be defined as smaller editions
of intercalations. Instead of one pericope being inserted within another, something in some way foreign is "inserted" into one
pericope. Stein sees them as Mark's way of commenting on a
tradition to the reader, therefore as important to Mark's theology. He uses the examples of Mark 14:28 and 16:7.[62] Donahue
attempts to establish criteria for identifying "insertions":
a) close verbal agreement in the material framing the insertion;
b) redundant quality to one of those phrases; and c) synoptic
alteration.[63] According to Donahue, Mark uses this technique
to call attention to the inserted verse "much in the same fashion that a modern writer would use italics or an asterisk."[64] [64]

The inserted material gives "an added dimension" to the narrative into which it is inserted.[65] Donahue's definition of an insertion is useful. And here, at least in his appendix listing markan insertions, Donahue appears to approach the use of the device less rigidly and from a more literary perspective:

> Continued study of this phenomenon in Mark has convinced me that it is a very important compositional technique used by Mark for a variety of functions, and not simply to call attention to the "inserted" material.[66]

Framing techniques. The outside material of both intercalations and insertions can be called "framing" material. Scholars have noticed that Mark will also frame larger blocks of material. The two stories of the healing of blind men frame the midsection of the gospel which centers on the themes of christology and discipleship.[67] The first healing of a blind man and the healing of the epileptic boy form an inner frame around the extended concentric structure of 8:27-9:13.[68] In the following rhetorical analyses other framing materials besides miracle stories will be noticed.

As matters of style at some point pass over into literary techniques, so also at some point, such as frames around an extended concentric structure, literary techniques become Mark's methods of putting his gospel together.

How Mark Put the Gospel Together

If our conception of Mark's style has remained much the same since our first investigation of it, our picture of the extent of Mark's editorial activity and of his sophistication as a writer has changed drastically. We still accept K.L. Schmidt's conclusion that Mark has strung together many individual stories.[69] We still agree with Bultmann's description of markan techniques for linking materials: 1) simple linking in succession above all with the connective καί, sometimes εὐθύς or πάλιν;[70] 2) the use of spatial and temporal links; 3) the occasional expanded transitions or situation indications which correspond more or less to Schmidt's *Sammelberichte*; and 4) the use of motifs such as the lake, boat, house, mountain, disciples, crowds, opponents, motifs which Mark found in

individual pieces of tradition and then used to incorporate
other pieces of tradition.[71] But we no longer see these as the
simple or simple-minded techniques of a not very adept compiler.
Johannes Sundwall's excellent study, *Die Zusammensetzung
des Markusevangeliums* (1934) is the only detailed literary study
of how each pericope is fitted into its place in the text.[72]
He pays particular attention to word repetitions, and observes
the great frequency of catchwords between pericopes, words that
recall what has gone before, and bracket words occurring at the
beginning and end of pericopes. He believes that these word
repetition techniques were common in the oral tradition available
to Mark, which Mark took over and greatly expanded, in order to
bind his gospel together.[73] Sundwall's observations are the
starting point for any literary analysis of the composition of
the text. Sundwall, however, did not look beyond the immediate
connections between individual pericopes or premarkan collections
to possible larger structural patterns in Mark.

For we no longer assume that the gospel of Mark contains
no more elaborate structures than the simple linking of episodes
in succession. The midsection, 8:27-10:45, clearly is structured
around the threefold repetition of the pattern: passion pre-
diction--misunderstanding of the disciples--teaching on discipleship. Various structures, more or less elaborate, have been
proposed for Mark 13. Extended concentric structures have been
observed by various people in many sections of the gospel.[74]
The analysis of markan structures is an ongoing activity of
scholars at present. It is evident, however, that in many if
not all parts of the gospel, pericopes are organized into larger
wholes or structures which serve to interrelate the material.

We also no longer agree with Schmidt, Bultmann and Taylor
that Mark was a simple compiler who abstained from much if any
editorial work on the traditional material itself.[75] As a
result of the studies of redaction critics, we now conclude that
Mark has made extensive editorial modifications within individual
pericopes, and even in the passion narrative.[76] We have come
to believe that far more of the pericopes than just the
Sammelberichte were composed by Mark. Mark is truly an author
as well as an editor.

Form

The relevance of previous research on Mark's style, literary
techniques, and methods of composition to a rhetorical analysis
of the markan text is self-evident. The relevance of form criticism is less evident, for the aims of the rhetorical critic and
the form critic are different. The form critic seeks to discover
the typical forms in which the synoptic material clothed itself
in the oral tradition; he/she attempts to dissolve the final
text into its constituent elements, one or more originally independent traditions, later accretions, editorial additions and
emendations; the form critic seeks to determine the *Sitz im Leben*
of the form or its particular exemplar. The rhetorical critic,
on the other hand, is not concerned with the *Sitz im Leben* or
the tradition history of the pericope; he/she seeks to interpret
the meaning of the final text, and to understand how each individual element contributes to that text.

Yet, as the above discussion of Muilenburg's approach indicated,[77] rhetorical criticism builds precisely upon an understanding of the typical form. A rhetorical critic uses one of
the major results of form-critical investigation,'the description
of the form itself, as a preliminary guide to the literary techniques and structure employed in a text.

Such a use of form criticism presupposes that biblical
scholars have achieved some agreement on the form lying behind
the markan public debate material. And that is indeed the case.
The major form-critical works dealing with the controversy
material are the monograph of Martin Albertz;[78] the studies of
Martin Dibelius[79] and Rudolf Bultmann,[80] the first editions of
which were all published about 1920; Vincent Taylor's study,
The Formation of the Gospel Tradition,[81] first published in
1933; and Arland J. Hultgren's 1971 dissertation, "Jesus and
his Adversaries: A Study of the Form and Function of the Conflict Stories in the Synoptic Tradition."[82] The form critics,
except for Dibelius, agree that there is a controversy form,
however they may choose to name it. And they all, including
Dibelius, classify most of Mark's public debate material as be-
longing to that form.[83]

To state that the form critics agree on the characteristics
of the form is true only in the most general sense. They disagree

not only on nomenclature but also on some of the defining characteristics and on whether or not certain pericopes belong to it.
The following discussion describes the understanding of the form
that will underlie the rhetorical analysis, plus a summary of
selected aspects of the form critics' thinking which seem particularly useful for the rhetorical critic. No attempt is made to
give a comprehensive overview or analysis of the form critics'
work on controversy stories.[84]

Hultgren's description. Hultgren's description of the oral
form, which he calls "conflict story," seems to be the most adequate description of the material. A conflict story consists
of a brief narrative introduction and a "dialogue" between Jesus
and his contemporaries, and the latter are depicted as adversaries.[85] It is a "form of narrative and dialogue material showing *conflict* between Jesus and his adversaries."[86] Hultgren,
in agreement with the other form critics, emphasizes the con-
ciseness of the form and the fact that it climaxes in the final
saying of Jesus.

Hultgren has abstracted four formal characteristics of the
form: 1) *the dominical saying* dominates, appearing at the close
of the dialogue;[87] 2) *the opponents' question*, whether real or
imaginary, is of great importance and is sometimes the means
whereby material is fashioned into the conflict story form;[88]
3) *narrative* always precedes the dialogue and may occur in the
middle or at the end. At its most concise, the narrative element merely links the story to the preceding pericope and gives
a brief setting for the dialogue. When the narrative is more
extensive, it is employed to increase the dramatic effect.[89]
4) Finally, the *opponents* represent one party only--that is,
they function as a single character in the conflict story form.
"The interchange is between two parties only: Jesus on one side,
his opponents (individually or collectively) on the other."[90]
The opponents are described only in the most general terms,
"sufficient to set up the necessary polarity for the conflict
dialogue."[91]

Hultgren's description of the form seems to fit the synoptic
material best because of his consistent emphasis on conflict as
an essential ingredient of the form without overspecification of

the occasion of conflict[92] or the technique of argumentation.
Dibelius, Taylor and Albertz all to varying degrees deny or lose
sight of the element of controversy.[93] Bultmann maintains the
element of conflict, but in defining the starting point as "some
action or attitude which is seized on by the opponent,"[94] and
in defining Jesus' argument as one leading the opponent *ad
absurdum*,[95] he defines the material more narrowly than the data
warrant.

Albertz' description. Hultgren's definition of the conflict
form, although more systematic than Albertz', draws heavily on
Albertz' work.[96] Since Albertz' description follows the narrative sequence of the form, it provides the rhetorical critic
with convenient categories for analyzing the public debate
material in Mark's gospel.

According to Albertz, the form consists at most of three
parts: the opening *exposition*, the *dialogue*, and when present,
the *closing remarks*.[97] The exposition corresponds to Hultgren's
narrative elements. It serves to introduce the questioner and
prepare for the question.[98] Then follows the dialogue, corre-
sponding to Hultgren's question of the opponents and the dominical saying. The dialogue is the focus of interest. In its
simplest and most usual form, it is a question followed by Jesus'
answer—word and counterword. In a few instances, there is more
extended dialogue, ending with Jesus' word. Jesus' final word
is the climax of the story. Only in those instances where Jesus'
final action is not a word but a healing miracle is the form
concluded by closing remarks.[99] Otherwise the story ends with
Jesus' word. As Albertz noted, however, the dialogue may consist of more than one interchange between the questioner and
Jesus.

The dialogue. All the form critics agree that Jesus' final
answer is the climax of the story.[100] As Albertz noted, however,
the dialogue may consist of more than one interchange between
the questioner and Jesus.[101] C.H. Dodd has posited that a true
dialogue form exists which may be distinguished from the
apophthegm.[102] He cites five instances in Mark, and two in
Luke.[103] According to Dodd, these dialogues differ from the

apophthegms in that the intermediate steps of the dialogue are
either necessary to the final answer or in themselves constitute
at least implicitly the answer. Therefore the questioner is not
simply a foil to elicit Jesus' pronouncement, but a significant
contributor to the discussion. The emphasis is not solely on
Jesus' answer. Dodd's idea of a separate dialogue form has not
been generally adopted. His observation, however, that extended
dialogue changes the emphasis and balance in a pronouncement
story is helpful.

The occasion and content of the conflict. Bultmann analyzes
the controversy apophthegms according to three different categories: those "occasioned by Jesus' healing," those "otherwise
occasioned by the conduct of Jesus or the disciples," and "questions asked by opponents."[104] Although Bultmann does not refer
to these categories in his general discussion of controversy
and scholastic dialogues, they nonetheless appear to represent
real subgroups within the controversy form. A controversy is
concerned *either* with Jesus' healing (on the sabbath, by
Beelzebul) *or* with some other behavior of Jesus or his disciples
(eating with tax collectors and sinners, not fasting) *or* with
some question asked Jesus by opponents (about divorce, taxes,
resurrection).

The division reflects the content as much as it does the
occasion of the conflict. A healing controversy, for example,
is about Jesus' use of his healing power. The division also
reflects variations in the controversy *form*. Bultmann's second
category, those to do with some behavior of Jesus or the disciples, generally follows the simple or "typical" form. The
exposition provides the setting: some action of Jesus or the
disciples. The behavior is questioned, and, in a brief response,
Jesus triumphantly justifies it. The pattern is behavior-question-
justification.

In Bultmann's third group, questions asked Jesus by opponents, the starting point is not any behavior of Jesus or the
disciples. Thus the exposition is usually minimal. The dialogue, however, is generally developed beyond simple question
and answer. Here, as Dodd suggests, the emphasis falls on the
process of the dialogue, not just on Jesus' final word.

The situation in the first group, controversies in which
Jesus' healing plays some role, is more complex. The sabbath
healing in Luke 13:10-17 and the Q version behind the Beelzebul
controversy (Mt 12:22-32/Lk 11:14-23)[105] follow the pattern of
Bultmann's second group: behavior-objection-vindication. The
others, the sabbath healing of Mark 3:1-5 (and par) and the
healing/forgiveness dispute of Mark 2:1-12 (and par) do not.[106]
The objectionable behavior, the healing, occurs at the end, after
Jesus' sayings. This dislocation naturally disturbs the normal
dialogue form. For example, Jesus may take the initiative asking
the question, and the opponents may remain silent throughout.
Thus the synoptic gospels record two healing controversy types:
those in which the objectionable healing begins the controversy
and those in which the healing comes at the end of the controversy.[107]

Thus, in summary, there appear to be three types (or one
type and two variants) of the controversy form. The basic form
is the action-objection-justification type. The conflict arises
out of some behavior of Jesus or the disciples; the opponents
question it and Jesus vindicates it. Some but not all of the
controversies arising out of Jesus' healing conform to this type.
In the first variant the opponents simply question Jesus: there
is no preceding objectionable act. In this variant, the dialogue
is usually extended. In the second variant, Jesus' objectionable
act occurs at the end of the story, after the debate. In this
variant, the objectionable behavior is always Jesus' healing
activity.

Literary Techniques

Before turning to the definition of literary techniques,
some general issues need to be mentioned. The first issue concerns whether the rhetorical devices are phenomena of oral or
written literature. Unquestionably, many if not all of them
have their origin in oral literatures.[108] Even extended symmetrical patterns are well documented in oral composition.[109]
But they are also techniques which can be used in written composition. And to assert a clear difference between oral and
written composition for popular literature in the first century
C.E. seems out of place. For even if a work was written, it

was meant to be read aloud and to be heard. Most of those who
became acquainted with the gospel of Mark undoubtedly heard it
read. Thus the distinction between oral and written techniques
does not appear applicable from the point of view of the audience.

The second question concerns whether the techniques are
basically Greek or Semitic in inspiration. They are, of course,
attested in both literatures. Inclusios and hook words are
characteristic of virtually all oral literatures studies. Ring
composition and chiasm are also to be found in both Greek literature and the Old Testament. But the frequency of extended symmetrical structures, introverted parallelism, in the Old Testament, combined with our knowledge of the extensive influence of
the Old Testament on the New in other respects, makes it seem
probable that a major influence for such patterns comes from
Hebrew rhetoric.[110]

The last general issues are perhaps the most difficult to
speculate about with any accuracy. These are the question of
how conscious or unconscious an author is of his use of literary
techniques and the question of how and to what extent a hearer
is consciously or unconsciously aware of or affected by the use
of such techniques. The use of inclusios and hook words (catchwords) is so pervasive that an author could use them consciously
or unconsciously, and the hearer would probably sense them in
terms of completion and transition. Mark's intercalations and
insertions seem to be deliberate--but that is only because it
is difficult for us to see how they could occur without some
deliberate intent. They are sufficiently obvious that it seems
safe to assume that the audience would be aware of them also.

The questions become particularly difficult and also particularly important in regard to extended symmetrical patterns.
It is hard to believe that elaborate, elegant concentric structures which have been documented in many literatures occurred
without the authors deliberately intending them. Some of the
looser structures may have been less fully conscious.[111] The
question of if and how the audience was aware of such structures
is more difficult to answer. C.H. Talbert, who has perhaps done
the most study of the issue, concludes that the greater sensitivity to form in the first century and the widespread existence
in literature and art of the principle of balance and symmetry

are such that "the architechtonic patterns would have been immediately sensed or felt but not consciously and rationally per-
ceived until after reflection."[112]

Classification and Definition
of Literary Techniques

The following is a rough classification and definition of
literary devices that appear likely to be found with some frequency in the gospel of Mark. The terminology is basically that
in use among biblical scholars, although rhetorical works have
been consulted.[113]

Classification of Word or Phrase Repetitions

Inclusio. The repetition of the same word or phrase at or
near the beginning and ending of some unit, a sentence, a pericope, or a larger section. The form of the word need not be
repeated exactly. For instance, one might find a noun and a
verb from the same root. Inclusio is by definition an indication of structure, the beginning and end of a rhetorical unit
of any size. It is a recognized technique of oral literatures.[114]
So the rhetorical critic by designating certain repetitions as
inclusios is making a judgment about the limits of some unit
of narrative.

Hook words. The repetition of the same word or phrase in
two successive or parallel units, clauses, verses, or pericopes.
In the technical terminology of Greek rhetoric,[115] anaphora is
the use of hook words at the beginning of each unit:

    Fear not, O land; be glad and rejoice,
      for the Lord has done great things!
    Fear not, you beasts of the field,
      for the pastures of the wilderness are green....
                        (Joel 2:21-22a, RSV)

Epiphora is the use of hook words at the end of each unit.
Anadiplosis is the repetition of the same word or phrase at
the end of one unit and at the beginning of the following one.
Hook words may also occur in the middle of verses or pericopes.

Hook words indicate some structural relationship between
the materials they "hook" together. The same statements about
variation and the critic's judgment made about inclusios apply

to all hook words.[116] The term "hook word"[117] rather than catch-word is employed, since it is a more neutral and descriptive term, without catchword's overtones of editorial compilation. Both uses of a hook word or phrase may have been in the tradition, or one or both may be the redactional or compositional activity of Mark.

Key words. In addition to word repetitions which are indica-tive of structure, a word may be used repeatedly as the leit-motif or theme of a passage or longer section of narrative. Examples are "to fast" in Mark 2:18-20 or "bread" in Mark 6-8. Such key words help to give thematic unity to a narrative, with-out demarking any structural pattern.[118]

Anticipation and retrospection. A word or phrase may be used to prepare the reader for later events in the narrative, to foreshadow developments to come. The same word or phrase is then used later in the narrative to recall to the reader's mind incidents that have gone before. Such devices help to inter-connect the parts of a narrative, to give an episodic work a sense of unity.[119]

Repetition for rhetorical effect. Word repetition is also frequently employed for rhetorical effect. Repetition may be used to indicate emphasis, as a means of retarding action, or as a way of indicating climax.[120] Repetition may also be used to highlight or stress unrepeated material, new information sur-rounded by redundancies.

Lack of word repetition. The use of word repetition is so pervasive in the gospel of Mark, that its absence should be observed as well.

Other Rhetorical Techniques

Chiasm. Chiasm, from the Greek letter *chi*, means "crossing." In its narrowest sense, it refers to repetition of words in inverted order: a b : b' a'. As such, of course, it is an instance of word repetition for rhetorical effect. However, chiasm also refers to a broader range of literary devices in

which crossing occurs. Syntactical chiasm--e.g., subject, verb:
verb, subject--occurs frequently in Mark. A chiasm may also
consist of content parallels in inverted order:

> I will pour out my spirit on all flesh:
> Your sons and your daughters shall prophesy,
> Your old men shall dream dreams,
> and your young men shall see visions.
> Even upon the menservants and maidservants
> in those days, I will pour out my spirit.
>   (Joel 2:28-29, RSV)

As in the above example, a chiasm may consist of more than two
elements. Also a chiasm may contain a middle element which is
not repeated: a b c b' a'. A chiasm may be made up of larger
content elements, even of whole pericopes. In such cases, the
chiastic elements often contain hook words. The essential
feature of all chiasms, of whatever dimension, is that of crossing or inversion.

   Ring composition. Ring composition is a circular technique,
an a b a pattern. In its simplest form, it is the device of
inclusio, the repetition of a word or phrase at the beginning
and end of some passage marking it as a rhetorical unit.[121]
However, ring composition, like chiasm, may be defined by content rather than verbal repetition and may encompass larger
sections of narrative, parts of a pericope or three or more
pericopes. As in the case of chiasm, hook words are often employed.

   Extended concentric structure. The symmetrical arrangement
or introverted parallelism of four, five or more pericopes or
items of narrative.[122] An extended concentric pattern may have
a single unparalleled element in the middle of it: a b c b' a';
or it may consist entirely of balanced elements: a b c c' b' a'.
An extended concentric structure may often contain chiastic elements, and it may often be grouped or collapsed into a ring
composition, e.g., (a b) c (b' a'). Extended symmetrical patterns are recognized by multiple congruent parallelisms of content, of form and structure, of vocabulary repetitions (hook
words), etc. A more extended discussion of such patterns follows
the definition of terms.

The foregoing three rhetorical devices are standard terms
employed in rhetorical analysis.[123] The following two devices
have been arbitrarily named and defined for use in the rhetorical analysis of Mark.

Interposition. A foreign narrative element interposed into
a larger narrative. Insertions and intercalations discussed
under the review of previous work[124] would both be interpositions.
However, the term "interposition" is a neutral definition of a
rhetorical device; it does not imply interpolation or lack there-
of. An interposition always breaks in some way with the preceding and following narrative. The central element of a ring
composition will be an interposition only if it in some fashion
disrupts the natural flow of the narrative. An interposition
may be of any size, from the interposition, "And the curtain of
the temple was torn in two, from top to bottom," between Jesus'
death on the cross and the centurion's reaction to that death
(15:37-39), to an extended section of narrative. Longer interpositions are often marked off by a frame.

Frame. A frame is defined as something that frames another
unit at its beginning and end, but which itself is not part of
the unit framed. For example, the two healings of blind men
constitute a frame for Mark 8:27-10:45, but the two miracle-
controversies beginning and ending Mark 2:1-3:6 are not a frame
because they themselves are part of the controversy section.

Extended Concentric Structures

Some further preliminary observations about detailed or
extended symmetrical structures need to be made. For unlike
the other literary techniques described, the technique is not
familiar to us either from our general knowledge of rhetoric,
ancient or modern, or as a specific literary technique of Mark's.
Furthermore, the structure is discerned by the twentieth century
reader only through detailed study of the text. One wonders if
the structure is not the brainchild of some twentieth century
critic determined to obfuscate matters.   .
    If it is the latter, we may be said to have that type of
obfuscation on the brain. Scholars are identifying symmetrical

structures, introversion, structure by envelopment, and extended chiasms in a wide variety of literatures.[125] In classical litera-ture, it has been found in Homer,[126] Herodotus,[127] and Vergil[128] among others. In biblical literature, the question is becoming, where is it not found? It has been recognized in Hebrew prose[129] and poetry:[130] in the creation stories in Genesis,[131] in Deuteronomy,[132] in the court succession narrative,[133] in Jeremiah,[134] Zephaniah[135] and Zechariah,[136] in Jonah[137] and Ruth,[138] in Psalms,[139] Proverbs,[140] Song of Songs,[141] and Lamentations.[142] The Aramaic section of Daniel has a concentric pattern.[143] It has been observed in the Hodoyat of Qumran.[144] It has been suggested as one of the organizing techniques of the rabbis for the oral Haggadah.[145]

It is just as ubiquitous in New Testament writings. It has been identified in Matthew,[146] Mark,[147] and John.[148] It has been found in Luke-Acts.[149] It has been studied in sections of the Pauline corpus[150] and Colossians.[151] Hebrews and many of its sections are symmetrically constructed.[152] And the Book of Revelation is not immune to the phenomenon.[153]

The compositional purpose of the technique has not been systematically studied and there is little consensus. Its ori-gins undoubtedly were in oral composition.[154] It has been con-sidered a mnemonic device for remembering oral tradition.[155] It has been used to argue unity of authorship in both oral literature (Homer)[156] and written (the Pentateuch and Historical Writings).[157] Other scholars have viewed it, on the contrary, as a method for a redactor to put together disparate bits of tradition.[158] Or it has been considered a sophisticated method of original written composition.[159] In fact, the technique has probably been used in all these ways. The primary interest of this study, however, is not in the reason for the use of the technique in Mark but in how such concentric patterns help to illuminate the meaning of the gospel of Mark.

Two other issues raised by recognition of symmetrical rhythms do require attention. First, what are sufficient cri-teria for identifying a concentric pattern? For scholars do not always agree when a particular unit is concentrically con-structed, or if they agree that far, they may offer different patterns of parallelism. Two methods of identifying such

structures have predominated: the strategic use of word repetition, and content. Content is a broad subject, covering everything from theme deduced from the content (e.g., eschatology),
to manifest content, such as throwing money changers out of the
temple, to repetition of narrative details, such as the coming
or going of messengers, to changes in audience or setting. In
synoptic studies, I would argue that it is appropriate to add
a third method: parallelism of form. This does not imply that
a concentric pattern need consist of material of only one form-
critical type, but rather symmetrical parallelism of form is an
added criterion. Parallelism of subsidiary structural elements
--as distinct from form-critical classification--can also be an
important element in recognition of extended symmetrical patterns.

The discussion of adequate criteria will continue to be of
concern throughout the following discussion.[160] As a preliminary
statement, manifest content should probably be considered the
primary criterion. If there is merely a pattern of word repetition, without any correspondence to content, then probably the
rhetorical device of key word repetition is being used to provide
thematic unity, continuity, etc.--not hook words to define structure. A concentric structure based on content, however, should
be confirmed by hook words, form and/or structural similarities,
symmetry in details of content, etc. The more different congruent symmetries a text contains, the more certain we may be
that a text really has a concentric structure.

The second issue which will be of concern throughout the
following rhetorical analysis is the question of the literary
or rhetorical function of a (particular) concentric structure.
Nils Lund in *Chiasmus in the New Testament* has endeavored to
establish laws of chiastic structure (in most instances what is
here defined as concentric structure). The most important are

1) "The centre is always the turning point."

2) There is often a change in the trend of the argument
in the center, and an opposite idea is introduced, before the
original trend is resumed. Lund names this "the law of the
shift at the centre."

3) Similar ideas are often distributed so as to be found
in the extremes and the center of a concentric system and nowhere else within it.[161]

Lund describes these laws as characteristic of the "form" of symmetrical patterns. And it is surprising how often at least some of his "laws" do occur in concentric structures of Mark. But rather than viewing them as laws, it seems preferable to view them as indicators of those rhetorical functions which a concentric structure may serve, that a simple linear structure or repetitive parallelism does not serve as well or in the same way. In this light, Lund's laws might be restated as follows:

1) A concentric structure may serve to emphasize its central element.

2) A concentric structure may serve to hold opposite ideas in tension with one another for the audience. It may be a way of expressing contrast or paradox.

3) A concentric structure may serve to interrelate ideas in a more complex fashion than permitted in a non-symmetrical structure.

A concentric structure *may* serve any or all or none of the above functions. Frequently, as Lund emphasizes, the emphasis is on the center. Sometimes, however, it does not appear to be. Sometimes, especially in chronological narrative, it appears to fall equally throughout the structure.

Lund virtually ignores linear development within concentric structure. Yet it almost always exists, at least to some degree. And in some instances, such as in the telling of stories, the linear development may be as important as the symmetrical development. For example, the stories of the rape of Tamar, and of David and Bathsheba are well-articulated concentric structures.[162] Yet the symmetry hardly suppresses the chronological development; rather it adds depth or another dimension. Thus a fourth way concentric structures may function rhetorically may be posited:

4) A concentric structure may serve to integrate additional dimensions or emphases into a chronological or linear narrative.

Any description of the actual functions of concentric structures in Mark must await the analysis of particular examples. But the general principle may be stated: concentric structure is a way of interrelating material in a variety of ways and with greater complexity than is possible in straight-forward linear narration, whether it be based on logical argument or chronology.

Postscript

Three reminders or cautions that perhaps have not been sufficiently stressed in the foregoing discussion should be made:

First, concentric structures are not the only extended literary or rhetorical patterns in Mark. Mark uses units of three in organizing small sections of his gospel[163] and in structuring larger sections such as the entire midsection, Mark 8:27-10:45. The entire gospel has a loose chronological geographical structure, based on the literary formula of a journey from Galilee to Jerusalem. Structures in the gospel are not necessarily entirely discrete, but may overlap or interpenetrate one another. As Sherman E. Johnson has written:

> One may contrast the rhetorical method of Mark with that of Hellenistic and Roman writers by saying that it is oriental; in fact the gospel can be likened to an oriental rug in which many patterns cross one another. They are not made up with mathematical exactitude but developed spontaneously as the author writes. The result is a colourful piece of folk art, sometimes symmetrical, rich, and full of endless fascination, and exhibiting the vitality of early Christianity.[164]

Second, literary-rhetorical criticism is not the only, or even necessarily the primary, methodology by which to reach an understanding of the gospel of Mark. Rhetorical analysis is but one aspect of the larger enterprise of general literary criticism. Source, form, and redaction criticism remain the important tools for answering historical questions about the markan material and the gospel's *Sitz im Leben*. Their limitations are not so much in their method as in the lack of sufficient data from which to draw sound conclusions, and the restricted range of questions they are designed to answer. Newer methodologies such as structuralism also help us to approach the core of the thought of Mark. No one methodology can answer all questions, and all are needed to assist and correct and control each other. Nonetheless, any interpretation of the gospel of Mark should not ignore Mark's means of expression and his rhetorical structures.

Last, literary-rhetorical analysis is *not* an exact science. It is as much art as science. How much it reveals about the gospel depends on the skill of the practitioner as well as on

texts studied. Such a statement can and should be made about
most methodologies appropriate to biblical criticism.[165]   But
it is particularly true of literary criticism. For in literary
criticism, although there are interpretations which are clearly
wrong, not supported by the text, there is not necessarily a
single correct interpretation. A good one, however, will illumine
the meaning of the text for the reader.

CHAPTER II

MARK 2:1-3:6 AND 11-12:

PRELIMINARY CONSIDERATIONS

It was observed in Chapter One that rhetorical criticism,
although a new methodological approach, builds upon the results
of other methodologies. In regard to the structure of sections
encompassing several pericopes, rhetorical criticism builds primarily upon the work of source critics and form critics who have
investigated larger blocks of traditions. The relevant scholarly
studies consist mainly of hypotheses of premarkan collections.[1]

Scholars who have proposed premarkan collections have not,
of course, been investigating the structure of the markan text,
per se. They have been attempting, rather, to account historically for the occurrence or arrangements of blocks of material
found in Mark. The work of such scholars, however, often proves
helpful for a rhetorical analysis of the material. For the
arguments for (or against) a collection are often in fact arguments about the literary nature and interrelationships of the
material. Further, the arguments also serve to highlight the
issues of theological interpretation raised by a text, that the
rhetorical approach in turn must consider, using its own methodology.

If the literary structure of a section is to be used as a
guide to the section's meaning or theology, as is proposed in
this study, and if that meaning or theology is to contribute to
our overall understanding of Mark, then it is necessary to determine that the literary structure is substantially due to Mark.
At a minimum, if it is impossible to disprove the existence of
a hypothetical source, the theology highlighted by the structure
must be consistent with what is known of Mark's theology. If
the theology is consistent, and if the literary techniques un-
covered in the rhetorical analysis are found to be fairly common
in Mark, then it is unnecessary to assume any premarkan source
or collection.

Thus, the following survey and critique of previous research has two purposes. First, it will review those arguments

41

which are relevant to the rhetorical analysis to be made. And
second, it will evaluate hypotheses of premarkan collections and
patterns to see if they in fact account for the final structure
of the markan text, and if they are necessary assumptions for
the explanation of the text.

The discussion of Mark 2:1-3:6 will deal only with studies
arguing for or against premarkan collections, since the few
other studies relevant to its structure will be considered in
Chapter Five, following the rhetorical analysis. The discussion
of the public debate material in Mark 11-12 will begin with an
overview of the structure of all of chapters 11-13, as an introduction to the problem of determining the limits of rhetorical
units in that portion of the gospel. It will include two brief
literary analyses of its structure, as well as the proposals for
premarkan collections or patterns of arrangement.

Mark 2:1-3:6

In Mark 2:1-3:6, Jesus is shown engaging in five controversies with the scribes and/or the Pharisees concerning his own
actions or those of his disciples: Jesus addresses the paralytic,
"Your sins are forgiven" (Mark 2:5); Jesus eats with tax collectors and sinners; unlike the Pharisees and the disciples of John,
Jesus' disciples do not fast; the disciples, in plucking grain,
do unlawful work on the sabbath; Jesus heals on the sabbath. In
each conflict, Jesus emerges triumphant, silencing his opponents.
They, however, are far from reconciled to him: the fifth and
last controversy in the sequence concludes with the statement:
"The Pharisees went out, and immediately held counsel with the
Herodians against him, how to destroy him" (3:6). The series
of conflicts is set off from the surrounding material in which
people are portrayed flocking to Jesus, and in which there is
no hint of conflict.[2]

The obvious topical unity of the section, in contrast to
the more episodic appearance of much of Mark's gospel, is such
that scholars, almost without exception, have believed that Mark
drew upon an earlier written collection of conflict stories for
this portion of his work. First, the seminal theory of Martin
Albertz will be considered, then the reactions to Albertz, then
alternate proposals, and finally the possibility of no collection
at all preceding Mark's organization of the material.

Martin Albertz

While K.L. Schmidt had earlier suggested that Mark might
be dependent upon a controversy source for Mark 2:1-3:6,[3] Martin
Albertz in 1921 was the first to argue extensively for Mark's
use of an earlier written collection.[4] Albertz views Mark 2:1-
3:6 as an early collection of like material, similar to the
parable collection in Mark 4.[5] His arguments for the existence
of a collection are primarily literary: the section consists
of a series of stories showing Jesus in conflict with the Jews
over matters of Jewish law, in which the hostility of the opponents gradually increases from silent to direct questioning,
climaxing in open hostility in 3:1-6.[6] Mark 3:6, the plotting
to destroy Jesus, is the original conclusion to the last story
and to the entire collection.[7] The purpose of the collection
was to demonstrate the necessity of Jesus' death by showing an
overview of the historical conflict between Jesus and his enemies.[8]

The collection is a concatenation of originally independent
stories made without any attempt to reach a climax through the
order of questions or of the questioners,[9] and without any formal
assimilation of the stories to one another, except for the growing opposition to Jesus.[10] At some point, the sayings in 2:21-
22 and 27-28 were added to the individual stories or the collection and the call of Levi, 2:14, was inserted into the collection.[11] Then Mark took over the expanded collection, and by
means of the clamps of 2:1 and 13, gave the source a local setting
in Capernaum and by the Sea of Galilee.[12]

Albertz' reasons for rejecting the complex as markan are
based on his theological understanding of Mark. The title, Son
of Man, used in 2:10 and 28, is not employed in Mark's usual
eschatological sense; 2:20, the taking away of the bridegroom,
alludes to Jesus' death, which Mark himself does not have Jesus
unveil until 8:31 in the first passion prediction; and the mention of the plot against Jesus in 3:6 comes too early in Mark's
plan.[13] Nonetheless, the place Mark chose to insert the collection was not clumsily selected. It prepares the way for the
rejection of Israel in 4:12.[14]

Albertz does not interrelate his literary reasons for a
collection with his theological reasons against its markan

provenance. So the literary and theological arguments need to
be evaluated separately and both must be valid for his hypothesis
to stand. The literary arguments--the series of conflicts with
increasingly overt hostility between the opponents--remain valid
observations on the narrative and imply that the section has
some sort of unity or structuring. They do not in themselves
indicate whether that unity is due to an earlier collector or
the final redactor[15] and Albertz does not so use them. But
Albertz has established the first part of his argument: Mark
2:1-3:6 has a certain literary coherence.

Albertz' theological objections to markan provenance are
not self-evidently valid. They depend on one's theological
understanding of the gospel of Mark, and our understanding of
Mark has changed drastically since Albertz' day. The very points
that Albertz found troublesome, some recent scholars have seen
as indicators of Mark's thought. For example, Theodore J. Weeden
uses the taking away of the bridegroom in 2:20 virtually as a
prooftext for Mark's belief in the absence of Jesus from the
community between the resurrection and the parousia.[16] Perrin
cites the use of Son of Man in 2:10 and 28 as evidence for one
of Mark's three characteristic uses of the term, authority on
earth,[17] and notes that every major section of the gospel ends
on a note pointing ahead to the passion.[18]

Further, Albertz' theological arguments, insofar as they
are valid, apply to the individual pericopes rather than to the
section as a whole, and therefore do not demonstrate that Mark
did not compile the section. Albertz makes no attempt to determine a general theological outlook different from Mark's for -
his collection, or to relate the content of his various objec-:-
tions to each other. As a consequence, even if one accepts
Albertz' objections, one could argue that Mark has taken over
the alien content from the individual pericopes which he then
combined, using the narrative device of the increasing opposition
of the opponents. The fact that Albertz finds objections in all
but one of the five pericopes (2:13[15]-17) does not enhance the
probability of a collection, unless the objections can be shown
to relate to each other.

Thus one must conclude that Albertz has not demonstrated
his hypothesis of a premarkan collection in 2:1-3:6. His work,

however, remains important. The issues he raised, about the existence and development of a collection, about the literary structure of the section, and about the relation of some of its contents to the theology of Mark, remain issues to this day. And Albertz' literary analyses of the individual materials are frequently valid and illuminating, often unsurpassed in later research. Finally, it should be noted that the fact that Albertz has not proved his case does not in itself dispose of the possibility of a premarkan collection of the five controversy stories.

Critical Reactions to Albertz' Hypothesis

Albertz' theory has been widely praised, frequently adopted, amended as to where it begins and/or ends, sometimes ignored, but rarely challenged until the 1970's. It should be noted that while scholars may disagree over the beginning and ending of the collection, they have generally agreed that Mark 2:1(2), 13, 14, sometimes 21-22, and either 25-26, or 27-28, have been added or inserted into the individual pericopes or the collection, prior to or by Mark.

Acceptance of Mark 2:1-3:6 as a Premarkan Unit

The view that 2:1-3:6 is a premarkan collection has been held by Taylor,[19] Hultgren,[20] and Jan Willem Doeve[21] in dependence upon Albertz.[22] It has also been advanced by Schmid[23] and Willi Marxsen.[24]

Perrin and Taylor introduce another method into the discussion, with differing conclusions: the presence or absence of typical markan word usage and style. Perrin cites the lack of typical markan connecting links between the pericopes of Mark 2 as evidence that they were joined before Mark.[25] Taylor, while noting the absence of any connecting links between pericopes, except for 2:13, finds the vocabulary and style of the section to be typically markan.[26] Taylor reconciles this fact with his acceptance of Albertz' arguments by suggesting that Mark himself may have compiled the section before he wrote his gospel.[27] As Trocmé writes, "One can admire this harmonious compromise; it is more difficult to support it."[28] The case for a premarkan collection of 2:1-3:6 remains unproved.

The Problem of Mark 3:6

Mark 3:6, in its present setting, functions not only as the
conclusion to its own pericope, but also as the conclusion to
the controversy section as a whole. Albertz' argument for the
literary unity of 2:1-3:6 based on the increasing hostility of
the opponents is largely dependent on the climax of 3:6. For
this unity to be premarkan, 3:6 itself must be premarkan. Most
scholars, however, have argued that the verse is markan redaction.[29] Those positing a premarkan Galilean conflict collection
must argue for the premarkan provenance of 3:6.

For Albertz, that presented no problem. Mark 3:6, coming
too early in Mark's plan, was one of his reasons for arguing
that the controversy section could not be markan.[30] It can be
argued, however, that it is Mark's intention to show Jesus
standing under the shadow of the cross from the beginning of
his ministry, and that Mark ends the major sections of his gospel
on a note of rejection or misunderstanding.[31] While Albertz'
argument has some weight--the "plot" against Jesus does not
reach the intensity of 3:6 again until 11:18--it is insufficient
by itself to prove premarkan composition.

More recently, Ingrid Maisch has attempted to demonstrate
that 3:6 is premarkan on the basis of its literary and theological differences from the similar statements in 11:18, 12:12, and
14:1.[32] She notes that the last three all employ the verb ζητέω
while 3:6 does not. Further the opponents in 11:18 and 14:1,
and by inference in 12:12 as well, are the chief priests and
scribes; while the opponents in 3:6 are the Pharisees.[33] The
Pharisees, according to Maisch, can hardly be markan "death
enemies" since they are mentioned neither in the passion predictions nor the passion narrative.

Maisch's argument does not survive critical scrutiny. Her
theological argument that the association of the Pharisees with
Jesus' death cannot be markan is difficult to maintain in light
of such passages as 8:15 and 12:13. They are not directly associated with bringing about Jesus' death in Mark, because they
lacked the legal political authority of the chief priests, elders,
and scribes, the membership of the Sanhedrin. Further, the fact
that ζητέω is not found in 3:6 would not appear to argue against
markan composition of 3:6. The first two death sayings (3:6 and

11:18) both employ the verb, ἀπόλλυμι while the last two are
connected by the use in each of κρατέω (12:12, 14:1). Further,
Mark might well have avoided ζητέω in 3:6 since the events of
2:1-3:6 do not directly precipitate the passion, while the latter statements follow events which do.

Moreover, 3:6, as it is expressed, is not complete in itself; it raises the question of the further progress and outcome
of the plot against Jesus.[34] It does not appear to be a suitable
end for a source.[35] W.L. Knox suggests, therefore, that the
source may have continued with 12:13-17, followed by a passion
account, however brief.[36] If Mark, however, has separated the
parts of his source so widely in the gospel, he may well also
have rearranged and added to or deleted from the source to compile the material now found in 2:1-3:6. Knox's proposal cannot
be used to account for the structure of 2:1-3:6.

The difficulties in demonstrating that 3:6 has a premarkan
provenance, and in viewing it as the conclusion of an independent
source, militate against acceptance of Albertz' hypothesis of a
Galilean controversy collection.

One or Two Collections

If Mark 3:6 is considered markan redaction, there is no
particular reason to limit the collection of the five stories
of 2:1-3:6. A catena of controversy apophthegms could include
the debate on Jesus' source of healing power (3:22-30)[37] or the
controversies of 11 and 12.[38] The fact that the Pharisees and
Herodians are mentioned both in 3:6 and 12:13--and only there--
has suggested to some critics that 12:13-37(44) may once have
followed the earlier stories in a single collection.[39] The
double mention of the Pharisees and Herodians, however, may be
explained equally well (or inadequately) on the rhetorical
hypothesis that their use in 12:13 serves to recall to the
reader's mind the controversies of 2:1-3:6.

The existence of a general concatenation of conflict stories
is difficult to prove--or disprove. Since Mark has not incorporated such a collection as a whole, and since he might easily
have selected and rearranged material from a loose collection,
it cannot be used to explain the rhetorical structure of 2:1-3:6
or 11-12.

Alternate Theories of Premarkan Collections

Scholars, although not fully convinced by Albertz' theory
or its modifications, have been loathe to abandon the idea of a
premarkan conflict collection lying behind 2:1-3:6. Finally,
two new proposals appeared in 1971: 1) Maisch's for a collection
consisting of 2:15-3:6[40] and Heinz-Wolfgang Kuhn's for one consisting of 2:1-28.[41] Their methods as well as their conclusions
are different. Maisch seeks to show the literary means and
theological intentions of each stage in the development of the
healing of the paralytic (2:1-12).[42] The last stage--the pericope in its markan context--leads her into a consideration of
the issue of a premarkan collection. Her emphasis on the literary and theological aspects, though drawing on the techniques
of form and redaction criticism, is reminiscent of Albertz' fifty
years before. Kuhn, on the other hand, doubts the validity of
literary-critical arguments,[43] and stresses instead the applica-
tion of form criticism, particularly the determination of *Sitz
im Leben*.[44]

Ingrid Maisch: Mark 2:15-3:6

Maisch assumes as her starting point the scholarly consensus that a collection exists behind 2:1-3:6 and then proceeds
to test for its beginning and ending points.[45] For Maisch,
2:1-12 cannot form part of the original collection because
1) it is told in the style of a true miracle story in contrast
to the terseness of the four following conflict dialogues;
2) the Pharisees are not mentioned in it as they are in the
other four; and 3) the Pharisees' questions are about correct
teaching, not miracles. Mark 3:1-5, the sabbath healing, in
her opinion, is not comparable to 2:1-12 since it is not told
in the miracle style, and the healing is a necessary part of the
conflict; whereas the forgiveness controversy could stand without a healing.[46] If 2:1-12 is excluded, then Mark's editorial
introduction in 2:13 and the call of Levi "insertion" (2:14) also
fall away. The collection cannot begin earlier than 2:15.[47]
As already noted, Maisch argues that Mark 3:6 is the original
ending of the collection.

Thus, a premarkan collector has taken four stories similar
in form and theme, already linked by overlapping catchwords, in

which the emphasis is on the victorious word of Jesus, and added
3:6 in order to stress the enmity of the Pharisees to Jesus which
will lead to his death.[48]

Maisch is certainly correct that 2:1-12 bears more of the
marks of a miracle story than 3:1-5(6).[49] Her other reasons for
excluding 2:1-12 appear less valid. The absence of the mention
of the Pharisees from the first pericope appears to be part of
the pattern of shifting groups of opponents presented in 2:1-
3:6. The issue of authority to forgive sins in 2:5-10 could also
be considered a matter of correct teaching. Further, her pattern of overlapping catchwords includes 2:1-12 as well: sinners/
sin connects 2:1-12 with 2:(13)15-17 just as sabbath connects
2:23-28 and 3:1-5. Furthermore, the similarities in form between
2:1-12 and 3:1-6--both healing controversies with the miracle
at the end--in contrast to the three middle pericopes, which
contain no healing and are of the standard behavior-question-
justification type, would seem to indicate that one cannot exclude 2:1-12--and not 3:1-5(6)--on the basis of its participation
in the miracle form alone. Nor, as has been noted above, can
her arguments that 3:6 is premarkan, therefore the end of a collection, be sustained. The evidence does not support her hypothetical collection.

On the other hand, Maisch is quite correct in her literary
observation that the conclusion in 3:6 shifts the emphasis of the
material in 2:1(15)-3:5 from Jesus' triumph over his opponents to
the opponents' implacable hostility to Jesus. Mark 3:6 serves to
underline the opposition to Jesus throughout all the controversies.

Heinz-Wolfgang Kuhn: Mark 2:1-28

Kuhn alone attempts to delineate a clear methodology for
establishing collections. He argues for the extension of the
methodology of form criticism, especially the determination of
the function of a tradition in the life of the community, from
individual pericopes to possible collections.[50] A premarkan
collection may be posited when a series of pericopes of similar
form have the same *Sitz im Leben* in the community, individually
and collectively, and when the collection serves the practical
needs of the community but does not serve the intention of the
evangelist.[51]

Kuhn concludes that there was an earlier collection of four units: the healing of the paralytic, the eating with tax collectors and sinners (without vv. 13-14), the question about fasting, and the plucking of grain on the sabbath without its Old Testament reference (vv. 25-26).[52] All four concern Christian practice opposed to Jewish: the Christian claim to forgive sins, table fellowship with sinners, fasting praxis, and not keeping the sabbath law. And all four conflicts are settled by christological arguments: the Son of Man's authority to forgive is grounded not in Jewish argument, but in Jesus' miracle-working power; association with sinners is permissible because Jesus' (the Christian) mission is to sinners; fasting is related to the presence and absence of the bridegroom; and finally the sabbath law is abrogated by the authority of the Son of Man.[53] Verse 28, "the Son of Man is lord *also* of the sabbath," serves as the conclusion not only to its own pericope, but also concludes the entire collection, referring back to the Son of Man's authority to forgive in the first story.[54]

Such arguments would only be useful against those who already accept Jesus, who are already Christians. A Jew would consider the answers irrelevant. These four pericopes, as Kuhn reconstructs their premarkan form, individually and collectively serve the needs of the community against Jewish Christians who accept the full power of the earthly Son of Man.[55]

The final pericope in Mark's section, 3:1-5, is also on the subject of sabbath observance. The argument justifying breaking the sabbath law, however, is grounded not on Jesus' authority but on a "Jewish-type argument," the general principle of good over evil, life over death.[56]

According to Kuhn, the collection is not markan. Mark is not interested in arguments against Jewish Christians. Rather, Mark uses the collection to show the objections of the Jewish authorities to Jesus, and he places the conflicts in connection with the death of Jesus.[57] The earlier collection accounts for the unusual appearances of the title, Son of Man, and also the "too early hints of Jesus about his death" in 2:20.[58]

Kuhn's proposal for a premarkan collection in 2:1-28 contains many helpful observations. His emphasis on the function of the material in the life of the community has led him to make

a useful distinction between the content of the conflict--what
it is all about, forgiveness, sabbath law, etc.--and the type
of argument used to settle the conflict, here appeal to Jesus'
authority *or* "Jewish type." The first four pericopes in Mark
2:1-3:6 presuppose that the opponents accept Jesus' authority;
the last does not. This would seem to be a legitimate basis
for including one healing controversy but excluding the other.
Kuhn has indeed met the first part of his criteria for a collection: several pericopes which individually and collectively
have the same *Sitz im Leben*--controversy with Jewish Christians.

On the other hand, it is less certain that Kuhn has met
the criterion of showing that the collection does not reflect
markan interests. It has already been noted that the use of
Son of Man and the early hints about Jesus' death may well reflect markan concerns.[59] Furthermore, Mark's concern with the
Jewish war, his arguments against Jerusalem and the temple, his
interest in Galilee as the place of the kingdom of God, both
before and after Jesus' death, and his treatment of the disciples,
seem to indicate that Mark is indeed engaged in controversy with
at least some Jewish Christians.[60] In fairness to Kuhn, however,
anti-Jewish-Christian polemic does not appear to be the focus
of 2:1-3:6 as a whole.

Moreover, to say that the function of individual pericopes
and a group of pericopes is the same, is only partially true.
It has already been observed in the discussion of Maisch's proposed collection that the inclusion of 3:6 shifts the emphasis
away from the triumph of Jesus onto the opposition to him. The
literary emphasis also shifts as a result of aggregating the
stories. In the individual story, the stress is on the particular content--e.g., Jesus authorized violation of the sabbath,
therefore we do not have to keep the sabbath. By combining the
four stories, the emphasis shifts in a large measure to the common factor: the authority of Jesus. The collection, although
certainly useful in debate with Jewish Christians, becomes in
itself a proclamation of the "full authority of the Son of Man,"
as Kuhn himself implicitly realized.[61] Kuhn could have strengthened his argument by providing a *Sitz im Leben* for the collection
as a whole--a community or redactor interested in exalting or
defending the earthly authority of the Son of Man.

Kuhn's hypothesis, however, cannot be dismissed outright.[62]
His proposed collection does stress the earthly authority of the
Son of Man, an emphasis which does not occur elsewhere in Mark.
Further, the use of Son of Man in 2:10 and 28 would serve as an
inclusio for such a collection, giving it a rudimentary literary
structure of its own.[63] The presence of a literary structure
which is not the structure of the final text is, for a rhetorical
critic, a strong argument for the existence of an earlier collection. The possibility of Kuhn's collection would seem tenable.

Summary

Maisch's and Kuhn's studies have several implications for
understanding the rhetorical structure of Mark 2:1-3:6. First,
they demonstrate that a shift in literary emphasis occurs when
material is combined and thereby placed in a larger context.
Kuhn, unwittingly perhaps, has shown that individual arguments
useful for a preacher/teacher in a polemic addressed to Jewish
Christians who seem to him too closely bound to the old way,
become a powerful plea for the earthly authority of the Son of
Man when they are combined. And Maisch has shown the shift in
literary emphasis from the triumph of Jesus to the continued
opposition of the opponents, accomplished by the inclusion of
3:6. Second, Kuhn's recognition of the christological emphasis
present in 2:1-28 but absent from 3:1-6, raises the question of
whether Mark's (or a prior redactor of 2:1-3:6) major interest
in presenting the material is christological or whether the
christology is something the redactor accepted, even took for
granted, and used to show the basis of opposition to Jesus, or
for other reasons.

The Possibility of No Premarkan Collection

Although not all scholars explicitly accept the hypothesis
of a premarkan collection (of whatever extent) behind Mark 2:1-
3:6, very few scholars have gone so far as to imply that Mark
compiled the five pericopes himself. J. Weiss in 1903 did suggest that Mark was the compiler.[64] Taylor, as noted, suggested
that Mark compiled 2:1-3:6 prior to his composition of the gospel.[65] E. Trocmé suggests another variant: that Mark composed

2:1-3:6 on the model of Albertz' Jerusalem controversy collection, which Mark used in chapters 11-12.[66]

Recently, scholars have begun to argue against a premarkan Galilean controversy collection. G. Minette de Tillesse, for example, holds that Mark grouped and arranged the stories in 2:1-3:6 on the grounds that the stories reflect Mark's overall theology--his veiled christology or "messianic secret."[67] However, the christology Minette de Tillesse finds so prominent in 2:1-3:6 is found in, and only in, the material Kuhn includes in his proposed premarkan collection.[68]

Anitra Bingham Kolenkow, as a byproduct of her argument for a "healing-controversy gospel" source used independently by Mark and John, has argued against a controversy collection of 2:1-3:6 on form-critical and redactional grounds as well as on theological grounds.[69] Her major thesis is that, in the proposed source, miracles and passion--that is, gospel--are tied together through healing controversy culminating in death threats against Jesus.

Kolenkow observes that the single healing controversy story in John 5:1-18 deals with the same material that Mark covers in the two healing conflicts, Mark 2:1-12 and 3:1-6. There are verbal and content parallels (the "pallet" command to the sick man, sabbath healing, claiming divine power) and both conclude with the Jews attempting to destroy Jesus.[70] The connection to the passion is strengthened by the fact that in Mark the words κατηγορέω and συμβούλιον occur only in Mark 3:1-6 and 15:1-4.[71]

In the proposed source, the tie between controversy and death is found in the healing controversies only. According to Kolenkow, Mark has transformed the healing controversies in form and content from the proto-gospel in order to depict a Jesus who is not legally guilty, a markan interest.[72] Mark has then used the healing controversies of 2:1-12 and 3:1-6 as "passages enclosing and reinforcing the non-healing controversies of 2:15-28."[73] This may well be an example of the markan technique of beginning and ending sections with miracles, as seen in the miracles surrounding 9:30-10:45.[74] The middle stories in 2:1-3:6 are eating controversies, and would help clear the way for inclusion of Gentiles, also a markan interest.[75] Thus, Kolenkow would argue that Mark has composed 2:1-3:6 for his own purposes. Whether or not one accepts Kolenkow's proto-gospel source theory,

the fact that she can propose an explanation of the markan development of traditional material in 2:1-3:6, which excludes the
hypothesis of a Galilean controversy collection, suggests that
no such hypothesis may be necessary.

Kuhn's and Kolenkow's conflicting hypotheses both seem
tenable. However, the feasibility of explaining the theology
and the markan redactional development of the structure of 2:1-
3:6, without positing a premarkan collection, suggests that the
assumption of a premarkan collection may be an unnecessary one.
A redaction critic should perhaps begin by attempting to explain
the material in Mark 2:1-3:6 on the basis of markan compilation,
not on the basis of Mark's use of a prior controversy collection.

Precisely this point was put forward by D.-A. Koch in 1975.[76]
He argues that all the reasons put forward for a collection can
easily be explained without any such assumption:

(1) Neither 3:6 [Albertz and Maisch] nor 2:28 [Kuhn] need
to be explained as premarkan redactional conclusions to a collection. Mark 3:6 is not only a conclusion but points ahead to
the passion, a redactional technique of Mark. Mark 2:28 shows
no recognizable difference from other passages considered to be
markan redaction.

(2) The use of Son of Man in 2:10 and 28 is indeed unusual.
However, neither use is in contradiction with the construction
of the gospel, and both are in conformity with the major theme
begun in Mark 1:21--that of the authority of the earthly one.

(3) The fact of the form-critical and content similarities
of the traditions in 2:1-3:6 is not a proof for a premarkan collection. To place together related traditions would occur to
an evangelist as well as to any other compiler of tradition.

(4) The loose construction of Mark 2:1-3:6 can be understood without difficulty as markan compilation. It does not
point to a markan insertion into a larger narrative.[77]

Koch's first three points are well-taken, although they do
not definitively exclude Kuhn's hypothesis. The fourth cannot
be so readily accepted. The following rhetorical analysis of
Mark 2:1-3:6 will show that the section is in fact a closely
interwoven and tightly constructed literary unit. Further, it
is set in a frame (1:45; 3:7-8) which contrasts sharply with the
material in 2:1-3:6. Mark 2:1-3:6 can certainly qualify for

consideration as a markan insertion or interpolation into a
larger entity. Thus the rhetorical critic wishing to use the
results of the rhetorical analysis of Mark 2:1-3:6 for understanding the literary techniques and theology of the gospel of
Mark as a whole, must be able to argue that 2:1-3:6 is not a
markan insertion into a preexisting narrative but Mark's own
handling of tradition. This question will be returned to in
Chapter Six, following the detailed rhetorical analysis of 2:1-
3:6 and a brief consideration of some rhetorical structures
similar to 2:1-3:6 found elsewhere in Mark. Before turning to
the rhetorical analysis, however, it is necessary to give some
preliminary consideration to structural issues in Mark 11-12.

Mark 11-12
Jerusalem Public Debate

In chapters 11 and 12, Mark once again portrays Jesus
participating in a series of public controversies: Jesus debates the source of his authority (11:27-33); he argues whether
or not taxes should be paid to Caesar (12:13-17), whether or not
there is individual resurrection (12:18-27); he publicly dis-
cusses what is the fundamental demand of God (12:28-34); and he
inquires how the scribes can say that the Christ is the son of
David (12:35-37).

The Jerusalem public debate material presents a different
problem for the literary critic investigating rhetorical structure than did the Galilean public debate in Mark 2:1-3:6. The
Galilean section, as we saw, constituted a coherent literary
sub-unit within Mark's gospel as determined by form, content,
and contrast with surrounding materials. The only major preliminary issue, still unresolved, is whether the unity is markan
or premarkan.

The Jerusalem debates, on the other hand, are not a literary unit on the basis of form, content, or contrast with surrounding material. They are not even all contiguous. Further,
the climax of conflict between Jesus and his opponents in chapters 11-12 is not primarily associated with the public debates.
As in 3:6, twice in 11-12, the reader is informed of Jesus' opponents' desire to destroy or arrest him. The first instance
follows Jesus' cleansing of the temple (11:18), and the second

follows his teaching of the allegorical parable of the wicked tenants (12:12). Most of the debate material follows 12:12. Indeed, why the public debates are placed during the Jerusalem public ministry is not obvious.[78] Between the opening confrontation between Jesus and the Jewish leaders in the temple cleansing and the parable of the wicked tenants at the beginning, and the great eschatological discourse to the inner circle of disciples in Chapter 13, fall the public debates with the attached warning against the scribes and the story of the widow's mite. This material appears to destroy the topical and dramatic narrative development of Mark 11-13. It seems rather miscellaneous in content and definitely tame in comparison to the rest of Jesus' Jerusalem ministry.

Yet, the public debates are the second major block of such material in Mark, and they occupy a substantial portion of the Jerusalem ministry. As in the case of 2:1-3:6, scholars have resorted to hypotheses of a premarkan collection or literary pattern to explain the Jerusalem debate material. Before turning to a brief review and critique of their theories, an overview of the narrative of Mark 11-12 from a literary perspective will be made to provide a basis for further discussion.

Overview of the Narrative of Mark 11-12 From a Literary Perspective

As has long been recognized, the Jerusalem ministry in Mark is divided into three days: the day of the entry into Jerusalem (10:46-11:11), the day of the cleansing of the temple (11:12-19), and the third day, which includes public debates, public teaching, private teaching, and Jesus' long, private discourse on the future (11:20-13:37). Following the three day chronology, the overview will focus primarily on narrative interconnection and structure.

Day One

Day one contains two incidents, the healing of the blind Bartimaeus on the way to Jerusalem (10:46-52) and the triumphal scene at the entrance to Jerusalem (11:1-11).[79] These two scenes provide a transition from the predominately private teaching of the way section (8:27-10:45) to the public Jerusalem ministry,

and serve as a prologue to the Jerusalem ministry itself.[80]   In
both pericopes, the reader is reminded of Jesus' popularity with
the crowd, and is prepared for the role of the crowd in the
Jerusalem ministry proper.[81]

Secondly, the motif of Davidic messianism occurs in both
pericopes. Bartimaeus, while still blind, twice addresses Jesus
as "Son of David" (10:47-48). The crowd cries out as Jesus rides
on the colt towards Jerusalem: "Blessed is the coming kingdom
of our father David" (11:10). These are the first mentions of
Davidic messianism in the gospel of Mark, and they occur precisely at the point when Jesus is about to enter the city of
David.

Day Two

Day two contains the first major event of Jesus' public
ministry in Jerusalem, Jesus' acting out the proleptic fall of
the temple.[82]   Jesus casts out those buying and selling; he
overturns the tables and seats of the money changers and dove
sellers (11:15). Alluding to Jeremiah's speech that God will
once again permit the temple to fall, Jesus accuses the cult
leaders of making the temple "a den of thieves" (Jer 7:11, Mk
11:17). In the temple cleansing, Jesus takes the initiative
strongly against the Jewish authorities, and they indeed take
offense. The reader is told that the chief priests and the
scribes wish to destroy Jesus but fear the crowd (11:18). In
the gospel of Mark, Jesus' dramatic act in the temple is the
precipitating cause of his death.

The temple cleansing is framed by--or, in other words, it
is an interposition in--the story of the cursing and withering
of the fig tree, "for it was not the season for figs" (11:12-14,
20-25).[83]   It is no longer the time of Israel. The incident of
the fig tree and its associated teaching is private, witnessed
by the disciples only. It is not part of the public Jerusalem
ministry. By the device of the shift in audience, and the interposition-frame technique, the fig tree material is rhetorically
set apart from the main development of the narrative of Jesus'
public ministry.[84]

Day Three

The second half of the fig tree episode begins day three.[85]
This fact, plus the overloading of material on day three, indicates that the rhetorical structure of the Jerusalem ministry
does not coincide with the chronological division into days. Day
three continues with seven pericopes, either debates or teaching,
all set in the temple and witnessed by the crowd.

The controversy apophthegm on authority (11:27-33). When
Jesus enters the temple the next day, the chief priests, scribes
and elders, the representatives of the full Sanhedrin, question
Jesus on his authority to do "these things" (11:28). The logical narrative antecedent of "these things" is Jesus' acts and
words in the temple cleansing.[86] Jesus, by bringing up the
question of John the Baptist's authority, avoids answering the
question.

The parable of the wicked tenants (12:1-12). Jesus, however, immediately proceeds to tell the allegorical parable of
the wicked tenants, in which the owner of the vineyard "will
come and destroy the tenants, and give the vineyard to others"
(12:9). They--the priests, scribes and elders of 11:27--recog-
nize that the parable is told against them and wish to arrest
him. But again they fear the crowd and leave Jesus (12:12).
The first three pericopes recounting Jesus' public ministry
in Jerusalem--the temple cleansing, the question on authority,
and Jesus' parable against the tenants--constitute a dramatic
and thematic unity.[87] In all three, the characters are Jesus,
the crowd, and the legitimate Jewish authority, members of the
Sanhedrin. In all three, the authorities fear the crowd (11:18,
32; 12:12). In structure, the pericopes may be considered an
extended controversy apophthegm of the action-objection-vindication type. Jesus' objectionable behavior is the cleansing of
the temple; the opponents question his authority for so doing;
Jesus avoids a direct answer, but through the parable condemning
the tenants, implicitly claims to have God's authority.
The issue of the controversy is a fundamental one: essentially whether Jesus or the legitimate temple authorities speak
for God. This is brought out even in Jesus' counter-question on

authority: τὸ βάπτισμα τὸ 'Ιωάννου ἐξ οὐρανοῦ ἦν ἢ ἐξ ἀνθρώπων;
The level of conflict is high: Jesus prophesies God's destruction of the authorities, and they, on the other hand, seek to
destroy Jesus. The confrontation, however, is not yet to be
resolved. The authorities fear to act because of Jesus' popularity with the crowd. For the moment, Jesus is left unharmed
in the temple and the atmosphere of confrontation fades away.

Three questions (12:13-17, 18-27, 28-34). First, the opponents of the preceding pericopes, the legitimate Jewish political
authority, send the Pharisees and Herodians to try to catch Jesus
in his talk. The introduction of the Pharisees and Herodians
recalls to the reader's mind the earlier controversies in 2:1-
3:6, and the Pharisees' and Herodians' determination at that
time to destroy Jesus. In their question about the legitimacy
of paying taxes to Caesar, an attempt to discredit Jesus with
the crowd, Jesus adroitly avoids the horns of the political
dilemma. The Sadducees, another Jewish religious group, then
question Jesus about the resurrection, and Jesus informs them
their understanding is wrong. Finally a single scribe questions
Jesus about the fundamental commandment, and Jesus and the scribe
agree on the basic demands of God. At this point, Jesus is
triumphant and no one dares question him further (12:34).

Public teaching (12:35-37, 38-40). Immediately after the
school debate in which Jesus and a scribe are portrayed in agreement with each other, two examples of Jesus' teaching criticizing
the scribes are appended. First, Jesus questions the scribes'
understanding of the Christ as the Son of David; then he warns
against them, criticizing their behavior and prophesying their
condemnation.

Private teaching (12:41-44, 13:1-2, 3-37). In 12:41-44,
Jesus points out to his disciples the good example of the poor
widow contributing to the temple treasury. Next, Jesus and his
disciples leave the temple, and Jesus prophesies the destruction
of the temple. Jesus' earlier act of cleansing the temple is
recalled to the reader's mind. Finally the third day ends with
Jesus' extended discourse on the future with the inner circle
of disciples, the apocalyptic discourse.

Summary

The first day forms a prologue to the Jerusalem ministry.
The second day, and the first incidents of the third day, spell
out the conflict, between Jesus and the legitimate Jewish power,
over who truly represents God. The conflict is not resolved
because of the presence of the crowd. Then the obvious coherence
of the narrative and its dramatic effect are dissipated in a
series of questions and public teachings of Jesus. In one
scholar's words, "The stories do not form any easily recognizable
pattern nor do they rise to a climax."[88] Then, after an apparently unrelated episode of private teaching, the narrative reverts
to the theme of the destruction of the temple and future events.
The problem for the rhetorical critic is to explain or account
for the two controversies over taxes and the resurrection, the
school debate on the first commandment, and the assorted public
and private teaching in the temple.

Proposed Explanations of the Jerusalem Public Debate Material

Solutions External to the Text

Martin Albertz. As well as positing a Galilean controversy
collection, Albertz also posited a Jerusalem one, collected by
a different circle.[89] It too consists of five controversies,
the debate on authority, the questions on tribute, resurrection,
the great commandment, and David's son (11:27-33; 12:13-37).
Albertz based his argument for a collection on the inner uniformity of the material which concerns the five most important
issues of the Judaism of the day, and in which Jesus as teacher
triumphs over all opponents in turn.[90] For the collector, the
question was Jesus or the Rabbis?[91] The collection, he argued,
could not be markan because it contains no hint of the coming
suffering and death of Jesus, and so stands in sharp contrast
to the other material found in Mark 11-12.[92]

Albertz' hypothesis, although accepted by some,[93] has not
received the wide acceptance that his proposed Galilean controversy collection did. Neither Knox,[94] who delighted in sources,
nor Kuhn,[95] saw sufficient grounds to posit any premarkan collection in Mark 11-12. The inner uniformity of the collection
is to be doubted. The diversity of forms has already been noted.

Only the first, the question on authority, is a controversy
apophthegm arising out of Jesus' behavior. The second and third
(taxes and resurrection) belong to Bultmann's category of "questions asked by opponents." They might better be described as
hostile school debates. The fourth is a friendly school debate,
and the last is not a debate at all.

In terms of content, the first story of the proposed collection, the demand for the source of Jesus' authority, and the
last, the question of David's son, do not concern the most important issues of first century *Judaism*. And, strictly speaking,
the sequence of opponents ends with the third story. The fourth
debate is initiated by a single scribe--who, as an opponent, is
already included among the opponents of the first story; the
last story has no opponents.[96] Thus, while Albertz is certainly
correct that at least some of the debates are in sharp contrast
to the other contents of Mark 11-12, the debate material does
not have sufficient unity or coherence to be considered a collection.

David Daube. Daube argues that the four pericopes, 12:13-
37, are modelled on the Alexandrian pattern of four questions,
particularly the questions of the four sons at the Passover
Haggadah.[97] (He does not argue whether it was Mark or an earlier
compiler who structured the material in this way.) Daube's
theory cannot be sustained. It is questionable whether the
Passover Haggadah pattern was so fixed a pattern at the time.[98]
The more serious problem is that the questions in Mark do not
really fit the types of the Haggadah questions. Above all, the
issue of the Christ as David's son is not a comparison of two
scriptures both of which are true in some sense, but rather a
contrast between the views of scripture and those of the scribes,
similar to that found in Mark 7.

Summary. In analyzing the public debate material in Mark
11-12, the rhetorical critic who wishes to generalize from the
results to the gospel of Mark as a whole need not be concerned
with the possibility that the rhetorical structure is due to a
premarkan collection or pattern.

Internal Solutions

The lack of viability of the suggestions for a premarkan
controversy collection and a nonmarkan structural pattern in
Mark 11-12, combined with the trend in America for redaction
criticism to move towards general literary criticism, has led
two scholars to look briefly at the markan text to see if any
structure is to be discerned in it.

John Donahue. Donahue, in his brief investigation of the
literary structure of 11-12, views 11:1-27 as the introduction,
built up by a careful sequence of temporal and geographical
units; 11:27-12:12 as the "midpiece" of the section, culminating
in the second reference to the Sanhedrin's desire to arrest
Jesus; and 12:13-44 as a "loose Marcan construction by means of
sequential appearances of adversaries and catchwords."[99] The
great commandment, the question of David's son, and the denunciation of the scribes are connected by the catchword, "scribe,"
while the story of the widow's mite is joined to the denunciation
of the scribes because of the catchword, "widow."

Donahue has noted the connection between the question on
authority and the parable of the wicked tenants, and the new
beginning in 12:13. He has noted the hook word sequence, but
not that such construction in Mark is often an indicator of more
complex structural relationships.

Norman Perrin. Perrin, in his brief exegetical remarks on
Mark 12 in his New Testament *Introduction*, has noted some rhetorical units within 12:13-44.[100] Mark 12:13-34 is a unit of
three controversies in which the first two questioners are
hostile and the last sympathetic. Perrin suggests that the contrast is deliberate. Mark 12:35-40 reports two stories critical
of the scribes. Finally, the chapter closes with the story of
the widow's mite, which points ahead in the gospel to the sacri-
fice of Jesus.

Perrin, like Donahue, notes that a new beginning is made in
12:13. He goes beyond Donahue's "loose Marcan construction" to
note structural groupings of the material in 12:13-44. Perrin's
analysis suggests a rudimentary pattern or coherence to Mark 12.
It remains for the rhetorical critic to analyze the material from

a rhetorical perspective to find out if the structure is more
than rudimentary, and to see how the rhetorical structure (or
lack of it) helps to illumine the function of the debates in
the Jerusalem public ministry. The subject will be taken up
again in Chapter Five.

CHAPTER III

FIRST READING OF MARK 2:1-3:6

It is now time to turn to the detailed rhetorical analysis
of Mark 2:1-3:6, to see how the methodology outlined in Chapter
One--that of first studying the text for its use of rhetorical
techniques and its indications of literary structure, and then
seeing how this analysis helps us to understand the meaning of
the text--helps to illumine the meaning of 2:1-3:6 for the
reader. For it is the task of the rhetorical critic to educate
and sensitize the reader/hearer to the experience of reading--
or listening to--the text of the gospel of Mark.

The following rhetorical analysis of 2:1-3:6 consists of
two parts: first, an analysis of the literary techniques and
rhetorical structure in each of the five individual pericopes,
and, second, a study of the structure of 2:1-3:6 as a whole.
The two parts may be better described as two successive readings
of the text. The first reading is a linear or progressive reading, stressing the major rhetorical features and smaller structural units as they occur in the narrative. The second reading
is an architectonic or rhythmic reading of the text as a whole.
The second reading will build upon the first, and call attention
to new--and in this instance, elaborate--interrelationships of
the material. It will discuss what light the rhetorical analysis
sheds on the meaning of the section as a whole. The first reading will be presented in this chapter; the second in the following one.

In the course of the rhetorical analysis, various exegetical,
and upon occasion, redactional conclusions will be drawn. However, no systematic attempt will be made to address redactional
questions. The rhetorical approach is not a branch of the redactional enterprise. The rhetorical critic is not asking the
historical question of how and why Mark has redacted the tradition to form the present text. The rhetorical critic is asking
the *literary* question of how the rhetorical features of the
present text--structure, pattern, rhythm--affect the reader's
response to and understanding of that text.

65

Since the rhetorical approach builds upon form criticism,
the first reading, the analysis of the individual pericopes,
will begin with a consideration of the form of the pericope.
It will then continue with a discussion of the rhetorical structure and other rhetorical features to be found in the individual
elements of the pericope and in the pericope as a whole. The
rhetorical interconnections of a pericope with the one that
preceded it will be noted. Exegetical conclusions will be
pointed out, as the analysis warrants.

Mark 2:1-12: The Healing of the Paralytic

The story of the healing of the paralytic with its controversy over Jesus' authority to forgive sins is, in form, a healing
controversy of the second type, with the healing at the end.
The exposition or narrative introduction is unusually long and
detailed: vv. 1-2 serve as a general introduction, setting the
scene; vv. 3-4 set up the healing situation; and v. 5 starts
the actual healing. Then, for vv. 6-10a, the healing is sus-
pended, while some scribes and Jesus enter into conflict.[1]
Verses 10b-12a resume and complete the healing, and v. 12b concludes the narrative, presenting the crowd reaction. Thus, vv.
6-10a are an interposition in the miracle narrative, giving the
pericope a circular rhythm.[2]

The narrative may be outlined as follows:

> a   Introduction (vv. 1-2)
>   Healing (vv. 3-5)
>
> b   Controversy (vv. 6-10a)
>
> a' Healing (vv. 10b-12a)
>   Conclusion (v. 12b)

As the text now stands, Mark 2:1-12 is a complex, carefully
constructed story, characterized by abrupt shifts in the plot
line *and* careful rhetorical intertwining of the elements of the
story. The individual elements will first be discussed separately.

Rhetorical Analysis of the Individual Elements

Verses 1-2. The opening of the story is itself an abrupt break in the plot line from the preceding pericope. The first chapter of Mark ends with Jesus' healing the leper, and the leper spreading the news "so that Jesus could no longer openly enter a town, but was out in the country; and people came to him from every quarter" (1:45b, RSV). Mark 2 opens with Jesus returning to Capernaum. According to the gospel of Mark, the first thing Jesus does after not being able openly to enter a city is to enter a city. The contrast (or contradiction) emphasizes the new narrative beginning.[3]

Yet Mark 2:1-2 is carefully tied to 1:45 by the use of three hook words (or hook phrases) presented in chiastic order:[4]

1:45   τὸν λόγον, ὥστε μηκέτι...εἰσελθεῖν

2:1-2   εἰσελθὼν...ὥστε μηκέτι...τὸν λόγον

These are the only two occurrences of the phrase ὥστε μηκέτι in Mark, and the first two uses of λόγος which does not recur until 4:14. Thus the reader/hearer is presented with a sharp disjunction in content,[5] and by means of the hook words, continuity in sound. The audience is given the double message: Mark 2:1 is a break in the narrative and a new beginning; at the same time, the content following the break is in some way related to the material preceding it.

It is conceivable, of course, that hook words occur here simply to bridge or form a transition between otherwise disparate material. That in fact they indicate some interrelationship of the material in Mark 1 and 2 is confirmed by the number of other words in 2:1-2 that recall the first chapter. Πάλιν εἰς Καφαρναούμ reminds the reader of the first time Jesus entered Capernaum (1:21). The "house" presumably refers to Simon and Andrew's house in Capernaum which Jesus first entered in 1:29. On that occasion, the whole city gathered (ἐπισυνάγω) "at the door" (1:33); on this occasion, so many gathered (συνάγω) that there was no room "even at the door" (2:2). The numbers of people seeking out Jesus have steadily increased in the interval.

Mark 2:1-2 is a typical introductory or transition scene, complete in itself. Jesus appears at some place; a crowd, variously described, collects around Jesus; and Jesus teaches them--

here, "speaks the word"--without any specific teaching being
given.[6] The little scene emphasizes both Jesus' popularity with
the crowd--that the people sought him out--and that Jesus' typical response on such occasions was to teach them.[7]
In this instance, the summary scene also sets the stage for
the episode to follow. Mark's audience knows that Jesus is in
a house, and that the doorway is blocked by people. The audience
is prepared for the coming story in which people will dig through
the roof as the only way to approach Jesus.
Thus, vv. 1-2 accomplish multiple functions in terms of the
narrative of Mark. From the abrupt shift in setting from 1:45,
from the hook words and the other ties to Mark 1, the hearer
knows that there has been a definite break in the narrative, and
also some connection to what went before. Jesus' popularity and
teaching activity have been stressed. And the scene has been
set for the next event. A great deal has been packed into these
two transition verses.

Verses 3-5. These verses do not continue with the content
of Jesus' "word," but begin the healing narrative proper. Verses
3-4 are full of picturesque detail, often characteristic of the
miracle form.[8] Four people carrying a paralytic cannot reach
Jesus "on account of the crowd." Here, for the first time, Mark
uses the word ὄχλος. So, the four with the paralytic climb the
roof, dig through it, and lower the paralytic upon his pallet
before Jesus. Jesus responds by addressing the sick man directly:
"Child, your sins are forgiven."

Verses 6-10a, the interposition. Verse 6 presents another
abrupt plot shift. The story is interrupted to inform the
hearer that there are some scribes present in the house who
wonder about Jesus' statement. For the moment, the paralytic
is forgotten, and Jesus holds a theological debate with the
scribes. Then in v. 10b, equally abruptly, employing an anacoluthon, the plot shifts back. The scribes are forgotten, and
Jesus is speaking to the paralytic. Jesus' two addresses to
the paralytic serve as a frame for the interposition:

> v 5:   λέγει τῷ παραλυτικῷ, Τέκνον, ἀφίενταί σου αἱ
>   ἁμαρτίαι

vv 10b-11a: λέγει τῷ παραλυτικῷ, Σοὶ λέγω, ἔγειρε ἆρον
τὸν κράβαττόν σου καὶ ὕπαγε εἰς τὸν οἶκόν σου

A frame, it may be remembered, is defined as something which
frames another unit at its beginning and its end, but which itself is not part of the unit framed.[9] In the final narrative,
both speeches to the sick man are not part of the theological
debate with the scribes, but are part of the healing in which
the scribes do not appear. The repetition of λέγει τῷ παραλυτικῷ
may or may not indicate compilation of sources or traditions.[10]
The repetition does, however, function for the hearer as a frame
to block off the theological debate from the healing, and it
also functions to stress the parallelism of the two speeches to
the paralytic.

The interposition itself is a nicely balanced unit making
extensive use of repetition for varying purposes. The text laid
out to reveal its structure will help to illustrate the point:

6 ἦσαν δέ τινες τῶν γραμματέων ἐκεῖ καθήμενοι καὶ διαλογιζόμενοι
      ἐν ταῖς καρδίαις αὐτῶν,

7 Τί οὗτος οὕτως λαλεῖ; Βλασφημεῖ·
      τίς δύναται ἀφιέναι ἁμαρτίας εἰ μὴ εἷς ὁ θεός;

8 καὶ εὐθὺς ἐπιγνοὺς ὁ Ἰησοῦς τῷ πνεύματι αὐτοῦ ὅτι οὕτως
      διαλογίζονται ἐν ἑαυτοῖς λέγει αὐτοῖς,

   Τί ταῦτα διαλογίζεσθε ἐν ταῖς καρδίαις ὑμῶν;
9 τί ἐστιν εὐκοπώτερον,
      εἰπεῖν τῷ παραλυτικῷ, Ἀφίενταί σου αἱ ἁμαρτίαι,
      ἢ εἰπεῖν, Ἔγειρε καὶ ἆρον τὸν κράβαττόν σου καὶ
      περιπάτει;

10 ἵνα δὲ εἰδῆτε ὅτι ἐξουσίαν ἔχει ὁ υἱὸς τοῦ ἀνθρώπου ἀφιέναι
      ἁμαρτίας ἐπὶ τῆς γῆς--

The scribes, new characters on the scene, are described
debating in their hearts two unspoken questions beginning with
τί and τίς respectively (vv. 6-7). Then Jesus is described
knowing that the scribes are debating among themselves, and responds with two spoken counter-questions, both beginning with
τί (vv. 8-9). The scribes first question why Jesus speaks like
like this; Jesus first asks why the scribes debate these things.
So far the form and content are parallel to each other.

Jesus' second question introduces a new element: "Is it
easier to say to the paralytic, 'your sins are forgiven,' or to
say, 'rise and take up your bed and walk?'" (v. 9). Of course,
it is as easy--or as hard--to say the one as to say the other.[11]
The counter-question may serve to emphasize that the two sayings
are in fact equivalent in meaning.[12] Finally, however, Jesus
does answer the scribes' questions directly:[13] ἵνα δὲ εἰδῆτε.
Οὗτος--the one they spoke of contemptuously[14]--is in fact the
Son of Man (vv. 7a,10); he is able (δύναται v. 7b); he has
authority (ἐξουσίαν v. 10a) to forgive sins (ἀφιέναι ἁμαρτίας
vv. 7b and 10a) on earth. He is the one besides God who forgives. The implication is clear: if one accepts the authority
of the Son of Man, what Jesus speaks is not blasphemy. The
interposition is completed. The presence of the scribes and
the theological argument over who may forgive are ended.

Verses 10b-12. The story, however, is not. Without grammatical transition, the healing is resumed. Jesus commands the
paralytic by word to rise and take up his pallet. The paralytic
does so and leaves. Then the reaction of the crowd is given.[15]
The action of the paralytic and the response of the people are
joined by the repetition of the hook word πάντων/πάντας: the
paralytic went out before everyone so everyone is amazed (v. 12).
The story ends with the crowd glorifying God.

The Ring Composition as a Rhetorical Unit

The devices giving unity to the theological debate, the
interposition or middle part of the ring composition have already been noted: the addresses to the paralytic framing the
interposition, the shift in content, the balanced questions and
counter-questions of the scribes and Jesus, and finally, in
v. 10a, Jesus' direct answer, introduced as such, to the scribes'
questions.

Likewise the outer parts of the ring, the beginning and
ending healing segments, have their own unity and balance--in
this instance introverted parallelism.[16] The healing begins
with the crowd pressing around Jesus; into this scene the paralytic is lowered upon his pallet. The healing ends with the
paralytic rising and leaving, carrying his pallet; the crowd

then responds, "We have never seen anything like this." The
crowd brackets the coming and going of the paralytic, but plays
no part at all in the interposition.

Word repetition serving to unify the ring composition.
Further, the parts of the ring composition are rhetorically interconnected. The junctures between the healing and the debate are
bridged at the beginning and end by the repetition of hook phrases:
the content of the first address to the paralytic is repeated in
the debate and the reverse occurs at the other end. Unlike the
hook words which connect 2:1-2 with 1:45 which provide continuity
of sound but not narrative or content continuity, the hook phrases
here provide continuity in content as well as aural continuity.[17]
Jesus' declaration of the forgiveness of sins to the paralytic
gives way to the scribes' question over who has the ability to
forgive sins (vv. 5-7). Jesus' question to the scribes, "Is it
easier...to say, rise and take up your pallet," leads into Jesus'
command to the paralytic to rise and take up his pallet (vv. 9-
11). The repetitions serve to interconnect the narrative--and
the thought--of the interposition and the outer ring.

The second juncture, that between the debate and the completion of the healing, is especially complex because there is
the grammatical disjunction of the anacoluthon *and* the continuity
in thought. The first direct coupling of forgiveness and the
command to rise occurs entirely within the debate (v. 9). The
second bridges the anacoluthon (vv. 10-11), and is only fully
completed when the paralytic rises and collects his pallet in
v. 12. The debate is set off from the healing, but at the same
time interwoven with it.

Word repetitions serving other functions. Λέγω, in connection with Jesus' speaking, serves as a key word or motif bringing out the thought of the pericope.[18] Three times Jesus engages
in direct speech: in the frame before the apophthegm, he *says*
to the paralytic; near the middle of the apophthegm, he *says* to
the scribes; and in the frame after the apophthegm, he *says* to
the paralytic (vv. 5,8,10b). In all three instances the form
is λέγει. These uses do help to structure the composition. In
addition, Jesus uses the word three times in direct discourse:

Jesus asks the scribes if it is easier to *say* this or to *say* that (εἰπεῖν both times, v. 9). He does not ask which is easier to do or accomplish. And finally, Jesus opens his second address to the paralytic with the emphatic *and* redundant Σοὶ λέγω (v. 11). The emphasis throughout is on Jesus' speaking or saying. Jesus is the one who speaks; since the paralytic does rise, Jesus' words may indeed be words of power.[19]

The use of λαλέω might be seen as part of the motif of Jesus as speaker. In v. 2, Jesus "was speaking the word" to the crowd.[20] However, the second use of the word suggests that its function may be to point up contrast. After Jesus has told the paralytic his sins are forgiven, the scribes debate (silently): Τί οὗτος οὕτως λαλεῖ; Βλασφημεῖ; (v. 7). This use of λαλέω--which could be omitted without affecting the sense of the line[21]--recalls v. 2. On the one hand, Jesus speaks "the word,"--that is, the gospel or good news. On the other, what the scribes hear him speak is "blasphemy." Here, for the first time in Mark, the reader (and Jesus) are made aware that there is opposition to Jesus and his message. The opposition is still tentative: it is only "some of the scribes" (v. 6); they only debate in their hearts, not out loud (vv. 6,8a,b); they do not yet question Jesus or his disciples directly; they are still far from the point of moving against Jesus. But opposition has arisen. And the basis for the opposition concerns a fundamental matter: Jesus is either speaking for/as God when he says, "Your sins are forgiven," or, as the story is told, he is speaking blasphemy.[22] There is no possible compromise.

Nor, as the story is told, is compromise or evasion Jesus' way. Rather he asserts directly that the Son of Man has authority on earth (v. 10a). Here repetition is used in yet a different way to highlight the Son of Man saying. The saying is almost entirely surrounded by repetitive material--that is, information already known to the reader. Three times we have been told that the scribes are debating in their hearts; four times we are told about forgiveness of sins; three times we hear about the paralytic rising and taking up his pallet, first in a question, then in a command to the paralytic, and finally in the report that the paralytic does so. In the midst of all this reiteration,[23] the statement that the Son of Man has authority on earth stands out. The effect of the repetitiveness is to stress the new information--the Son of Man saying.[24] Neither the scribes within the story nor the reader hearing the story is likely to miss Jesus' claim. Either Jesus has legitimate authority as the Son of Man or he is blaspheming; the scribes--and Mark's audience-- must choose.

However, although no middle ground is possible, the issue need not yet be joined. The use of the ring composition technique enables the narrator to revert to the healing, thereby avoiding immediate confrontation on the issue of Jesus' authority, while still completing the story. The issue of the grounds for conflict has been stated, but the conflict does not yet dominate the stage. This is confirmed by the response of the people at the end of the story. They are amazed and glorify God (not Jesus) saying they have never seen anything like this. They react to the healing/forgiving of the paralytic, not to the conflict with the scribes.[25]

Summary of the rhetorical analysis. The rhetorical analysis of Mark 2:1-12 has shown it to be a carefully constructed narrative that fits together into a literary whole. The introduction brings out both the discontinuity and the continuity of the following material with Mark 1. The employment of the ring composition, the healing encircling the debate, enables the narrator to reinforce the parallelism of forgiveness of sins and healing, and to raise separately the question of Jesus' authority to forgive.

The frame-interposition technique also in effect brackets the theme of opposition to Jesus within the already established theme of his popularity. Hostility to Jesus' healing/forgiving activity--and its implied claim--is made known to the reader by the objections of the scribes in the center. The popularity of Jesus is reflected in the crowd streaming to him at the beginning of the narrative and in their response to the miracle at the end. By means of the interposition, the hostility toward Jesus by the scribes and the popularity of Jesus with the crowd are placed side by side before the reader, in tension with each other. The reader is aware of both characters--the scribes and the crowd; the reader knows that the same words/deeds of Jesus

aroused both serious opposition and immense popularity. The
interposition blocked off by a frame has been used to separate
the reactions of the scribes and the crowd. Neither character
is shown dominating the course of the whole narrative; each is
dominant in its own portion.[26] So the reader is left to keep
both (conflicting) realities in mind. He is not told how to
reconcile the two, or which, if either, will eventually prevail.

Lastly, the motif of Jesus' speaking (keyword λέγω, see
also λαλέω) is found throughout the ring composition. It stresses
the power of Jesus' word and also points to the basis of the
conflicting attitudes toward Jesus: is Jesus' word from/of God
or not?

Exegetical Notes on Mark 2:1-12

Rhetorical analysis as a methodology does not claim to
answer all exegetical questions. Since its concern is with the
final text, it is not designed to answer historical questions
of tradition and redaction, although upon occasion it may offer
additional arguments. A rhetorical analysis should, however,
shed light on how a text is to be understood. If it is a useful tool, it should resolve some exegetical problems. Above
all, it should serve as a control limiting the possible ways in
which a text may be interpreted.

The following discussion, then, indicates some ways in
which the rhetorical analysis of Mark 2:1-12 may aid or clarify
its exegesis. The story of the paralytic with its interwoven
theological debate is a good test case for the usefulness of
the rhetorical method since the story bristles with form-critical
and exegetical difficulties. The relevance of the rhetorical
analysis to three areas will be discussed: first, the stylistic
or narrative "clumsiness" of the passage; second, the relation
of forgiveness to healing; and third, the occurrence of "Son of
Man" in v. 10.

Stylistic and narrative "clumsiness." Many scholars have
noted the "clumsy" style of the pericope--the "awkward"[27] repetition of λέγει τῷ παραλυτικῷ in vv. 5 and 10; the fact that
the scribes are not introduced into the story until v. 6; the
grammatical disjunction of v. 10; the fact that the ending

appears to have nothing to do with the debate, and that the hostile scribes, instead of reacting to Jesus' claim in v. 10a, appear to be among the "all" who glorify God in v. 12. And most have explained this "clumsiness" on the grounds that at some point in the development of the pericope the apophthegmatic material was interpolated into a simple healing story.[28]

In fact, most of the so-called literary "difficulties" of the narrative are the result of the failure of the critics to recognize the literary structure of the passage, its ring composition. The repetition of λέγει τῷ παραλυτικῷ within the rhetorical pattern is an effective aural device (conscious or unconscious) to call the reader's attention to the parallelism of Jesus' two addresses to the paralytic, and to frame the debate in the center.

The fact that the scribes do not appear until v. 6 and have disappeared completely in the ending is also the result of the ring composition. In a and a', the characters are Jesus, the crowd, and the paralytic; in b, the interposition, the characters are Jesus and the scribes. Thus each part of the story conforms to Olrik's law of no more than three characters. The paralytic is the subject of the debate, but not at that point a character in the plot.[29] Since the scribes play an active role only in b, it is appropriate that they should be introduced at the beginning of it (v. 6), and fade out at the end. The "character" who responds to the healing in a' is the "character" who witnessed the beginning in a, the crowd. The "all" of v. 12 recalls the "many" of v. 2. The crowd's response also fits with the ring composition: they react to the miracle, a and a', their part of the story, and not to the content of the debate with the scribes.

The grammatical difficulties of v. 10 remain. The shift from direct to indirect discourse is not necessarily clumsy: it is permissible Greek[30] and both Matthew and Luke keep the basic syntax.[31] As E. Lohmeyer writes, "wie sollte der Erzähler ein Wort an den Lahmen anders einführen."[32] The result, however, is to bind the interposition closely to its setting, which does produce a problem. "That you may know" in v. 10a, addressed to the scribes, implies clearly that they witness the healing described in vv. 11-12a, and so form part of the "all" of v. 12.[33]

Nonetheless, the reaction of "all" in v. 12 appears to be a
typical crowd response to a miracle--what one would expect given
the circular structure of the pericope. The scribes are no
longer in the narrator's mind.[34]

Thus rhetorical analysis can offer an explanation for most
of the stylistic phenomena which have been deemed awkward and
have been adduced as evidence for interpolation or two-stage historical development. The rhetorical analysis of Mark 2:1-12 reveals the present text to be a literary unity, a carefully constructed ring composition in which the outer parts and the center
are extensively interwoven and in which these stylistic phenomena
have their place. Of course, the rhetorical explanation of the
phenomena does not exclude the possibility of an interpolation;
it simply means that stylistic clumsiness is not a valid reason
for arguing for an interpolation. The style is not clumsy.

The relationship between forgiveness and healing. Only
here in the synoptic tradition is forgiveness associated with
healing;[35] and only here and in the story in Luke 7:36-50 about
the sinful woman annointing Jesus' feet does Jesus explicitly
forgive (or announce forgiveness). So exegetes have been
troubled to explain why the issue of forgiveness is debated in
the midst of a healing narrative. The question may perhaps best
be approached through a consideration of the form of the pericope. Bultmann considered it a mixed form, part apophthegm and
part miracle story.[36] He argued that the subject matter of
forgiveness was interpolated into an ordinary healing narrative
in which Jesus' only command to the paralytic was the command
to rise and take up his pallet.[37] According to this interpretation, both the fact that Jesus forgives and the question about
his authority to do so belong to the controversy apophthegm.
For Bultmann, the apophthegm is inserted into a healing narrative so that the miracle may serve as proof of the otherwise
invisible forgiveness. There is no inherent connection between
healing and forgiveness. In this understanding, the controversy
is about forgiveness and the right to forgive, and the miracle
functions as Jesus' final, triumphant retort. The story, strictly
speaking, would not be a healing controversy in form since the
conflict is not about healing.

Dibelius, on the other hand, does not view the pericope as a mixed or hybrid form. He classifies it as a paradigm of the "pure" type, not as a miracle tale.[38] Dibelius' classification scheme does not concern us; his analysis of the pericope that led to his classification does. Dibelius like Bultmann divides the narrative into two content issues. However, he makes the split between healing and the fact of forgiveness on the one side, and the issue of the right to forgive sins on the other.[39] "The first issue, forgiveness of sins, or healing, is crossed by a second: Who can forgive sins?"[40] In this view, the miracle is not an extraneous act brought in to justify the forgiveness; rather the argument moves from Jesus' healing/forgiving activity to his authority to heal/forgive. The outer story tells the miracle, the center deals with the "worth of the miracle worker."[41] Here we have a healing controversy of the second type, with the healing at the end. The controversy, in this understanding, is like the other healing controversies in Mark (3:1-6, 22-30) in that the controversy is over some aspect of Jesus' healing, acting unlawfully on the sabbath, or acting by the power of Beezebul not God.

To this day, the large majority of scholars agrees with Bultmann, not Dibelius.[42] However, the rhetorical analysis of the pericope indicates that Dibelius was correct.[43] The outer ring includes both healing and forgiveness;[44] the interposition contains the debate about Jesus' authority to forgive. Healing and forgiveness are equated both in the outer ring by means of the two parallel addresses to the paralytic, and in the center by the question to the scribes, "Which is easier to say...?" Since forgiveness is essentially equated with healing, virtually as a healing formula,[45] the healing naturally confirms the reality of forgiveness.[46] It is not an extraneous display of power or an *a minori ad majus* proof, but the expected outcome of the authoritative statement, "Your sins are forgiven."[47]

The occurrence of "Son of Man" in v. 10. Perhaps the most debated issue in scholarship on Mark 2:1-12 is the question of how to understand the use of Son of Man in v. 10. It is the first use of the term in Mark; it is not prepared for in the text; it is not explained. The Son of Man as pardoner of sins

does not occur elsewhere in the synoptic or Jewish tradition.
Further, Mark 2:10 and 28 (and par) are the only instances in
the synoptic tradition which refer to the earthly authority of
the Son of Man. Unlike many later uses of the title, the use
here is public, before hostile witnesses. And the term does
not occur again after 2:28 in Mark until 8:31 in the first passion prediction. Scholars have felt that 2:10 is in need of
explaining.[48]

Rhetorical analysis of the individual story of the healing
of the paralytic can offer some limits to possible explanations
of Mark 2:10. It can affirm that the title as a title is indeed
unheralded in Mark's narrative--unlike Christ or Son of God.
At the same time it must affirm that the narrative as it now
stands in Mark stresses the phrase "the Son of Man has authority
on earth." It is made to stand out and given emphasis by all
the repetitive material surrounding it. If this use of Son of
Man is "unmarkan" then it must be said that Mark has left the
text with the phrase strangely prominent. Mark's audience would
be unlikely to ignore it.

Rhetorical analysis of the pericope also has the negative
use of eliminating as a possibility one explanation of v. 10
that many scholars have recently put forward. Here is a clear
instance of rhetorical analysis serving as a control. Many have
attempted to resolve the problems of 2:10 and the passage as a
whole by saying that the phrase, "but that you may know that the
Son of Man has authority to forgive sins on earth" (v. 10a), is
a parenthetical aside by Mark to his Christian readers over the
head of the scribes. In their opinion, the "you" of εἰδῆτε refers not to the scribes whom Jesus is apparently addressing, but
to the Christian audience of the gospel. This view has been
recently and independently advocated by scholars of such diverse
viewpoints and traditions as C.E.B. Cranfield,[49] E. Trocmé,[50]
E.J. Mally,[51] W.L. Lane,[52] and N. Perrin.[53]

Their view is attractive since it explains why the term is
used so early in the gospel, why it is used in a public address
to opponents, and why the reaction in v. 12 takes no account of
the saying.[54] And Mark does use the device of parenthetical
addresses to his reader.[55] However, the explanation cannot be
valid for 2:10 since the saying forms an integral part of the

rhetorical structure of the debate with the scribes found in
vv. 6-10a.[56] It directly answers both questions posed by the
scribes in v. 7, and is therefore addressed to them. The scribes
now know that not only God but someone known as the Son of Man
claims to have (God's) authority on earth to forgive sins.

Seeing v. 10a as the answer to v. 7 also suggests a way the
Christian readers of the story might have understood the unex-
plained and unheralded use of "Son of Man." This chap who speaks
blasphemy is actually, according to Jesus, the Son of Man who
has legitimate authority to forgive sins. And by means of the
grammatical disjuncture in v. 10 and the emphatic Σοὶ λέγω to
the paralytic, Jesus is clearly identified to the hearer as the
Son of Man. The ring structure results in the identification
of the Son of Man with Jesus without any direct statement to
that effect in the narrative. Thus, the person who acts by for-
giving/healing, this Jesus, is the "Son of Man." This is sufficient definition for the narrative to be coherent. What other
ideas Mark's readers and/or Mark held about the Son of Man cannot be deduced from this pericope.[57]

Mark 2:13-17:
The Call of Levi and Eating with Sinners

In terms of form, the pericope reports à controversy apophthegm of the usual action-objection-vindication type. However,
the form appears pushed out of shape by its abnormally long prologue. Not only is the narrative exposition part of the controversy form unusually long and redundant (vv. 15-16a), but it
is prefaced by a general introduction (v. 13)[58] and the call of
Levi (v. 14). Form critics have generally viewed 2:13 as editorial, 2:14 as a biographical apophthegm, some or all of v. 15
as editorial, and 2:17b as an attached saying.[59]

Moreover, the various elements of the pericope appear to
be joined in an awkward manner; the narrative does not read
smoothly. Scholars have not been impressed by the unity or coherence of this passage. C.E. Carlston, for example, writes that
it is "fruitless to seek a literary or catechetical unity in
vv. 13-17, since the connections are unclear and since some of
the material probably comes from a pre-Markan collection in any
case."[60]

Yet, it is a presupposition of rhetorical criticism that
literary analysis may be applied to any text, and that it may
help us to understand that text. Indeed the following rhetorical analysis, while confirming (once again) that the narrative
is rather disjointed, also shows, as in 2:1-12, careful intertwining of the elements of the pericope. Extensive use is made
of verbal and content repetition in order to unify the passage,
for emphasis, and to interrelate disparate material. Awareness
of these rhetorical features helps to give unity or focus to the
narrative as a whole. Each verse will first be discussed separately, then the passage as a whole considered.

Rhetorical Analysis of the Individual Elements

Verse 13. Verse 13, the introduction, is very similar in
content and function to the introduction to the healing of the
paralytic. Like 2:1-2, it is a typical introductory or transition scene, complete within itself: Jesus appears at some particular place, the crowd gathers around him, and Jesus teaches
them.[61] Here the scene appears in its simplest version: only
the words πάλιν and πᾶς could be eliminated and still have the
scene complete.

Like 2:1-2, 2:13 reports an unmotivated shift in geography
(setting), providing a new narrative beginning.[62] Unlike 2:1-2,
however, 2:13 is not connected to the end of the preceding pericope by a chiastic pattern of hook words. Nor does the content
of 2:13 run counter to the content of the preceding pericope,
as 2:1-2 had Jesus entering a city immediately after being unable to enter one openly. Thus, in 2:13, the reader's attention
is not called to a break in narrative continuity as it is in
2:1-2.[63]

And, as in 2:1, the πάλιν in 2:13 refers the reader to a
place Jesus has already been in Mark 1, παρὰ τὴν θάλασσαν (1:16,
2:13). In 2:14, Jesus calls a disciple; the first time he was
beside the sea, he also called disciples.

Verse 14. As commentators have frequently noted, 2:14, the
call of Levi, is a call to discipleship similar to the calls of
the brothers in 1:16-20, although the word "disciple" is not
used in Mark until 2:15.[64] Jesus calls a person working at his

occupation; the person immediately follows Jesus. As v. 13 is
the simplest version of its general scene, so v. 14 is a bare-
bones version of a call. Levi, the son of Alphaeus, is described
only as sitting at the tax office and as getting up (καθήμενον/
ἀναστάς).[65] In 2:14, ἀκολουθέω is stressed, used both for Jesus'
call and for Levi's response.

Verse 15. This verse presents a challenge for the rhetorical critic's ingenuity, for it has several syntactical ambiguities: whose house is referred to? Does the second πολλοί refer
to the disciples or to the tax collectors and sinners? Is the
subject of ἠκολούθουν the ambiguous many or the scribes of the
Pharisees of v. 16?[66] Rhetorical criticism as a method may be
an additional tool to help resolve such syntactical ambiguities.[67]
By viewing the alternative grammatical possibilities from a
rhetorical perspective, certain possibilities may be seen to
fit the rhetorical pattern of a verse or passage better than
others.

The basic procedure of rhetorical analysis is to observe
rhetorical features in the text and argue from them to the understanding of the text. To attempt to use rhetorical criticism
to clarify syntactical ambiguities in a text is to apply the
method in reverse. One hypothesizes a particular understanding
of the text into which one or another alternative then fits better rhetorically. Such a procedure is hazardous since it is
projective and highly amenable to the subjective biases of the
interpreter. The attempt, however, seems worth making.[68]

Verse 15 once again presents Jesus in a new place, indoors
reclining at a meal in a house which may refer to Jesus' or to
Levi's house.[69] A specific meal appears to be in progress.
There would seem to be some rhetorical justification for con-
sidering Levi's house the more probable setting. First, Levi
provides a narrative connection between vv. 14 and 15: Jesus
calls Levi and then eats a meal in Levi's house just as earlier
Jesus had called Simon and shortly thereafter ate at Simon's
house (1:16-18, 29-31).[70]

Second, the pleonasm of v. 15ab then serves a rhetorical
function:

15a Καὶ γίνεται κατακεῖσθαι αὐτὸν ἐν τῇ οἰκίᾳ αὐτοῦ,

15b καὶ πολλοὶ τελῶναι καὶ ἁμαρτωλοὶ συνανέκειντο τῷ Ἰησοῦ καὶ
τοῖς μαθηταῖς αὐτοῦ·

Verse 15a would picture two individuals, Levi and Jesus, dining;
v. 15b extends the number dining to two whole groups, "many tax
collectors and sinners," and "Jesus and his disciples."[71] In
each case, there is an implied contrast between those viewed as
sinful and those not.[72] The two groups are distinguished from
each other.

In v. 15c, ἦσαν γὰρ πολλοί καὶ ἠκολούθουν αὐτῷ, ἠκολούθουν
αὐτῷ at the end of this verse serves as a hook phrase recalling
ἠκολούθησεν αὐτῷ at the end of v. 14.[73] The parallelism of con-
tent--following Jesus--as well as the verbal repetition suggests
that on rhetorical grounds the verb should be understood with
the preceding material, not with v. 16, and therefore its subject would be πολλοί.[74] The question remains, does πολλοί refer
to the disciples or to the tax collectors and sinners?[75]

Rhetorically, v. 15 seems to make better sense if πολλοί
is understood to refer to the disciples. Then the entire verse
achieves some coherence. As 15b has extended 15a, Jesus' association with Levi to his association with many tax collectors and
sinners, so 15c extends 15b, the number of disciples from the five
individuals already named in the text who are following Jesus, to
"many" who have responded to Jesus' call. The *many* tax collectors and sinners are balanced by the *many* disciples. Nor are the
groups fixed: Levi began as a tax collector and became a disciple.

The above understanding of v. 15 remains, of course, an
hypothesis based on rhetorical considerations. The rhetorical
argument, however, would be seen as support for the arguments
of those scholars who see the theological importance of v. 15
in the extension from the individual specific case to everyone[76]
and of those scholars who view 15c as an aside to the reader
defining "disciples" and extending their number.[77]

Verse 16. Finally, in v. 16, the opponents appear on stage
to ask their question.[78] The scribes of the Pharisees[79] ask the
disciples a general question: why Jesus eats with tax collectors
and sinners. The participle ἰδόντες[80] connects the presence of

the disciples with the meal described in v. 15. The phrasing
of the verse stresses the involvement of the disciples in the
narrative:

> καὶ ἰδόντες ὅτι ἐσθίει μετὰ τῶν ἁμαρτωλῶν καὶ τελωνῶν
> ἔλεγον τοῖς μαθηταῖς αὐτοῦ
> ῞Οτι μετὰ τῶν τελωνῶν καὶ ἁμαρτωλῶν ἐσθίει;

The reader already knows from v. 15 that Jesus eats with tax
collectors and sinners. In v. 16 the information is repeated
twice again, in chiastic order (eats, sinners, tax collectors/
/tax collectors, sinners, eats). And interposed between the two
repetitions, the reader is told, the opponents asked the disciples. The phrase stands out from the repetition surrounding it.

Verse 17. Verse 17 presents Jesus' answer in two parallel
sayings of the form, οὐ...ἀλλὰ.... In each saying, two groups
are contrasted: first the well and the sick, then the righteous
and the sinners. The distinction between the two groups mirrors
the distinction of v. 16 between the scribes of the Pharisees
and the tax collectors and sinners, and the distinction implied
in v. 16 and stated in v. 15 between Jesus and his disciples,
on the one hand, *and* the tax collectors and sinners. Thus far,
Jesus' answer builds upon the preceding narrative, contrasting
two groups of people.

Neither saying, however, has any direct connection with the
question of eating. The first saying, "Not the well but the
sick have need of a doctor," is a generally applicable proverb.
It applies to Jesus' associating with sinners, but it is hardly
a specific justification of table fellowship.[81] The second saying, "I came not to call righteous ones but sinners," seems more
clearly to justify the call of Levi in v. 14, than to justify
the eating questioned in v. 16.[82] As in the call of James and
John (1:20), so here in 2:17b, the verb καλέω is used.[83] In
2:17b, however, the call is not limited to Levi, or other particular individuals, but refers to sinners in general. The call,
like the meal in v. 15, is extended from an individual to a
general situation.

Verses 13-17 as a Rhetorical Unit

Verse 13 is a semi-detached scene preparing for what follows by placing Jesus beside the lake. Verses 14-17 are connected by the common subject matter of Jesus' relationship to tax collectors and sinners. In v. 14, Jesus calls Levi from his tax office. In vv. 15-16, the fact that Jesus eats with tax collectors and sinners is repeated three times. And finally in v. 17, Jesus announces his call to sinners. A formal pattern of repetition of the words τελώνιον/τελώνης and ἁμαρτωλός runs throughout the passage, providing a rhetorical continuity. First the tax office is mentioned alone; then both groups of people are mentioned three times, each time reversing the order, and finally the sinners are mentioned alone. The pattern is as follows:

$$x \:/\: x + y \:/\: y + x \:/\: x + y \:/\: y^{84}$$

Second, vv. 14-17 are connected by the interrelated themes of eating and calling. The two middle verses strongly stress Jesus' eating as well as his relationship to outcasts.[85] Twice in v. 15, Jesus is reclining at table (κατάκειμαι, συνανάκειμαι). Twice in v. 16, Jesus eats (ἐσθίει). On the other hand, neither v. 14 nor 17 explicitly mentions eating at all. Rather, v. 14 describes a specific call and v. 17 contains Jesus' affirmation that he came to call sinners. Thus, this pericope, like the healing of the paralytic, has a symmetrical rhythm, in this case, calling/eating/calling.

Rhetorically, however, 2:13-17 is not a ring composition as is 2:1-12. Unlike healing and debate, the motifs of calling/following and eating are intertwined throughout the pericope. Verses 14 and 17, as noted, concern Jesus' call to discipleship. Verse 15c in the middle concerns following in discipleship.[86] Moreover, the disciples as a group are explicitly mentioned in connection with eating: in v. 15 they participate in the meal; in v. 16, they are asked about Jesus' behavior in eating with sinners. Thus the rather disjointed interweaving of narrative elements in vv. 14-17 serves, at the time of the first mention of "disciple" (v. 15), to define who a disciple is. A disciple is a person who is called by Jesus, who follows him, and who eats with him.

Further, the disciples are defined in relation to other
groups of people. A disciple may have been a sinner or tax
collector before he accepted the call to discipleship (vv. 14,
17). The disciple, along with Jesus, eats with tax collectors
and sinners (v. 15). Thus the disciples are both sinners themselves, and after their call to follow, still associate with
sinners. And the opponents, by addressing their question to
the disciples, acknowledge the disciples' relationship to Jesus.

The primary literary focus of the pericope remains on Jesus'
behavior in calling and eating with sinners, and his concluding
teaching. However, the employment of the discipleship motifs
of calling and following, and the presence of the disciples
throughout the pericope, serve to establish the disciples in
the foreground of the narrative, in association with Jesus.

Relation of 2:13-17 to 2:1-12

Mark 2:13-17 continues the thematic concern of 2:1-12 with
sin.[87] In 2:1-12, the subject was forgiveness of sins; here
the subject is calling/eating with sinners. Άμαρτία was used
four times in the healing of the paralytic (2:5,7,9,10);
άμαρτωλός is used four times in this pericope (2:15, 16 bis,
17).[88] The two pericopes are presented in a logical order:
first, Jesus demonstrates his power over sin and only then does
he associate with sinners.[89] The relationship between the two
pericopes is also ironic: in the first, Jesus is accused of
blasphemy when he heals by forgiving sins; in the second, Jesus,
in defense of his association with sinners, in effect claims
to be like a doctor whose business is to be about the healing
of the sick.

There are also major differences between the two pericopes.
The first is a healing controversy; the second contains no
miracles. The two stories involve a different cast of characters: in the first, the paralytic, the crowd, Jesus, and the
opponents; in the second, the tax collectors and sinners (Levi),
the disciples, Jesus, and the opponents. The disciples are not
mentioned in the healing of the paralytic and they play a major
role in the second controversy.

The opposition is also presented differently in the two
pericopes. In 2:1-12, the opponents were "some of the scribes";

in 2:13-17, the opponents are designated more formally as "the scribes of the Pharisees." In the first, the opponents mumbled in their hearts; in the second story, they openly ask the disciples about Jesus' behavior. Opposition is more overt. On the other hand, the accusation is much less serious. In the first controversy, the charge is blasphemy, which can lead to death (see 14:64). In the issue of eating, Jesus is breaking the Pharisaic tradition but not the Torah; he is certainly not liable to a death penalty.[90] And the atmosphere is much more friendly than in 2:6-10a. The question of the opponents assumes that Jesus himself is not a sinner or tax collector. And Jesus' answer in v. 17, even if it does not really answer the question, is positively irenic.[91] Within the story level, the scribes of the Pharisees are naturally assumed to be among "the well" and "the righteous"; even if Mark's later Christian readers standing outside the story might consider these designations ironic.[92] Thus 2:13-17 continues the theme of Jesus' dealing with sin from 2:1-12, and picks up the element of opposition from 2:6-10a. The conflict is not as serious, but it is overt rather than held to one side by means of the interposition technique. And it now involves the disciples as well as Jesus.[93]

Notes on Mark 2:13-17

The implications that rhetorical analysis has for exegesis have been discussed during the course of the rhetorical analysis itself (e.g., v. 15, the role of the disciples). Here I shall only point out two implications that the rhetorical analysis may have for the tradition history of the pericope.

Verse 14. Contrary to most scholarly opinion,[94] v. 14 may well be a redactional composition designed to fit a combination discipleship/eating controversy. Verse 14 does not seem viable as an independent piece of tradition.[95] As noted in the analysis, the story of the call is about as simplified as it can be, and is constructed according to the model of 1:16-20, using much of the same vocabulary. It is uncertain that the verse by itself, without either 1:16-20 or 2:15-17, would be understood as a call to discipleship. The purpose of "following" is not given within the verse.

Further, τελώνιον is needed for the narrative and rhetorical
structure of vv. 15-17. Τελώνιον has been considered the catchword that led to the connection of v. 14 with vv. (15)16-17.[96]
If this were the case and v. 14 had an independent existence,
then one would expect more originality--new information or descriptive details--in v. 14. As it is, only the name, "Levi,
son of Alphaeus," is added information--that is, not derived
from the model in 1:16-20 nor needed for the following story.
And the name "Levi" for a disciple is suspect. For Levi is not
listed as one of the twelve in the gospel lists, and the tribe
of Levi was not counted among the twelve tribes of Israel.[97]

The occurrence of the disciples in v. 16. It is questionable if the disciples should be considered an integral part of
the eating controversy in vv. 16-17a(b). They appear on the
scene in order to receive the opponents' question. However,
Jesus apparently responds directly to the opponents, in normal
controversy fashion. In terms of the apophthegm form, the disciples do not fit well. They are an extra and non-essential
character--the story already has three, the scribes of the
Pharisees, the tax collectors and sinners, and Jesus. Indeed,
it seems unlikely that the scribes of the story would distinguish,
for example, between Levi the tax collector and Levi the disciple.[98]

On the other hand, the disciples fit well into the rhetorical structure of the whole of vv. 14-17 (see above). Thus the
disciples seem to be a secondary addition to v. 16, most likely
at the point vv. (13)14-17 were constructed as a unit, to emphasize the disciples' association with Jesus. It would appear
that Bultmann is wrong in viewing the presence of the disciples
in v. 16 as evidence that the controversy apophthegm necessarily
originated in the life of the church, in defense of the church's
behavior.[99] For whenever the eating controversy apophthegm may
have originated, it appears to have existed before the disciples
were added to it.

Mark 2:18-22:
The Question About Fasting

The question about fasting is a controversy apophthegm of
the usual action-objection-vindication type. Verse 18 presents
the exposition and the question about the disciples' behavior,
while vv. 19-22 present Jesus' answer. In terms of controversy
form, v. 19a completes the form, giving Jesus' pithy answer to
the question raised. Jesus' answer, however, does not end here.
The content of v. 19a is rephrased in 19b, and reversed in v. 20.
Two additional sayings unconnected with fasting are added in
vv. 21-22.[100]

The fasting apophthegm differs from the two earlier controversies in the Galilean controversy section in its lack of
specificity. The pericope opens without a notation of Jesus'
setting, such as a house in Capernaum or beside the lake. The
reader is not told where the story happens. Second, the question to Jesus is not connected to any specific event, such as
Jesus' address to a paralytic, or a meal at Levi's house.
Rather, the question (and answer) deal with the pious practice
of fasting in general and not with Jesus' or the disciples'
violation of a specific fast. Lastly, there are no specific
opponents, i.e., some scribes, or the Pharisees. The verbs
ἔρχονται and λέγουσιν in v. 18 appear to be impersonal plurals,
meaning in effect, "Jesus was asked."[101] Thus, while the pericope retains the controversy form, conflict is virtually absent
from it, when it is considered in isolation from its context in
the Galilean controversy section.

Mark 2:18-22 also presents a different rhetorical structure
from the first two controversies. There is no symmetrical rhythm
at all. Rhetorically, the narrative falls into two approximately
equal parts consisting of the controversy over fasting in vv.
18-20; and the two sayings on the old and new in vv. 21-22. Each
part is again subdivided in half: in vv. 18-20, the exposition
and question (v. 18) is balanced by Jesus' answer (vv. 19-20);
in vv. 21-22, the two sayings balance each other. Here the pattern may be described as a a' + b b'.

As in the first two pericopes studied, word repetition is
used extensively to structure the content and to indicate emphasis. The shift in content from the issue of fasting in vv. 18-20

to the relation of the old and the new in vv. 21-22 suggests
that a major division in the pericope should be made between
v. 20 and v. 21. The patterns of word repetition confirm this
division: extensive use is made of repetition *within* each half
of the pericope, and virtually no use of repetition or other
rhetorical devices is found *connecting* the two halves of the
pericope. First, vv. 18-20 will be discussed, then vv. 21-22,
and finally, the relationship of the two parts. When the rhetorical analysis appears to have particular significance for
exegetical or redactional issues, it will be mentioned in the
text or footnotes; there will be no separate "exegetical notes"
section.

Verses 18-20

As already noted, vv. 18-20 are divided into two parallel
pairs: a, v. 18, the exposition and question about fasting;
a', vv. 19-20, Jesus' answer on fasting. This may easily be
seen by looking at the use of the key word "to fast." In a,
the reader is first told that the disciples of John and the
Pharisees *fast*. The information is given again in the question,
"Why do the disciples of John and the disciples of the Pharisees
fast?" Finally, at the end of the question, the contrast with
the behavior of the disciples is made: "but your disciples do
not fast?" Jesus' answer in a' shows a similar pattern. First,
Jesus asks, "How can the sons of the bridechamber *fast*?" Then
he reiterates the information as a statement, "they cannot *fast*."
Finally he notes the situation will change, "a time will come
when they *do fast*."

Thus, the verb "to fast" is repeated three times each in
a and in a'. In each case, the pattern of the content is repetition, then reversal: in a, fast, fast; not fast; in a', not
fast, not fast; fast. In neither instance is the repetition
necessary for understanding the narrative.[102] The repetition
may serve the rhetorical function of underlining the first position stated, so that the contrast, when it is made, is highlighted. A closer analysis of the rhetorical pattern of repetition in v. 18 and vv. 19-20 confirms the emphasis upon contrast.

Verse 18 (a)

Καὶ ἦσαν <u>οἱ μαθηταὶ</u> Ἰωάννου καὶ οἱ Φαρισαῖοι <u>νηστεύοντες</u>.
καὶ ἔρχονται καὶ λέγουσιν αὐτῷ,
Διὰ τί <u>οἱ μαθηταὶ</u> Ἰωάννου καὶ <u>οἱ μαθηταὶ</u> τῶν φαρισαίων
<u>νηστεύουσιν</u>,
<u>οἱ δὲ σοὶ μαθηταὶ</u> οὐ <u>νηστεύουσιν</u>;

The placing of the verb "to fast" in all three instances at the
end of its clause places the rhetorical emphasis of the pericope
on the issue of fasting. The repetition of οἱ μαθηταί four
times within such a short space also emphasizes the importance
of "disciples" in the story. The rhetorical stress on "disciple"
may be the explanation for the strange phrase, "the disciples
of the Pharisees."

The word order of the first three uses is the customary
one--noun followed by its genitive (of John, of the Pharisees).
In the final use, in regard to Jesus' disciples, the word order
is reversed. The more emphatic σοι is used instead of the usual
genitive σου, and it is placed before, rather than after, the
noun, "disciples."[103] A shift in word order for emphasis is a
common rhetorical technique of both oral and written literature.[104]
The use of repetition and the word order shift in v. 18 serves
to focus the hearer's attention on the contrast between Jesus'
disciples and others in regard to fasting.[105] As the preceding
pericope distinguished Jesus' disciples from tax collectors and
sinners, and from the scribes of the Pharisees, so here they are
distinguished from the disciples of John and the Pharisees.

Verses 19-20 (a')

Jesus' answer presents a similar use of repetition and
word order change:

Μὴ δύνανται οἱ υἱοὶ τοῦ <u>νυμφῶνος</u> ἐν ᾧ ὁ <u>νυμφίος</u> μετ' αὐτῶν ἐστιν
<u>νηστεύειν</u>;
ὅσον χρόνον ἔχουσιν τὸν νυμφίον μετ' αὐτῶν οὐ δύνανται
<u>νηστεύειν</u>.
ἐλεύσονται δὲ ἡμέραι ὅταν ἀπαρθῇ ἀπ' αὐτῶν ὁ <u>νυμοίος</u>,
καὶ τότε <u>νηστεύσουσιν</u> ἐν ἐκείνῃ τῇ ἡμέρᾳ.

The heavy emphasis on νηστεύω found in a, is continued in a'.
Twice more, a clause ends with the verb, "to fast." Five times,
in vv. 18 and 19, the reader has heard a major clause end with
some form of νηστεύω. Three times the hearers have been told
Jesus' followers do not fast (v. 18, v. 19 bis). Finally, in
v. 20, the sixth and last use of the word is placed before the
end of the clause. And here, the reader is told that the disciples *will* fast. Verse 20 is marked as the climax of vv. 18-
20 by means of the shift in word order and the coincident shift
in content.[106]

As "disciples" was employed four times in a, so the metaphor of the bridegroom's attendants is used four times in a'.
(The desire for rhetorical balance between a and a' may also
help to explain the phrase, "the disciples of the Pharisees" in
a.) First, οἱ υἱοὶ τοῦ νυμφῶνος are mentioned; then, twice, the
phrase, "those with the bridegroom" (in the order νυμφίος/ον
μετ' αὐτῶν), are mentioned (v. 19). Last, in v. 20, the bridegroom is taken away from them (απ' αὐτῶν ὁ νυμφίος). Again, in
the final instance of repetition (also a contrast), the word
order is shifted. The technique of word order shift in a final
repetition is used in v. 18 with "disciples," in vv. 19-20; with
"those with the bridegroom"; and in the larger unit, vv. 18-20,
with "to fast."

Thus, Jesus' answer in a' neatly balances the exposition
and question of a in the use of the word "to fast" and in the
parallelism of the sons of the bridechamber with disciples.
Jesus' answer, however, not only balances a, but itself falls
into two balanced parts, v. 19 and v. 20.[107] Verse 19 explicitly
answers the question posed in a, why Jesus' disciples do not
fast; v. 20 moves beyond v. 19 to posit a time when the disciples
will fast. Verse 19 is delimited by the use of μὴ δύνανται/οὐ
δύνανται at the beginning and near the end (just preceding
νηστεύειν)--the technique of inclusio. Verse 20 is delimited
by ἡμέραι/ἡμέρᾳ near the beginning and at the end, again an
inclusio.[108] Verse 19, describing the time when the bridegroom
is with the disciples, is thus clearly separated from v. 20,
the time after the bridegroom is taken away.[109]

Summary

Verse 18, (a), contrasts the fasting practices of groups of people at one period of time; vv. 19-20, (a'), contrast the fasting practice of the group named last in a, Jesus' disciples, at two points in time. Verses 19-20 not only answer the question raised in a, but also move beyond it to envision a new situation. The rhetorical unity and balance of vv. 18-20, the fasting controversy proper, is most impressive. Whatever the tradition history of Jesus' answer covering the two periods of time before and after his death may have been, the stages of its development are not visible in the text found in Mark. The allegorical allusion to Jesus' death in v. 20 is not just tacked on to the preceding material.[110] Rather, Jesus' answer in its entirety (vv. 19-20) closely parallels the statement of the issue in v. 18. The tradition history of these verses cannot be detected on the basis of literary joins.

Verses 21-22

The verses consist of two sayings parallel in form, οὐδεὶς ..., εἰ δὲ μή..., and similar in content, the incompatibility or discontinuity of the new and the old. The verses are connected rhetorically by the hook words, παλαιός and especially, καινός. Without the hook phrases employing καινός, the verses are almost exactly parallel in structure and content:

21a   οὐδεὶς ἐπίβλημα ῥάκους ἀγνάφου ἐπιράπτει ἐπὶ ἱμάτιον
              παλαιόν·

b   εἰ δὲ μή, αἴρει τὸ πλήρωμα ἀπ᾽ αὐτοῦ...

c   καὶ χεῖρον σχίσμα γίνεται.

22a   καὶ οὐδεὶς βάλλει οἶνον νέον εἰς ἀσκοὺς παλαιούς·

b   εἰ δὲ μή, ῥήξει ὁ οἶνος τοὺς ἀσκούς

c   καὶ ὁ οἶνος ἀπόλλυται καὶ οἱ ἀσκοί...

(The above schema is an artificial construct used to explicate the rhetorical features of the verses. It does not necessarily posit that the verses ever existed in that form.) In each verse, line a states that nobody puts something unshrunk/new into something old; line b states what will happen if someone does, namely that the new element will disrupt the old; and line c gives the final result--a worse tear is made, the wine and the wineskins are lost.

The point seems to be stronger than that the old and new do not mix; rather the new is an active threat to the continued existence of the old, and may itself be harmed in the destruction of the old. As B.W. Bacon wrote many years ago:

> The section concludes with two proverbs of unknown derivation whose application is a radical one. The new order cannot be treated as a patching up of the old (verse 21). The attempt to impose constraint on new forces will bring explosion (verse 22).111

The hook phrases employing καινός show that, given the danger of the new to the old, the new is to be established, not the old preserved. The interposition of τὸ καινὸν τοῦ παλαιοῦ between v. 21b and c is parenthetical, making explicit the new/old opposition. The final clause, ἀλλὰ οἶνον νέον εἰς ἀσκοὺς καινούς, at the end of v. 22, is in antithetic parallelism to 22a:

22a καὶ οὐδεὶς βάλλει οἶνον νέον εἰς ἀσκοὺς παλαιούς--
  b   εἰ δὲ μή, ῥήξει ὁ οἶνος τοὺς ἀσκούς,
  c   καὶ ὁ οἶνος ἀπόλλυται καὶ οἱ ἀσκοί--
  d   ἀλλὰ οἶνον νέον εἰς ἀσκοὺς καινούς.112

Line a repeats παλαιός from the interposition in v. 21; line d repeats καινός from it. Βάλλει serves as the verb for both lines a and d (an instance of prozeugma). The sense of d then is "Rather, [put] new wine into new wineskins!"

Verses 18-22 as a Whole

If the rhetorical structure and meaning of vv. 18-20 and 21-22 are each quite clear, the connection of the two parts of the pericope is not. The rhetorical links between the parts are minimal. First, the verses are an uninterrupted continuation of Jesus' sayings on fasting. There is no indication of a new beginning such as καὶ λέγει/ἔλεγεν. Secondly, vv. 21-22 as a whole follow a rhetorical pattern similar to that found in a and a' of vv. 18-20, the pattern of restatement followed by contrast or reversal. Verse 22d, employing the strong adversative particle ἀλλὰ contrasts the establishment of the new with the concern for the old shown in vv. 21-22c.

Both the continuation of direct discourse and the similarity of rhetorical structure suggest that some logical connection is intended between vv. 18-20 and 21-22. The facts that vv. 18 (a)

and 19-20 (a') present such a tight rhetorical unity, and that
vv. 21-22 follow a similar pattern to a or a', make it extremely
doubtful that the view held by Bultmann and others, that vv. 21-
22 are meant to be understood in light of vv. 18-19, excluding
v. 20, is correct.[113] Such an interpretation runs counter to the
rhetorical structure in which the entirety of a' (vv. 19-20)
parallels a (v. 18).

More probable is the suggestion that vv. 21-22 are a second
answer to the question posed in v. 18.[114] The rhetorical pattern might be described as a, a', a''. The logic would be not
unlike that found in Mark 12:18-27 where Jesus first answers
the specific issue about the woman's husbands, and then deals
with the general question of resurrection. Here Jesus answers
the specific question about fasting, and then speaks about the
fundamental change made by the coming of the kingdom or the new
age--of which not fasting is one consequence. The difficulty
here is that vv. 18-20 are a tight rhetorical unity, while vv.
21-22 are only loosely attached. This solution, however, appears
to have the most rhetorical support.

A third possibility for the relationship of vv. 21-22 to
vv. 18-20 would be to see vv. 21-22 as a continuation in time
after the death of the bridegroom.[115] Given the abundant references to time in vv. 19-20, and the dearth of them in vv. 21-22,
this view does not appear to be grounded in the text. Viewing
the individual pericope in isolation, it may be said that the
rhetorical approach has been more successful in pointing out
difficulties with proposed solutions to the question of the
logical relationship of vv. 21-22 to 18-20, than in propounding
a solution of its own.

Mark 2:23-28: Plucking Grain on the Sabbath

The controversy over plucking grain, like the two preceding
pericopes, is a controversy apophthegm of the action-objection-
vindication type. As in the preceding two stories, the narrative is developed beyond the basic requirements of the controversy form. In this instance, the exposition and question are
followed by two formally separate answers by Jesus.[116] Jesus
and the disciples are walking through fields on the sabbath,
and the disciples are plucking grain. The opponents ask Jesus

why the disciples are breaking the sabbath law. Jesus first
replies with the example of David who ate the bread of the presence and gave it to his followers; and then replies that the
sabbath was made for man, so that the Son of Man is lord of the
sabbath. The relationship of the two answers to each other and
to the question has been and remains a problem for exegetes.[117]

Here, rhetorical analysis will be applied, to see what light
it may shed on the interrelationships of the parts of the text.
The order of presenting the analysis will differ from that employed in discussing the three earlier pericopes. First, the
indications of overall rhetorical structure will be described,
and then the individual parts will be discussed. Finally, there
will be a short discussion of the title, Son of Man, in 2:28.

Indications of the Overall Rhetorical Structure

On the basis of content, the pericope consists of three
parts: the exposition and question (vv. 23-24), Jesus' first
answer (vv. 25-26), and Jesus' second answer (vv. 27-28). An
analysis of the use of word repetition in the text confirms the
division based on content. The use of word repetition is much
less extensive in this pericope than in the three pericopes already analyzed. There is some employment of word repetition
within each of the three parts of the text. The phrase τοῖς
σάββασιν occurs twice in vv. 23-24. The repetitions ἔφαγεν/
φαγεῖν and οἱ μετ' αὐτοῦ/τοῖς σὺν αὐτῷ occur in vv. 25-26. The
words "sabbath" and "man" are used three times each in vv. 27-
28.

Hook word repetition is also used to connect the three
parts of pericope. The opponents' question in v. 24 reads as
follows:

Ἴδε τί ποιοῦσιν τοῖς σάββασιν ὃ οὐκ ἔξεστιν;

Jesus answers the opponents: Οὐδέποτε ἀνέγνωτε τί ἐποίησεν
Δαυίδ (v. 25). He ate the bread of the presence, which it was
not lawful (οὐκ ἔξεστιν) for anyone but priests to eat (v. 26).
The first answer is connected to the question in that in both
someone disobeys the law. In the answer, however, David himself
disobeys the law, while in the opening scene sparking the controversy Jesus does not. Further, it is not clear how David's disobedience in eating justifies the breaking of the sabbath.

Jesus' second answer picks up the remaining word from the opponents' question, "sabbath," and asserts the Son of Man's lordship over the sabbath. The second answer is not connected to the first answer in content or by means of word repetition. It appears to refer directly back to the question in v. 24. Here also, the relation of the answer to the question is not clear: how does the lordship of the Son of Man justify the disciples' disobedience?

Thus the basic rhetorical structure of 2:23-28 is quite clear.[118] The text has a tripartite division in which the second and third parts are each joined to the first by means of hook words. The last part, vv. 27-28, does not continue the thought of the middle part, but rather answers directly the question raised in the first part. Thus the passage has a circular rhythm, the end recalling the opening. The repetition of the word "sabbath" in both the first and last parts emphasizes the connection and the importance of the sabbath issue. Recognition of the rhetorical structure, however, still leaves many questions unanswered about the logical progress of the argument in the pericope. A closer consideration of the individual parts of the structure is in order.

Analysis of the Individual Elements

Verses 23-24. The exposition and question presented in these verses conform more closely to the typical or "ideal" controversy form than those found in the earlier pericopes. The exposition is brief, describing a specific incident; specific opponents question Jesus. In the course of walking through a field on the sabbath, the disciples pluck grain, that is, violate the laws forbidding work on the sabbath. The normal translation of the Greek of v. 23b is "the disciples began to make a path (or make way), plucking the grain."[119] The reason for the plucking of the grain, insofar as it is indicated in the text, would appear to be to make a path for Jesus.[120]

In v. 24, the Pharisees, who are conveniently upon the scene as in 2:16, ask Jesus why the disciples are acting unlawfully on the sabbath. As in the preceding controversy over fasting, Jesus is questioned about the disciples' behavior. The sabbath violation raises a more serious issue, however, than not

fasting. Fasting was a matter of customary piety; working on
the sabbath was a violation of the written law. The question
of the opponents reflects the seriousness: "Look, why are they
doing something illegal...?" On the story level, the Pharisees
are holding Jesus responsible for the illegal behavior of his
disciples, even though Jesus himself is not breaking the law.[121]

   Verses 25-26. In his first answer, Jesus adduces the example of David eating the showbread. The hook words τί ἐποίησεν
and οὐκ ἔξεστιν indicate that the connection between the situation and Jesus' answer is that the disciples and David both engage in illegal activity. Using David as an example shows that
breaking the law is sometimes justified. The law that is broken,
however, differs. The disciples violate the sabbath, while
David's act is not a violation of the sabbath rest.[122] The
text stresses that David's illegal act is that of eating: David
ate the showbread which was not lawful for him to *eat* (v. 26).
The example of David's illegal eating would appear to be a good
answer to the question in 2:16 about Jesus' eating behavior. It
does not, however, appear to relate to the disciples' action in
v. 23. The plucking of grain is not presented as a step in the
gathering and preparation of food; nor is the reader told that
Jesus or the disciples were in any need or hungry.[123] The relevance of Jesus' answer to the question does not have to do with
eating.[124]
   A clue to the relevance of the answer may be seen in the
treatment of David's followers in vv. 25-26.[125] The verses
stress the primacy of David and the secondary and dependent role
of his companions. First, the reader is told that David is in
need and hungry, then αὐτὸς καὶ οἱ μετ᾽ αὐτοῦ. First, David eats
the showbread, then he gives it also (even?) to τοῖς σὺν αὐτῷ
οὖσιν. David's followers also act illegally, but only because
they are with David, and because David has authorized them to
do so. Jesus' answer may convey to the reader that the disciples
acted illegally on the sabbath because they are associated with
Jesus, and Jesus has authorized their action. Then, vv. 25-26
would seem to function in their immediate context, first, as
a statement that illegal behavior is sometimes appropriate, and
second, as an indication that the disciples' behavior is dependent on their relationship to Jesus. The emphasis upon eating in

vv. 25-26, as will be argued below, is significant not in the
context of this pericope but in the structure of 2:1-3:6 as a
whole.[126]

Verses 27-28. Jesus' second answer in vv. 27-28 consists
of two sayings, first the general proverb, "The sabbath was made
for man, not man for the sabbath" (v. 27), followed by the christological saying, "Therefore, the Son of Man is lord of the
sabbath" (v. 28). From the rhetorical perspective, the two sayings are interrelated and function as a single answer to the
opponents.[127] They are connected by the conjunction ὥστε, by
the repeated use of the words "sabbath" and "man," and by the
play on words between "man" in v. 27 and "Son of Man" in v. 28.[128]

Jesus' second answer does not build upon the first answer
in vv. 25-26. The new introduction, καὶ ἔλεγεν αὐτοῖς, indicates
the break in the argument. The phrase is a literary device by
which "Mark [or an earlier editor] indicates that the statement
which follows has no direct relationship to the immediately preceding verses."[129] The answer, however, is connected with the
exposition-question in vv. 23-24 by the use of the hook word
"sabbath" and by the fact that it does present a justification
for ignoring the sabbath law. The saying in v. 27 most probably
refers to God's purpose in creating man and the sabbath.[130] If
so, the logic is similar to Mark 10:2-9 in which Jesus appeals
to God's intention at creation to override a Mosaic law.[131] The
saying in v. 28 asserts Jesus' sovereignty over the sabbath law.
The answer as such does not directly justify the *disciples'* illegal behavior in v. 23. However, the intervening answer about
David's eating the showbread has stressed that the followers'
behavior depends upon the master. If Jesus' authority over the
sabbath is accepted, then the disciples' behavior is justified.

Summary. The pericope then has a narrative logic. While
the full significance of vv. 25-26 can only be understood in
the larger context of 2:1-3:6, the verses function in their immediate context to stress the derivative role of the disciple
or follower, and to prepare the way for an answer to the original
question in terms of Jesus' authority. In narrative terms, Jesus
accepts responsibility for his disciples' behavior, and challenges

his opponents that if they wish to take issue on the matter, they must reckon with him, not merely with his disciples.

The lines of conflict are most sharply drawn in 2:23-28 than in any of the controversies since the question of blasphemy in 2:6-10a. On the one hand, the Pharisees assert the validity of the sabbath law; on the other, Jesus claims that, as Son of Man, *he* is lord of the sabbath. As in the controversy over forgiveness/blasphemy, so here the two positions are irreconcilable. This time, the disciples also are involved in the conflict, since it is they who break the sabbath law, and they whom Jesus defends by his claim over the sabbath.

The Use of "Son of Man" in 2:28

The use of the title, Son of Man, in 2:28 recalls to the reader the earlier use of the title in 2:10. Καί in 2:28 would appear to mean "also" and to refer the reader explicitly to 2:10.[132] The rhetorical structure of the two sayings is similar:

2:10 ἐξουσίαν ἔχει ὁ υἱὸς τοῦ ἀνθρώπου ἀφιέναι ἁμαρτίας ἐπὶ
         τῆς γῆς

2:28 κύριός ἐστιν ὁ υἱὸς τοῦ ἀνθρώπου καὶ τοῦ σαββάτου

In each saying, the claim of authority (ἐξουσία, κύριος) is placed first, followed by the verb, the subject, and at the end, the object of the authority--forgiving sins on earth, the sabbath. The reader is held in suspense until the end of the saying. In each instance, the object of the authority introduces an element of surprise. From our knowledge of the Son of Man figure from Daniel and Enoch, one would not expect the figure to have authority *on earth* or *over the sabbath*.

The saying in 2:28 not only recalls 2:10 to the reader's mind; it also builds upon information given to the reader in 2:10. The identification of Jesus and the Son of Man was made in v. 10; the identification is taken for granted in 2:28. Furthermore, the logic of vv. 27-28 assumes that the reader already knows that the Son of Man has authority on earth. The fact that God's purpose in creating the sabbath was for man, does not of itself imply that the Son of Man is lord over the sabbath. However, if the reader already knows that the Son of Man has authority on earth, then the idea that the Son of Man

has authority to carry out God's intention in regard to the sabbath follows quite naturally. The reader/hearer who has heard
v. 10 would not be surprised at the use of the conjunction ὥστε
at the beginning of v. 28.[133]

Verse 28 also points ahead to the following sabbath controversy. Lane has suggested that the question about the sabbath
in v. 24 may be the legal warning necessary before actual pro-
secution on a charge can be made (M. Sanhedrin 7:8, M. Makkoth
1:8,9).[134] In v. 28, Jesus asserts his authority over the sabbath, an answer not acceptable under Jewish law. Then in 3:2,
the opponents are watching Jesus in order to accuse him legally
if he violates the sabbath. Since Jesus has been warned in 2:24,
if he acts illegally on the sabbath in 3:1-6, he is liable to
arrest. Thus while rhetorically 2:28 is part of the unit, 2:23-
28, and 3:1 presents a new narrative beginning, there is a logical connection between the two pericopes. The claim of Jesus
in 2:28 prepares the reader for the higher level of hostility
and the greater stakes involved in 3:1-6.

Mark 3:1-6:
The Man with the Withered Hand

In content, the healing of the man with the withered hand
is a continuation of the debate over sabbath observance begun
in the story of the plucking of the grain. The hook words τοῖς
σάββασιν (2:23,24; 3:4) and ἔξεστιν (2:24,26; 3:4) connect the
two pericopes.[135] Further, 3:1-6 builds upon the narrative of
2:23-28. In 2:28, Jesus claims, as Son of Man, to be lord of
the sabbath. In 3:1-6, he demonstrates or illustrates his lordship by healing on the sabbath.[136] In addition, the fact that
the antecedent of "they" of παρετήρουν (3:2) seems to be the
Pharisaic group who questioned Jesus about the disciples' sabbath
behavior in 2:24, indicates the continuity of the narrative.[137]

In form, however, the last controversy has much more in
common with the healing of the paralytic, the first controversy
in 2:1-12, than with 2:23-28. Like the healing of the paralytic,
3:1-6 is a healing controversy with the actual healing at the
end. In 3:1-6 the characters are Jesus, the sick man and the
opponents. In both 2:1-12 and 3:1-6, the opposition of the
opponents is not voiced aloud.

Perhaps the most striking similarity between 2:1-12 and
3:1-6 is the rhetorical pattern: the miracle is begun, then
interrupted for Jesus' address to the opponents, and only after
that completed.[138] As the debate section in 2:1-12 is framed
by Jesus' two addresses to the paralytic, here Jesus' answer to
the opponents is framed by his two commands to the sick man,
introduced by λέγει τῷ ἀνθρώπῳ (3:3,5). Both are clearly delineated ring compositions. Unlike 2:6-10a, however, the central
portion of 3:1-6 should not be considered an interposition. It
is not sufficiently set off from the outer ring in which the
opponents also feature strongly. The three parts of the pericope will first be analyzed: 3:1-3, the beginning of the miracle; 3:4-5a, Jesus' interchange with his opponents; and 3:5b-6,
the completion of the miracle. Then, the pericope as a whole
will be discussed, in itself and as the conclusion to 2:1-3:6.

Rhetorical Analysis of the Individual Parts

Verses 1-3: Jesus once again enters a synagogue. The
opening phrase echoes the opening phrase of the controversy section in 2:1: Καὶ εἰσῆλθεν (εἰσελθὼν) πάλιν εἰς. Πάλιν, as in
2:1 and 13, refers specifically to a place Jesus has already
been in Mark 1; in this case a synagogue (1:21). The reader is
informed that there is a sick man present--a man with a withered
hand--and the opponents are watching Jesus to see if he will
heal on the sabbath, in order to accuse him. The description
of the opponents presumes, on the internal story level, that
they are aware of Jesus' healing powers and the likelihood that
he would heal on the sabbath.[139] Mark's readers have been well
prepared for these presuppositions by the narrative of the gospel thus far. Jesus' healings have played a prominent role
(1:21-27, 29-31, 32-34, 39, 40-44; 2:1-12). Two have occurred
on the sabbath: the public exorcism in the synagogue (the story
recalled by πάλιν,and the healing of Peter's mother-in-law.

Further, the description of the opponents emphasizes their
hostility or opposition to Jesus. The opponents' "watching" is
hardly neutral curiosity. They wish to accuse him, that is,
bring legal charges against him.[140] Sabbath violation could be
a serious charge, punishable by death (Exod 31:14-15; M. Sanhedrin
7:4).[141] The fact that the Pharisees are trying to find legal

grounds for accusing Jesus shows that, on the story level, they
do not accept Jesus' claim that, as Son of Man, he is lord of
the sabbath. In their eyes, Jesus does not have the authority
to change or ignore the sabbath law.

In v. 3, Jesus says to the handicapped man: Ἔγειρε εἰς
τὸ μέσον, literally, "get up to the middle." Jesus has commanded
the man to stand on center stage; whatever healing may occur will
be witnessed by everyone present.[142] The public nature of the
healing confronts not only the synagogue audience but also the
reader with the choice between Jesus and the Pharisees. The
reader may either accept that Jesus indeed has the authority to
dispense with the divinely ordained sabbath law, or he may agree
with the Pharisees that the sabbath law is binding on Jesus.

Verses 4-5a: As the narrative is recounted in Mark, vv.
4-5a are the central part of a ring composition, in which Jesus
concerns himself with his opponents, enclosed by an outer ring
which contains the miracle. Although the reader is not told
explicitly as he was in 2:8, Jesus appears to be aware of the
unspoken objection of the Pharisees--violation of the sabbath.[143]
For he responds with a double counter-question about what is
legal on the sabbath: to do good or to do harm (evil), and to
save life or to kill.[144]

Several features of the saying should be noted. In the
first place, the saying does not directly address the issue of
legality on the sabbath. It was not legal to do harm or kill
on any day of the week; saving life was permitted on the sabbath even if it violated the sabbath rest. The Pharisees would
consider Jesus' answer irrelevant to the issue of sabbath observance.

Second, the saying admits no middle ground; there are no
neutral acts. One must choose to do good *or* evil, to save life
or kill. The parallelism between the two pairs of alternatives
accentuates the seriousness of one's acts: doing good is in
effect saving life; failing to do good may be equivalent to
killing. Third, the saying in its narrative context is the assertion of a general principle which overrides the Mosaic law
concerning the sabbath.[145] As a general principle, it becomes
not only the principle by which Jesus acts, but also the principle by which the actions of Jesus' opponents will be judged and
condemned.

Last, unlike Jesus' answers in all four preceding apophthegms, here Jesus' response contains no direct personal claim.
In this pericope, Jesus does not justify his (or the disciples')
objectionable behavior on the basis of his own particular status
or mission. By means of a rhetorical question, he asserts a
universal principle applicable to all. In the gospel narrative,
Jesus' assertion of a principle which can override the law is
undoubtedly an indirect claim to be speaking for God. Nonetheless, the saying places the opponents in the position of grap-
pling with the issue of doing good, a goal they would accept,
rather than being able to attack Jesus on the basis of a potentially blasphemous personal claim.

The opponents remain silent. Jesus then reacts to the opponents with anger and grief at their hardness of heart (v. 5a),
one of the longest descriptions of Jesus' emotions to be found
in the gospel. The biographical interest, not characteristic
of the controversy apophthegm form, serves to intensify the element of conflict between the opponents and Jesus: not only do
the opponents seek to accuse Jesus, but Jesus is angry with them
and grieved at their reaction to his message.

Verses 5b-6: As in 2:10, the narrative reverts in mid-
sentence from consideration of the opponents to the healing.
Although 3:5 does not present the syntactical difficulties of
2:10, it does present the same shift from opponents to sick man.
Jesus commands the man to stretch out his hand, he does so, and
the hand is restored. The completion of the miracle balances
the beginning of the miracle in vv. 1b-3, forming the outer part
of the ring composition. In each part, χείρ is mentioned twice
(3:1,3,5 bis); in the first part, "withered" is repeated
(ἐξηραμμένην ἔχων, ξηρὰν...ἔχοντι); in the second, the verb
"to stretch out" is repeated (ἔκτεινον, ἐξέτεινεν). In addition,
λέγει τῷ ἀνθρώπῳ is used twice (vv. 3, 5), each time to introduce Jesus' command to the sick man. The commands frame the
central part of the ring composition containing Jesus' address
to his opponents.

Verse 6 reports the reaction of the opponents. They do not
accuse Jesus of sabbath healing as one might expect from v. 2;
perhaps because healing by word, not touch, is not illegal on

the sabbath,[146] perhaps because in this story Jesus does not
personally claim authority over the sabbath, or perhaps because
it is too soon in the gospel for a formal charge leading to
Jesus' trial and death. Rather the Pharisees leave the synagogue, the scene of the conflict. For the time being, Jesus is
the victor.[147] The reader is informed, however, that the Pharisees immediately held counsel with the Herodians,[148] how to destroy Jesus. The reader is now aware that the opposition to
Jesus has escalated to the point where some--the Pharisees and
Herodians--wish to kill him.

The Pericope as a Whole

As the first controversy was a ring composition in which
a healing framed a debate between Jesus and his opponents, so
also the last controversy is a ring composition in which a
miracle frames a debate. In the healing of the paralytic, however, the interposition of the debate within the miracle func-
tioned to isolate the conflict from the ongoing development of
the narrative. In the healing of the man with the withered hand,
the atmosphere of conflict dominates the entire narrative. In
comparison to 2:1-12, the opponents replace the role of the crowd
at the beginning and the end of that narrative. In the opening
miracle portion, the opponents seek to catch Jesus on a legal
charge (3:2), the first explicit indication in the gospel that
the opponents wish to move against Jesus. In the middle section,
Jesus virtually taunts the opponents with his question about
doing good and saving life, and is angered and grieved with their
lack of response.[149] Finally, after the healing, the Jewish
leaders go out to seek Jesus' death. Conflict per se, not sabbath observance, appears to be the major focus in the final controversy. Verse 6 is the climax not only to this pericope, but
to the entire section, spreading its note of impending doom over
all the controversies.

The conflict in the last pericope is explicitly a matter
of life and death: the opponents seek to accuse Jesus on what
may be a capital offense (v. 2); Jesus' question poses the alternatives of saving life or killing (v. 4); and finally the
opponents begin to plot to kill Jesus (v. 6). The ironic (and
tragic) interplay of life and death pervades this pericope. As

Albertz wrote, "Wie Jesus durch Unterlassung der Heilung Leben
morden würde, so sind die Gegner im Herzen wirklich erstorben
und finden daher nur den Ausweg des Mordanschlags."[150] From now
on in the gospel narrative, Jesus stands under the threat of
death. Jesus' healing act has become a step on the way to the
cross. And the Jewish leaders' rejection of Jesus and his message is a step on the way to their own destruction (12:1-12).[151]

The Frame Around Mark 2:1-3:6

It was noted above that Mark 2:1-2 introduced an abrupt
shift in the plot line from 1:45. In 1:45 Jesus was out in the
country, unable to enter a city, and people were coming to him
from everywhere. In 2:1, with no reason given, Jesus returns
to Capernaum. Mark 3:7, following the controversy section, again
presents a stark plot shift from 3:6: Jesus is in the country,
with people flocking to him, and with no hint of opposition to
him. Indeed, 3:7 picks up again exactly where 1:45 left off:

> Jesus withdrew with his disciples to the sea, and
> a great multitude from Galilee followed; also from
> Judea and Jerusalem and Idumea, and from beyond the
> Jordan and from about Tyre and Sidon, a great multi-
> tude, hearing all that he did, came to him. (3:7-8,
> RSV)

In 1:45, the people came to him πάντοθεν. In 3:7-8, the places,
"everywhere," are specifically named. In 1:45, Jesus was no
longer able to enter a city because of the crowds; in 3:9, Jesus
has the disciples prepare a boat for him, lest the crowd should
crush him on land. Opposition, conflict, the threat of death
are put to one side, and the theme of the overwhelming popularity
of Jesus is resumed.

The frame around 2:1-3:6 brackets the opposition in the
controversy section exactly as the beginning and ending of the
healing of the paralytic bracketed the conflict over blasphemy,
Jesus' authority to forgive sins (2:6-10a).[152] Indeed, rhetorically, 2:1-3:6 is one large interposition. And the rhetorical
function is the same: in each instance, the use of the rhetorical device of an interposition set in a frame has enabled the
narrator to make the hearer aware of the depth and seriousness
of the opposition to Jesus, without, at that point in the narrative, having to resolve the conflict. By means of the interposition of 2:1-3:6, the reader is now aware that some groups

opposed Jesus from the beginning. He knows that the Jewish
leaders reject Jesus and his message of the kingdom of God, to
the point of wishing to destroy him. The reader is invited to
side with Jesus and the kingdom or with the Pharisees. Mean-
while, the narrator, by bracketing or framing the controversy
material, can continue the narrative of Jesus' activities without yet carrying the conflict to its conclusion on the cross.

Summary

The analysis of the individual pericopes has highlighted a
variety of rhetorical techniques and structures occurring in the
text. Some of the rhetoric, such as the use of word repetition
and shifts in word order in 2:18-20, has been quite elegant.
Other rhetorical features, such as the interposition of 2:6-10a
in 2:1-12, strike most modern readers--though not Matthew or
Luke--as awkward. Upon analysis, each of the pericopes was
found to have a quite clearly defined rhetorical structure,
identified on the basis of content, form, and word repetition.
Mark 2:1-12, 13-17, 23-28, and 3:1-6 are all tripartite patterns;
2:18-22 has a balanced two-part structure. Mark 2:1-12 and 3:
1-6 are ring compositions; 2:13-17 and 23-28, while not strictly
delineated as ring compositions, show the third part in some
connection with the first part. The device of an interposition
set in a frame occurs both in 2:1-12 and 1:45-3:8.

Frequent and varied use of word repetition has been observed.
In 2:1-12, 23-28 and 3:1-6, word repetition (hook word usage)
aids in structuring the text. In 2:13-17, the repetition of
"sinners" and "tax collectors" serves to unify the diverse elements of the text. In 2:18-22, the absence of word repetition
between vv. 18-20 and 21-22--in contrast to the repeated use of
word repetition within each set of verses--helps to indicate the
rhetorical division of the pericope. Word repetition has been
used to connect the narrative retrospectively to Mark 1:16-45
(2:1-2,13,14; 3:1), and to interconnect the pericopes within
2:1-3:6. Repetition has also been used for rhetorical emphasis
in 2:1-12, 13-17 and 18-22. In regard to 2:10a, the first Son
of Man saying, extensive repetition has been used in order to
stress the new, unrepeated material.

The text of 2:1-3:6, however "unliterary" its Greek may be, exhibits a considerable range and sophistication of rhetorical usage. The analysis of the rhetoric of the texts studied should make the perusal of 2:1-3:6 a richer aesthetic experience for the reader.

Moreover, the rhetorical analysis is helpful for the exegesis of the texts. It serves as a control for exegetical interpretations. For example, the rhetorical analysis of 2:6-10a shows that the saying on the Son of Man in v. 10a cannot be a markan parenthetical aside to his reader for it is an integral part of the rhetorical structure and argument of 2:6-10a. Further, the analysis can help illumine the meaning and theological significance of a text. For example, attention to the rhetoric of 2:13-17 makes the reader aware of the emphasis on the disciples and the nature of their relationship to Jesus.

Finally, the rhetorical analysis provides upon occasion some assistance to redaction and form critics. Negatively, it demonstrates that 2:1-12 need not be explained as the interpolation of a controversy into a miracle narrative. The present form of 2:1-12 may equally well be explained on the hypothesis that the material was originally a healing controversy apophthegm. The "clumsiness" of the literary seams which modern readers usually adduce as evidence for interpolation may be the result of employing the interposition-frame technique to set off the controversy from the on-going narrative. Positively, the results of the rhetorical approach suggest, for example, that the emphasis upon the disciples in 2:13-17 is due to redaction not tradition. Thus, rhetorical criticism would seem to be a useful, indeed a necessary, tool for the redaction and form critic.

CHAPTER IV

SECOND READING OF MARK 2:1-3:6

In the first reading of Mark 2:1-3:6, the rhetorical techniques within the individual pericopes and between successive
pericopes were described and discussed. In the second reading,
the focus will be upon the rhetorical structure of 2:1-3:6 as
a whole. First, the concentric and chiastic rhetorical pattern
of 2:1-3:6 will be described. Second, the significance of the
overall rhetorical structure for understanding the meaning or
theology of the Galilean controversy section will be discussed.

The Rhetorical Pattern of
Mark 2:1-3:6 as a Whole

The Results of the First Reading

As noted earlier, the second reading builds upon the results of the first reading. Several of the major results of the
first reading are important indicators of the overall rhetorical
structure:

First, the opposition to Jesus, evident in all five stories,
climaxes in the last one in which the opponents seek grounds to
accuse Jesus, and at the end, plot to destroy him. Further, the
five controversies are framed by 1:45 and 3:7-8 in which Jesus'
popularity is stressed and opposition to him is absent. These
two observations suggest a linear or climactic development within 2:1-3:6 which is not the linear development of the larger narrative. This phenomenon will be returned to in the discussion
of the significance of the structure.

Second, the first two pericopes, the healing of the paralytic and the call of Levi/eating with sinners, are concerned
with Jesus' relation to sin and sinners. There is continuity
of subject matter and the presence of hook words between the two
pericopes. Similarly, the last two pericopes, plucking grain on
the sabbath and healing on the sabbath, both concern sabbath observance. Here also, there is continuity of content and the
presence of hook words. In contrast, the middle pericope is
concerned with fasting, not with sin or sabbath. It has no hook

words joining it to the preceding or following pericopes.[1] It
also differs from the other four in that no specific opponents
are introduced. These facts suggest that 2:1-3:6 may have a
three-part structure of sin-fasting-sabbath (2:1-17, 18-22, 23-
3:6).

Third, the first and last pericopes are both healing controversies with the healing at the end. The cast of characters
includes Jesus, a sick man, and the opponents. The three middle
pericopes, on the other hand, are all controversies of the action-
objection-vindication type. They report no healings. The cast
of characters includes Jesus, the disciples, and opponents.
These facts suggest that 2:1-3:6 may be a ring composition of
healing controversy, followed by non-healing controversies involving the disciples, followed by healing controversy (2:1-12,
13-28; 3:1-6).

The second and third groups of observations considered together suggest that the structure or rhythm of the Galilean controversy section is more complex than a three-part pattern or a
ring composition. The second reading or rhetorical analysis of
the interrelationships of the five pericopes will show that 2:1-
3:6 has a tight and well worked out concentric and chiastic structure. The pericopes may be labelled as follows:

A   2:1-12   The healing of the paralytic

B   2:13-17   The call of Levi/eating with sinners

C   2:18-22   The sayings on fasting and on the old and
               the new

B'   2:23-27   Plucking grain on the sabbath

A'   3:1-6   The healing on the sabbath

The two healings (A and A') are parallel to each other. The
call of Levi and the plucking of grain (B and B') have many
parallel elements. The question of fasting (C) is a middle
unit without a parallel pericope. It is related to B and B' in
one way and to A and A' in a different way. First, the rhetorical indicators connecting A and A', B and B', and defining C's
place in the structure will be described. Then the pattern as
a whole will be summarized.

Rhetorical Analysis of the Elements of the Concentric Structure

A and A'. The two healing controversies. As noted in the
first reading of 3:1-6, the parallelism of structure between
2:1-12 and 3:1-6 is striking. In both pericopes, the miracle
narrative is begun, interrupted for Jesus' address to his opponents, and then resumed. This rhetorical pattern, miracle initi-
ated-debate-miracle completed, is found only in these two narratives in Mark and their synoptic parallels.[2] In both stories,
the miracle portion of the narrative is ended and then resumed
by parallel addresses by Jesus to the man being healed. In the
first healing, the addresses are introduced by λέγει τῷ
παραλυτικῷ (2:5,10); in the second by λέγει τῷ ἀνθρώπῳ (3:3,5).
The repetition of λέγει τῷ... not only helps to structure each
pericope but also to emphasize the parallelism between them.

The parallelism of A and A' may be recognized as well in
various details of content, form and hook word usage. The pericopes open with virtually identical introductions: A, Καὶ
εἰσελθὼν πάλιν εἰς (2:1), and A', Καὶ εἰσῆλθεν πάλιν εἰς (3:1).[3]
Both occur indoors: A in a house, A' in a synagogue. In neither
story do the opponents of Jesus openly state their opposition.
Thus, in both, Jesus may be said to take the initiative. In the
first, A, Jesus knows that they debate in their "hearts"; in the
last, A', Jesus is grieved at their hardness of "heart." These
are the first uses of "heart" in the gospel[4] and the word is not
used again until 6:52 in which the disciples' hearts are hardened.
In both A and A', Jesus responds to unspoken opposition with a
counter-question: "Which is easier, to say...or to say...?"
(2:9), "Is it lawful on the sabbath to do...or to do...?" (3:4).

The healings are also similar. Both are accomplished by
word alone. Neither is a cleansing or an exorcism, but rather
the restoration of parts of the body.[5] These healings might be
described as resurrection-type healings.[6] The symbolism of
death-resurrection is implied in the narrative of the healing
of the paralytic as Farrer argues:

> The man is carried by four bearers, like the dead
> going to burial. Unable to come at Christ other-
> wise, they *dig out* (St Mark's word) a hole and lower
> him into his grave. Thus descending, he falls in
> the presence of the Son of God, and "stands up on
> his feet"... The miracle of the paralytic carries
> the symbolism of resurrection almost as far as it
> will go.[7]

The withered hand is also "resurrected." Bowman writes, "Life
has been given to his apparently dead hand."[8] The verb ἐγείρω
is used three times in the story of the paralytic and once in
the story of the withered hand, in the rather odd expression,
ἔγειρε εἰς τὸ μέσον (3:3). The expression serves to bring the
verb into the story.

Finally, each narrative closes with the description of the
reaction of the onlookers, "the impression the miracle creates
on the crowd." [9] The content of the reactions is not parallel
but antithetic. The crowd responds to the first with amazement
and glorification of God (2:12). The opponents respond to the
healing of the man with the withered hand by beginning to plot
to destroy Jesus (3:6). The reaction in 3:6 is hostile, not
admiring, but it seems nonetheless to fill the slot in the miracle
form of the response of the audience.[10]

Thus A, the healing of the paralytic, and A', the healing
of the man with the withered arm, are constructed in a closely
parallel manner as shown by structure, form, content and word
repetition. The detailed similarities seem well beyond any
parallelism which might result from the use of the same form.

*B and B'. The controversies over eating with sinners and
plucking grain on the sabbath.* As noted above, B is set in relation to A, and B' to A'. A and B concern sin/sinners. In
both, the crowd (and the larger group of tax collectors and sinners) plays an important role. B' and A' are concerned with
violation of the sabbath law. In these two pericopes, the crowd
no longer plays any part. Also, as noted earlier, B and B' share
several characteristics with C, over against A and A'. B, C
and B' are controversies of the action-objection-vindication
type; they report no healing; they include the disciples in their
cast of characters. Finally, B and B' have parallels of structure, form, content and word repetition with each other. The
multiple relationships of B and B' with A, C and A', and with
each other, should not surprise the reader. In the rising and
falling oral pattern of a symmetrical composition, the intermediate elements between the extremes and the center may well
balance each other as well as be related, each to what precedes
and follows it.

The parallelism between B and B' is strongly marked. Story B opens with Jesus out of doors, beside the sea, calling Levi from his tax office to be a disciple, calling a sinner who is in the middle of sinning (2:13-14). Jesus then enters Levi's house. It closes with a general proverb, "Those who are well have no need of a physician, but those who are sick," followed immediately by the implied christological or "I" saying:[11] "I came not to call the righteous but sinners" (2:17).

Story B' similarly begins out of doors, in the fields, with the disciples breaking the sabbath law by plucking grain (2:23). In vv. 25-26, David is pictured indoors in the house of God. It ends with the general proverb, "The sabbath was made for man, not man for the sabbath," followed immediately by the christological saying, "So the Son of Man is lord also of the sabbath." The content of B and B' is different (sin and sabbath) but the structure is the same. In both instances, the final proverb and christological claim may justify the initial action.

The central sections of B and B' (vv. 15-16, 25-26), moreover, are concerned *not* with sinners or sabbath; both are explicitly concerned with *eating*. In B, Jesus enters a house (as story A took place in a house) and eats with tax collectors and sinners. The fact that Jesus is eating is stressed four times, and the verb ἐσθίω is used twice in the present tense. In B', Jesus refers to the scriptural incident of David entering the house of God (as A' takes place in a synagogue), eating the bread of the presence and giving it also to "those with him." Ἐσθίω is used twice in the aorist. In story B, Jesus and his disciples eat with tax collectors and sinners, something not proper in the light of the rabbinic laws of ritual cleanliness. In B', David and his followers ate food which was not lawful for them to eat.

In story B, eating is an integral part of the controversy: the opponents question why Jesus eats with tax collectors and sinners (v. 16). Yet Jesus' answers in v. 17 do not explicitly justify *eating* with sinners. The opponents would agree that a doctor must go among the sick in order to heal them, but they would argue that his purpose in going is to heal them, not to catch the disease--to become a sinner--himself. In B', eating is not an essential part of the controversy. The relevance of

the example of David eating the showbread as a justification for
the disciples' breaking of the sabbath work laws is doubtful.
However, the Davidic example could be used as a justification
for eating with sinners. The story of Peter and Cornelius in
Acts 10:1-11:18 shows that the image of eating forbidden food
may serve to justify the reception of Gentiles into the church.
In Acts, the connection was that both the food and the people
were considered unclean. In Mark 2:15-16, 25-26, the connection
would be that both eating with sinners and eating the showbread
were unlawful. The function of the Davidic reference in B' may
well be to justify Jesus' eating with sinners in B, rather than
to justify the breaking of the sabbath law in B'.[12] David broke
the law when he had need (χρείαν ἔσχεν, v. 25); Jesus asserted
that the sick, not the well, need a physician (χρείαν ἔχουσιν,
v. 17). The inclusion of the Davidic reference in B' establishes
a strong chiastic relationship between B and B' *and* serves to
introduce the subject of eating into B'.

   C. The question of fasting and of the old and new. The
literary interrelationships and correlations of the first two
and the last two controversy stories seem sufficiently numerous,
significant and precise to establish that A,B and B',A' are a
well-worked out chiasm. Thus C is the middle section of the
literary pattern by definition.
   The rhetorical pattern of story C differs from the other
four. The others all fall rhetorically into three major parts.
A and A' are ring compositions, with the miracle at the beginning and the end. B might be described as two situations with
one dominical response (2:13-14, 15-16, 17), and B' as one situation with two dominical responses (2:23-24, 25-26, 27-28). Story
C, on the other hand, falls rhetorically into two halves: the
question and answer on fasting (vv. 18-20) and the sayings on
the old and the new (vv. 21-22). The other four pericopes are
connected to each other rhetorically by hook words; C is not.
   C also differs from the other controversies in its content.
Each of the other four has an explicit setting: in a house, by
the sea/in a house; in the fields/in the house of God; in a
synagogue. C is completely without indication of setting. In
the other four controversies, the opponents are specifically

named: scribes, the scribes of the Pharisees, then Pharisees,
and the Pharisees with the Herodians. In story C, the opponents
are not specified. Finally, in C alone, two time periods are
explicitly contrasted, the time before and the time after Jesus'
death.[13]

These rhetorical and content differences serve to set C
apart from the other four controversy stories. It stands alone
as the middle pericope of the five. It is not closely connected
rhetorically with any of the others, all of which are closely
interwoven with each other.

At the same time, however, C is set in relation to B and
B'. C shares with B and B' the absence of any healing and the
presence of the disciples. Further, it, like B and B', is concerned with eating. The verb "to eat" is not used in C; instead
the verb "to fast" is used--six times. Fasting in C is contrasted with eating in B and B'. Thus all three middle pericopes are concerned in some way with eating. In B, Jesus eats
with the wrong people. In C, the disciples do *not* fast. In
B', Jesus cites the example of David eating unlawful food. And
in all three stories, the disciples are associated directly or
indirectly with eating: they too eat with sinners; they do not
fast; David's followers were also given the unlawful food. Thus,
B, C and B' have a common content which A and A' do not share:
religiously or legally "objectionable" eating in which the disciples are included.

C also has a commonality of content with A and A'. However,
it is not a relationship of manifest content but of theme: death/
destruction vs. life/resurrection. Since the relationship is
one of theme, not of manifest content clearly evident in the
text, it will be discussed below as part of the significance of
the structure, rather than here as part of the argument for the
existence of the structure.

Summary of the Structure

Thus the five controversy stories of Mark 2:1-3:6 form a
tightly constructed literary unit which has a quite elegant symmetrical pattern: the first two stories have to do with sin;
the last two with the sabbath law; the first and last stories
describe resurrection-type healings; the second, third and fourth

in some way concern eating; the disciples play a role in the
middle three controversies but not in the first or last one.

The pattern may be observed not only in general content,
but also in structure, and details of content, form, and word
repetition. The parallelism of A and A' is extensive on the
basis of all the criteria. The relationships of B and B' are
elaborate. They are parallel to each other in their shift of
setting from outdoors to indoors, in their common content of
eating in the middle verses and their common structure in their
closings. Further, B is rhetorically related to A, and B' to
A', while both B and B' are related to C. The central pericope,
C, is in some ways set apart rhetorically from the other four
pericopes, and in other ways related to them. The sheer number
of congruent parallelisms, both major and minor, noted in the
text, demonstrates that the concentric literary pattern is
definitely to be found in the text itself.

The elegance of the pattern in all its detail need not imply that the composer or compiler of 2:1-3:6 constructed it with
a worked-out geometric model in mind. For the pattern at its
base is quite simple, a rising and falling rhythm of healing-
eating-healing developed in regard to the issues of sin and sabbath. This may suggest that the redactor worked from a preliminary plan, as many ancient authors did.[14]

Mark 2:1-3:6, however elaborate its pattern, remains a
series of conflict stories. The opponents move from silent
criticism of Jesus in the first story, to the questioning of
Jesus' disciples, to the questioning of Jesus himself, to trying to find grounds for a legal accusation, finally to plotting
to destroy him. This sequence may be a literary device to lend
a sense of progression and climax to an otherwise content-struc-
tured unit.

The Significance of the Structure
for the Meaning of Mark 2:1-3:6

Since the rhetorical structure of a literary text does not
exist apart from the content of the text; since the determination
of structure is based to a considerable degree on content (e.g.,
healing, sabbath, conflict, etc.), the discussion of the significance of the structure is basically a discussion of how the

structuring of the content helps the reader to interpret that content. The discussion will be in four parts: first, the contribution of the linear or climactic development to the understanding of 2:1-3:6; second, the contribution of the concentric pattern to its understanding; third, a consideration of the occurrence of the title, Son of Man, in 2:10 (A) and 2:28 (B'); and last, a consideration of the role of the disciples in 2:1-3:6.

Linear or Climactic Development in 2:1-3:6

Mark 2:1-12 as the introduction to the controversy section. In her introduction to her study of Mark 2:1-12, Maisch writes that it is not clear how to entitle the pericope: should it be "the healing of the paralytic," "the forgiveness of sins through Jesus," "the first controversy of Jesus with his opponents," or "the authority of Jesus as Son of Man"?[15] She concludes that the authority of Jesus is the most appropriate designation for the narrative.[16] Budesheim, on the contrary, opts for conflict,[17] while Hultgren sees the forgiveness of sins as the central issue.[18]

This scholarly debate need not be resolved. A controversy apophthegm, unlike a parable, does not have a single major point. Even as an independent unit in the tradition, a controversy apophthegm inevitably includes three major elements--conflict between adversaries, the actual subject matter of the conflict, and the vindication or triumph of the hero. The vindication of the hero may be demonstrated by a resolution of the actual issue under debate, by a dismissal or adroit avoidance of the issue, or by the hero's claim to be above the issue on the basis of his status or mission. In Mark 2:1-12, Jesus' healing begun by means of a forgiveness formula sparks the conflict with opponents over Jesus' right to act for God, which Jesus vindicates by his claim to be the Son of Man with authority on earth. All four of the aspects of 2:1-12 that Maisch describes are an integral part of the story of the paralytic.

Furthermore, all four aspects are resumed and developed in the ensuing controversy stories. A person hearing or reading Mark 2:1-3:6 might focus first on Jesus' extraordinary miracle-working power stressed in 2:1-12 then on Jesus' power over sin as he hears the story of the call of Levi and Jesus' eating with

tax collectors and sinners. The reader's attention then would
be drawn to Jesus' special status with God, the aspect introduced in the first Son of Man saying (2:10), reinforced by Jesus'
saying on his mission to call sinners (2:17) and by his metaphor
of the bridegroom (2:19-20), and climaxing in the second Son of
Man saying asserting lordship over the sabbath (2:28). Finally,
as the last controversy again involving a healing is heard, or
read, the reader's attention would turn to the continuing opposition to Jesus, first introduced in the story about the paralytic, reinforced by the continuing series of debates, and
climaxing in the last narrative, in which the opponents plot
to destroy Jesus (3:6). Thus, Mark 2:1-3:6 serves for the reader
as an introduction for the entire controversy section.

   The heightening of conflict. The earlier discussion of
possible premarkan Galilean controversy collections highlighted
the fact that any concatenation of controversy apophthegms serves
to stress both the opposition to the hero and the hero's triumph
over the opposition.[19] The predominant thrust of a series of
controversies depends on how the opposition is developed from
controversy to controversy and the note upon which the series
of controversies ends.

   In 2:1-3:6, the element of opposition is gradually heightened
for the reader until its climax in 3:1-6. In the first story,
the seriousness of the threat to Jesus, the possibility of a
charge of blasphemy, is muted for the reader by employment of
the interposition technique and the favorable reaction of the
crowd at the end. In the second story, the opponents question
the disciples. In the fifth, the reader is told that the opponents are watching Jesus in order to make a legal charge against
him, and finally that they begin plotting how to destroy him.
This sequence or linear development places the emphasis of the
entire controversy section on the *opposition* Jesus' actions have
aroused. Further, the fact that the notices of opposition in
3:1-6 are information given to the reader only and not to the
internal audience of the story,[20] indicates that a, if not the,
major function of the Galilean controversy section in the gospel
of Mark is to make the reader aware of the opposition to Jesus.
The emphasis in 2:1-3:6 is not upon Jesus' triumph over his opponents, but on their implacable hostility.[21]

Mark 3:1-6 as the conclusion to the controversy section.
The Galilean controversy section stresses not only the fact of
conflict but also the serious or fundamental nature of the conflict. The first story poses the alternatives of Jesus as
blasphemer or Jesus as the legitimate Son of Man. As noted in
the first reading, the final controversy makes explicit that
the outcome of the conflict is a matter of life or death.
Mark 3:1-6 adds no new subject matter for conflict. Rather it
serves as a conclusion to the whole series summing up the abso-
luteness of the conflict: what Jesus considers doing good or
making alive, his opponents consider sufficiently harmful to
warrant his death. Mark 3:1-6 also hints at the outcome of the
conflict--Jesus' death. Whatever else 2:1-3:6 in the context of
Mark's gospel may convey to the reader, it certainly conveys that
Jesus and the opponents are on a collision course leading towards
Jesus' death. Mark 2:1-3:6 might perhaps be compared in musical
terms to the statement, early in a musical work, of a major theme
which then hangs ominously over the composition, but which only
comes to dominate the music much later in the piece.

The Concentric Pattern as an Aid to Understanding Mark 2:1-3:6

Perhaps the most important function of the symmetrical pattern in 2:1-3:6 is to create a coherent literary unity out of
episodic incidents, to bind the incidents into an organic whole.
The controversy section is not just a concatenation of miscellaneous acts of Jesus to which the opponents increasingly take
exception. The effect of the literary unity of the section on
the reader is to emphasize that the opponents objected to Jesus'
activity as a whole, and to the messianic claim which was the
basis of Jesus' actions.

The literary unity of the Galilean controversy section means
that the individual parts of the section can only be fully understood in the context of the larger structure. Thus recognition
of the structural pattern can be of considerable assistance to
the twentieth century exegete in his attempt to understand Mark
2:1-3:6.

First, awareness of the pattern can help to elucidate the
meaning of individual elements in the section which are otherwise obscure or a matter of debate. Second, awareness of the

organization of individual elements into a larger structure leads
to recognition of themes which are brought out in the narrative
as a whole more forcefully than in the individual elements.
Third, awareness of the rhetorical pattern can make the reader
aware of contrasts or paradoxes implicit in the narrative, greatly enriching his experience of the text.

The usefulness of the rhetorical analysis of 2:1-3:6 for
interpreting the meaning of the text will be discussed under
three headings: exegesis of individual elements, the role of
healing and eating, and the theme of life vs. death. The issues
of the occurrence of the title Son of Man, and of the role of
the disciples, will be held for separate consideration.

Exegesis of individual elements. The concentric and chiastic
rhetorical pattern is particularly helpful in interpreting the
material contained in B and B'. As noted earlier, the meaning
of Jesus' citation of the scriptural incident of David eating
the showbread is more fully grasped when it is seen not only in
relation to its own pericope, B', the plucking of the grain on
the sabbath, but also in relation to its parallel pericope, B,
eating with sinners. Further, the parallel structure of the
ending of B and B', a general proverb followed by a christological or "I" saying (2:17, 27-28), suggests that the proverb about
the sick not the well needing a physician is to be understood as
a generally applicable saying. The physician is *not* to be interpreted as a christological metaphor analogous to the metaphor of
the bridegroom in 2:19-20.[22]

Retrospectively, A' helps to interpret A for the reader.
The fact that in A' the opponents are searching for legal grounds
on which to accuse Jesus recalls to the reader's mind the opponents' objection in A that Jesus blasphemes (2:7), and that
blasphemy can be a capital offense. In retrospect, A as well as
A' suggests the possibility (or inevitability) of Jesus' death
at the hands of his opponents. What is explicit in A' is implicit in A.

The role of healing and eating. The symmetrical pattern,
the ring composition of healing-eating-healing, emphasizes that
Jesus' objectionable behavior is associated with the activities

of healing and eating. Neither activity is in itself illegal
behavior. Both activities are a fundamental part of Jesus'
ministry in the proclamation and bringing of the kingdom. In
Mark 1, preceding the controversies, Jesus has already worked
three specific miracles, an exorcism, the "raising" of Peter's
mother-in-law, and the cleansing of a leper (1:23-27, 30-31,
40-44), as well as healing "many who were sick with various
diseases" and casting out "many demons" (1:34). In Mark 1, he
ate a meal with the four men he had called to be disciples (1:
29-31). Healings continue to be an important part of Jesus'
ministry in Mark 1-10, and eating is also stressed in the spec-
tacular feedings of the 5,000 and the 4,000 and in the institution of the last supper (6:30-44; 8:1-10; 14:22-25). Both healing and eating again become the subject of controversy (3:22-30;
7:1-23), and the feeding of the four thousand apparently provokes
the Pharisees' demand for a sign from heaven (8:1-13).

In 2:1-3:6, healing and eating are yoked together by the
concentric pattern. The issues of sin and sabbath are each
raised in regard to both healing and eating (A,B : B',A'). Thus
the structure of 2:1-3:6 helps to underline for the reader the
fundamental nature of the conflict between Jesus and his opponents. Opposition arises not because of Jesus' incidental violation of specific religious pieties or laws which could have been
avoided. It arises because Jesus' basic ministry includes as
prominent elements healing and eating behavior which could not
be accommodated in the wine skins of the Judaism of the time.[23]

The theme of life vs. death. In A and A', Jesus visibly
triumphs over his opponents in the two "resurrection-type" healings. The objections of the opponents, on the other hand, are
issues which could lead to death for the healer.[24] In A, the
charge is blasphemy, the charge upon which the Sanhedrin eventually condemns Jesus to death (2:7; 14:64). A healing on the
sabbath which was not necessary to preserve life could also be
a capital charge.[25] While Jesus avoids grounds for legal accusation in A',[26] the opponents nonetheless begin to plot how to
destroy him.

Thus both the first and last controversies contain at least
implicitly the themes of resurrection and death. These themes

are made explicit in Jesus' saying in A', in which he presents
the opponents with the either/or of saving life or killing (3:4).
Jesus chooses to save life in restoring the withered hand; the
opponents choose to kill in plotting against Jesus (3:5-6).

C, like A and A', reflects implicitly the theme of death
vs. life. In C, however, there are no specifically named opponents, and not fasting is not a legal offense, let alone a capital charge. In C, it is Jesus himself who alludes to his own
death (2:20). Then, without interruption, Jesus speaks of the
threat the new poses for the continued existence of the old (2:
21-22). Now it is the opponents, the guardians of the old way
of Judaism, who stand under the threat of destruction. It is
not until the parable of the wicked tenants that the reader (and
the opponents) is clearly told that the death of Jesus, the son,
will lead to the destruction of the opponents as well (12:1-12).
In 2:1-3:6, by means of the concentric structure, the reader is
alerted that 3:6, the climax of the linear development, may not
be the end of the story.[27]

The occurrence of the theme of death vs. life in A, C and
A' corresponds surprisingly well to Lund's "laws" of concentric
structure.[28] Similar ideas *are* expressed in the extremes and
center of the pattern and not elsewhere. The theme of death vs.
life is not found in B or B'. An opposite idea *is* introduced
in the center, before the original trend is resumed. The section
as a whole shows the growing opposition to Jesus, pointing ahead
to his death; C, the central section, points beyond Jesus' death
to the continued existence of the disciples, who will then fast,
and to the possibility of destruction for the opponents (2:20,
21-22). A great deal has been conveyed to the reader through
the five controversy stories--about Jesus' ministry, the objections to it of the Jewish opponents, the possibilities of Jesus'
death, the destruction of the opponents, and the continued life
of the new community.

Excursus on the Son of Man in 2:10 and 28

In this instance, the question is not, how does the struc-
ture of 2:1-3:6 help us to understand the meaning of the Son of
Man sayings in this section? The meaning seems evident enough:
Jesus as Son of Man has authority on earth over sin and the

sabbath. The question, rather, is how does the rhetorical structure of 2:1-3:6 help the reader to understand the function and
importance of the two sayings?

Rhetorically, the double use of the Son of Man title stands
outside of the symmetrical pattern of 2:1-3:6. Mark 2:10 occurs
in the interposition in A; 2:28 at the end of B'. This fact,
combined with the observations that these are the only two uses
of Son of Man in the sense of earthly authority in the synoptic
tradition, and the only uses in Mark prior to 8:31, may suggest
that the occurrences of the title in 2:1-3:6 are due to the redactor's unmodified incorporation of tradition.

Such a position is difficult to maintain, however, since
each individual saying is rhetorically stressed. Mark 2:10
stands out by virtue of the repetition in which it is embedded.[29]
Mark 2:28 is emphasized by virtue of its climactic place as the
punch line of the controversy form. Each individual saying calls
attention to itself. The double use would certainly strike the
listener or reader. A redactor who could create the rhetorical
richness of 2:1-3:6 would hardly overlook the rhetorical stress
on Son of Man in the composition.[30]

A single asymmetrical stressed element would not appear to
undermine the existence of a balanced concentric structure such
as 2:1-3:6. In the first place, balanced literary patterns
(whether symmetrical or repetitive parallelism) in the ancient
world normally contained asymmetric elements. Ancient authors
on rhetoric or literary criticism may be cited either praising
the lack of perfect balance or condemning too perfect balance.[31]
(The fact that it is apparently easier to find such statements
in ancient writings than statements arguing for extended balance
perhaps implies that balance in literary compositions was taken
for granted, consciously or unconsciously.) In the second place,
from a rhetorical perspective, an effective way to emphasize an
element is to make it stand out from the general rhetorical pattern. Third, while the two sayings are not rhetorically parallel
--one in the middle of A, the other at the end of B'--there is
an overall balance in terms of the manifest content of 2:1-3:6.
One saying is in regard to sin and healing, the other in regard
to sabbath and eating.

The sayings in 2:10 and 28 serve to stress Jesus' earthly
authority as Son of Man, that is to express an aspect of christology. The other christological material in 2:1-3:6, the "I came"
saying in 2:17b and the bridegroom image in 2:19-20, are also
connected with Jesus' earthly ministry expressing its mission
or the joy associated with it. Together with the Son of Man
sayings, they provide for the reader the basis for and the justification of Jesus' acts. Only the two Son of Man sayings, however, concern directly the issue of Jesus' authority.

The conflicts described in 2:1-3:6, however, do not appear
to center on the issue of Jesus' authority. Other controversies
in Mark are over the source or legitimacy of Jesus' authority
(3:22-30; 11:27-33). In 2:1-3:6, the issue of Jesus' authority
is raised by the opponents in the first story, when they say to
themselves that Jesus blasphemes (2:7). The opponents, however,
do not raise the authority issue again in 2:1-3:6. Instead,
they continue to object to Jesus' or the disciples' *behavior* re-
lating to healing and eating, sin and sabbath. In the final
controversy, the opponents are watching to see what Jesus will
do, and Jesus' saying contains no christological material at all.
The opponents are concerned with what Jesus does and not with
who he is or claims to be.

The linear development of 2:1-3:6 has shown that conflict
between Jesus and the Jewish leaders is a major theme of 2:1-
3:6. Since the conflict is over behavior, not christology, it
would seem that the narrator is not using the material in 2:1-
3:6 to argue for (or against) a christological position. The
emphases of the concentric structure on healing and eating and
on the theme of life vs. death also suggest that christology is
not among the major theological intentions of the narrator in
2:1-3:6.

Nonetheless, the section does contain considerable christological material. From the *rhetorical* perspective, the christological material seems to be assumed or taken for granted by
the narrator. The treatment of the christological material
would imply that the narrator intends his writing for an audience
which shares the christological assumptions of 2:1-3:6. Similarly, from the *redactional* perspective, W.H. Kelber writes in regard to this section, "Mark uses Son of Man to establish rapport

with his [Mark's] opponents because it was under this title that
Jesus was known to them."[32] It would not seem necessary to presuppose
markan opponents in 2:1-3:6. It is sufficient to say that the
author of 2:1-3:6 assumes that his audience shares his christology at this point; he does not argue for it.

The double use of the title Son of Man remains a striking
feature of 2:1-3:6, even if it does not appear to reflect any
of the narrator's major theological intentions in the controversy
section. Looking beyond 2:1-3:6 in Mark's gospel, the stress on
Son of Man with earthly authority appears to serve a useful rhetorical function in preparing the reader for the later (and
clearly polemical) uses of Son of Man for the suffering, death
and resurrection of Jesus. As Perrin wrote, the two sayings
"serve the function of equating the authority of Jesus with that
of the Son of Man."[33] This equation needs to be made before the
passion prediction in 8:31, if 8:31 is to be understood by the
reader. Thus the occurrence of Son of Man, both rhetorically
stressed and outside the rhetorical symmetrical pattern, serves
mainly to prepare the way for later developments in the narrative, not to illumine the meaning of the Galilean controversy
section.

Excursus on the Role of the Disciples in Mark 2:1-3:6

    In recent scholarly debate over the theology of Mark, much
attention has been paid to the role of the disciples, and to
their "misunderstanding" or "blindness."[34] However, neither in
studying the role of the disciples in Mark, nor in studying 2:1-
3:6 has much attention been paid to the disciples in this portion
of the gospel.[35] Yet the rhetorical analysis of Mark 2:1-3:6
has brought to light the prominence of the role of the disciples
in the Galilean controversy section.

    In the first reading of the individual pericopes, the promi-
nence of the disciples in B, C and B' was observed. In B, 2:13-
17, by means of the call of Levi, the first use of the term
"disciple," the statement that many were following Jesus, and
the fact that the question about Jesus' behavior is addressed
to the disciples not Jesus, the disciples are brought to the
forefront of the reader's attention.[36] In C, the fourfold use
of the terms "disciples" and of "those associated with the bridegroom" in vv. 18-20 again places the emphasis upon the disciples

in regard to the question of fasting. In B', 2:23-27, the stress
upon the disciples is sustained by the fact that it is they who
violate the sabbath rest and whose behavior is attacked, and by
the inclusion of David's companions along with David in the Old
Testament reference (vv. 23-24, 25-26).

In the second reading, the rhetorical structure of the
section as a whole, the role of the disciples is also stressed.
The presence--or absence--of the disciples is one of the determining features of the symmetrical pattern. The disciples are
involved along with Jesus in the three controversies over associating with sinners, over not observing the pious practice
of fasting, and over breaking the sabbath. Thus, they are joined
with Jesus in the three specific issues of the section--sin,
fasting, and sabbath. Further, they are joined throughout with
Jesus in his objectionable behavior in regard to eating. On
the other hand, they do not participate in Jesus' objectionable
healing behavior: they play no role in A or A'.

The rhetorical analysis, which has demonstrated an emphasis
upon the role of the disciples in the Galilean controversy section, indicates that scholars studying the role of the disciples
in the gospel of Mark as an avenue to understanding Mark's theology and *Sitz im Leben* should include a consideration of the
disciples in 2:1-3:6.[37]

The present concern of this study is not on the function
of the disciples in markan theology but on the significance of
the rhetorical structure of 2:1-3:6 for understanding the meaning and function of that text. Thus, the following discussion
will be limited to two issues: first, the portrait of the disciples presented in 2:13-28 as a whole; and second, the question
of whether the rhetorical structure sheds any light on the reason
for the disciples' exclusion from Jesus' healing activity in 2:1-
3:6.

The portrait of the disciples in 2:13-28. The rhetorical
emphasis upon the disciples in 2:13-28 and the disciples' place
in the symmetrical pattern of 2:1-3:6 suggest that the disciples
are not just incidentally characters in these controversies but
that the redactor of 2:1-3:6 is making some point about the disciples and the nature of discipleship. A closer consideration

of the role of the disciples in 2:13-28 may help to illumine
what that point is.

The picture of the disciples in 2:13-28 is indeed a consistent one. The disciples, with Jesus, engage in behavior characteristic of the coming of the kingdom--they eat with outcasts,
they do not fast, they ignore the sabbath requirements. The new
freedom is not Jesus' alone but extends to his disciples as
well.[38] Further, the disciples' participation in "kingdom" behavior brings them, like Jesus, into conflict with the Jewish
opponents. It is their behavior which is questioned in C and B'.

Perhaps the most striking feature, however, of the presentation of the disciples in 2:13-28 is not their inclusion in Jesus'
freedom and its consequences, but the presentation of their relationship to Jesus. Throughout the three pericopes, the disciples' dependence upon Jesus is stressed. The call of Levi to
become a disciple rests solely upon the initiative of Jesus.
The justification for Jesus' (and by extension, the disciples')
eating with outcasts is *Jesus'* mission to sinners. The disciples' practice of fasting or not fasting depends entirely upon
the presence or absence of Jesus. The citation of the incident
of David eating the showbread emphasizes the subordinate or derivative role of David's followers. The followers did not act
illegally on their own account; they did so because of their
association with David and because he in effect authorized them
to do so. Finally, the disciples' violation of the sabbath is
justified by Jesus' authority over the sabbath as Son of Man
(2:23-24,27-28).[39] The disciples' behavior is justified indirectly by their relationship to Jesus. Throughout 2:13-28,
the subordinate or derivative role of the disciples is emphasized.
Their actions depend upon the initiative and authority of Jesus.[40]

The picture of the disciples in 2:13-28 does not yet show
any hint of the motif of misunderstanding or blindness found
later in the gospel. That motif appears to be introduced first
in 4:13 in regard to the disciples' not understanding the parable (Jesus' teaching) and in 4:40 in regard to Jesus' miraculous
power over the storm. The picture presented in 2:13-28 is a
positive one of the disciples responding to Jesus' initiative
and unhesitatingly following in his way against the old way of
Judaism.[41] In the gospel, Mark first presents the disciples'

immediate response to Jesus' call (1:16-20; 2:14) and then their
dependence upon Jesus' initiative and authority in their participation in the life of the coming kingdom (2:13-28). Only after
these motifs have been established is the further motif of the
disciples' lack of understanding introduced.

   The disciples and healing in 2:1-3:6. In 2:1-3:6, the disciples participate in all aspects of Jesus' ministry except for
healing. One major reason for their exclusion from healing may
be seen in the order of Mark's gospel. Mark 2:13-28 emphasizes
the dependency of the disciples upon Jesus, their subordinate
or derivative role. Healing, like eating, is a manifestation
of the coming of the kingdom of God. But healing, more particularly, is a manifestation of Jesus' ἐξουσία from God. It is
not until 3:14-15 that Jesus formally appoints the twelve and
gives them authority over demons, and not until 6:7-13 that he
sends the disciples out to preach and heal. Given the derivative nature of the discipleship role, the disciples' participation in healing can only follow their empowerment and sending
forth by Jesus.[42]

   The life versus death theme brought out by the symmetrical
structure of 2:1-3:6 may provide an additional reason for the
exclusion of the disciples from A and A'. In A and A', Jesus
triumphantly accomplishes resurrection-type miracles. Also in
A and A', the threat of death hangs most closely over Jesus--
in the potential charge of blasphemy in 2:7, and in the opponents watching Jesus to make a legal charge against him, and
then plotting to destroy him in 3:2,6. But the possibility or
inevitability of death for Jesus is not an inevitability or
necessity for the disciples.[43] Indeed, in the central pericope
of the concentric structure, the debate about fasting in which
Jesus alludes to his coming death (2:20), the disciples are
explicitly excluded from the death which will overtake Jesus.
They remain to fast after the bridegroom has been taken away.
The confrontation of the way of life and death revealed in 2:1-
3:6 is first of all a confrontation between Jesus, whom the
reader knows to be the Christ and Son of God (1:1,11), and his
opponents. By excluding the disciples from A and A', where the
conflict is most serious, and affirming their continued existence

after the conflict culminates in Jesus' death in C, the redactor
of 2:1-3:6 has emphasized for the reader the focus of the life/
death theme upon the person of Jesus *and* the fact that the disciples, the adherents of Jesus, will not be destroyed in this
confrontation of life and death.[44]

Summary

The results of the second reading confirm and extend the
results of the first reading. The rhetorical structure of 2:1-
3:6 is indeed elegant, showing the hand of a redactor skilled
in structuring, interrelating and developing his material. Both
the linear pattern, the introduction of motifs in 2:1-12, their
development in the succeeding pericopes and climax in 3:1-6, and
the elaborate concentric and chiastic pattern of 2:1-3:6 reveal
the work of a redactor skilled in the art of narrative.

Awareness of the literary pattern helps the reader to understand and appreciate the text. The pattern helps to explain
the meaning and function of individual elements of the text such
as the relation of 2:25-26 to 2:15-16, and the role of the Son
of Man sayings in 2:10 and 28. The pattern helps to bring out
the meaning and emphases of the text as a whole: the fundamental
nature of the conflict between Jesus and his opponents, the role
of healing and eating, the theme of life and death, and the
nature of the discipleship role. The study of rhetorical structure, then, not only enriches the reader's experience of the
text, but is a useful aid to the redaction critic in determining
the theology of the text.

The rhetorical analysis also has important implications for
the methodology of form and redaction criticism. The multiple
interrelationships of the text indicate that the critic, who
attempts to determine the tradition history and redaction of a
pericope, may not restrict his study to the individual pericope.
He must also consider the larger rhetorical unit of which the
pericope is a part, since many details of the pericope may be
the result of modification of tradition to fit the larger structure. For example, the extensive parallelism of A and A' (2:1-
12, 3:1-6) suggests that one or both pericopes were modified
(or even composed) in order to make the two pericopes parallel.
The elaborate interconnections of A with B (2:1-12,13-17), B with

B' (2:13-17,23-28), and B' with A' (2:23-28; 3:1-6) show that
the individual traditions must have been redacted to fit their
place in the larger structure. For example, the fact that both
B and B' end with a general proverb followed by a christological
saying may be due not to the individual development of the separate pericopes but to the redactional activity of the compiler
of 2:1-3:6. Thus, rhetorical criticism is not only a useful
approach in its own right to elucidate the meaning of a text,
but also an additional tool for determining the tradition history and redaction of a text.

CHAPTER V

CONCENTRIC STRUCTURE IN THE GOSPEL OF MARK

In the previous chapter, after the rhetorical analysis of
Mark 2:1-3:6, the linear and the concentric patterns were discussed from the point of view of their contribution to understanding the meaning or theology of 2:1-3:6. In this chapter,
the focus of attention will be on literary structure itself.
For the recognition of the symmetrical parallelism or concentric
structure to be found in Mark 2:1-3:6 raises two questions re-
quiring consideration. First, if the concentric structure in
2:1-3:6 is as well-defined and elegant as has been argued, should
not the structure be a commonplace of biblical exegesis? Second,
is 2:1-3:6 an isolated occurrence of symmetrical patterning or
rhythm in Mark, or does it occur elsewhere, and frequently enough,
so that it may be considered one of Mark's literary techniques?
Since both these questions raise the issue of identification of
symmetrical patterns in a text, a major focus of this chapter
will be methodological, an analysis of adequate criteria for
isolating symmetrical rhetorical structures in a text. Although
the discussion will focus on concentric patterns, the methodology
should be generally applicable for identifying any rhetorical
pattern.

In this chapter, first the criteria actually used to identify the pattern of Mark 2:1-3:6 will be described. Then, the
recognition of the structure of 2:1-3:6 by modern biblical scholars and by Matthew and Luke will be discussed, and it will be
argued that at least Luke clearly recognized Mark's pattern.
After that, the gospel of Mark will be surveyed to see if extended symmetrical structures may be considered a markan literary technique. In this section, the opening of the gospel (1:
1-8), the parable discourse (4:1-34) and the Jerusalem public
ministry (11-12) will be discussed in some detail. It will be
concluded that indeed extended concentric patterns are one of
Mark's literary techniques for structuring blocks of material.
Finally, the issue of adequate criteria for identifying rhetorical patterns will again be reviewed.

Criteria for Identifying Concentric Patterns

In Chapter One, it was observed that content and/or word
repetition were the usual means employed for identifying symmetrical patterns. It was suggested that for the synoptic material, at least, parallelism of form provided an additional
criterion. It was stated that the more congruent symmetries a
passage contains, the surer one is that the pattern is one which
exists in the text rather than one imposed by the interpreter.[1]
The rhetorical analysis of 2:1-3:6 indeed disclosed multiple
congruent parallelisms based on content, form, and word repetition. The following is a more detailed analysis of the criteria
actually used in identifying the concentric pattern of Mark 2:1-
3:6.[2] The same types of criteria, of course, may be used to
identify any rhetorical pattern, whether linear, repetitive,
concentric, or for that matter, the absence of any clear rhetorical pattern.

Content. Parallelisms of content varied from the very general (Jesus heals, some reference to eating) to the highly specific (in each healing, Jesus restores a part of a man's body by
means of his word alone). The parallelism may be synonymous or
antithetic--e.g., the contrast of eating vs. fasting or the reaction of the crowd to Jesus' healing in 2:12 and of the opponents in 3:6.

Two particular types of content parallelism deserve special
mention for their usefulness in identifying structure: setting
and character roles. Setting includes indications of time and
place and generally occurs at the beginning of a pericope. In
2:1-3:6, place indications predominate. Character roles, as
has been seen, may be filled by the same person or group (e.g.,
Jesus or the disciples) or by different ones in turn (e.g., the
two disabled men, or the sequence of opponents). The narrative
or internal audience is a specific character role.

In using content parallels for identification of rhetorical
patterns, two methodological questions appear relevant. First,
is the content parallel objective--that is, can most readers
readily agree that the parallel really exists in the text?
Second, how does one establish the relative importance for identifying structure of various, sometimes incongruent, parallels

of differing specificity and salience? The second, while subject to the guideline of multiple congruent parallels, remains
dependent upon the literary sensitivity--and theological dispo-
sition--of the rhetorical critic. A rhetorical analysis may
be said to be successful to the degree that it sheds light on
the understanding of the text. The first issue is discussed
below.

     Content parallels involve varying degrees of abstraction.[3]
To say that in the healings in 2:1-12 and 3:1-6 Jesus restores
formerly handicapped parts of the body and employs the verb,
ἐγείρω, is descriptive. It reflects manifest content. To call
these two healings "resurrection-type" healings is to employ a
classification accepted by some scholars, not one self-evidently
contained in the text. To point out that blasphemy in A and
healing on the sabbath in A' are both potentially capital charges
is valid enough, based on our knowledge of the gospel of Mark
and the Judaism and Christianity of the time. But it is to
generalize beyond what is clearly stated in the text. To argue
on the basis of the above information (plus the manifest content
of 3:1-6) that both A and A' reflect the theme of death vs. life/
resurrection is to move beyond a description of manifest content
to an interpretation of the text. All of the above statements
are, in my opinion, helpful for understanding the text.

     However, for the purposes of *identifying* a rhetorical struc-
ture, it seems most objective and most subject to control to
limit the parallels used to those which are clearly descriptions
of manifest content or widely acceptable abstractions from manifest content. The death/resurrection theme should not be used
to help establish structure. Indeed, the argument at that point
has shifted from the first stage, the use of content to identify
pattern, to the second stage, the use of pattern to illumine the
meaning of the content. The second stage is indeed the aim of
the rhetorical enterprise. Methodologically, however, the two
phases should be kept as separate as possible.

     Form. Like content parallels, formal parallels may be very
general (pronouncement story, healing controversy) or quite specific (a general or secular proverb, a christological saying).
There is an obvious overlap with content: a healing controversy

contains the subjects of healing and conflict; a christological
saying says something about Jesus. Form, however, provides a
different perspective from content for viewing the text, and one
which may more readily be classifiable. Scholars may argue over
whether the disciples in Mark 2:23-24 are making way for Jesus
or are gathering food; they can, however, agree that the action
is the "objectionable behavior" which is the starting point of
the controversy apophthegm.

In the rhetorical analysis of the individual pericopes of
the Galilean controversy section, the internal structure of each
of the pericopes was found to differ in various ways from the
typical or basic "structure" of the controversy form. In the
second reading of the section as a whole, various parallels
were noted between the internal structure of one pericope and
another, parallels that cannot be attributed to form-critical
similarity. For example, both healing controversies, A and A',
not only were of the formal type with the healing at the end,
but both had the unusual structural pattern of healing, address
to opponents, healing. The apophthegms B and B' each climaxed
not with a single logion but with a double saying of Jesus, a
general proverb followed by a christological or "I" saying.
Thus, in addition to parallelisms of form-critical classification, the parallels found between the structures of individual
pericopes were a helpful tool in identifying the overall structure of the section.

Word repetition. The different types of word repetition
were spelled out in Chapter One. Here the question is, how does
one evaluate whether or not an instance of word repetition is
significant or merely coincidental. David J. Clark, in trying to
define criteria for determining the "variable significance" of
hook words, has written as follows:

> Rarer words are more significant then common words.
> Identical forms are more significant than similar
> forms. The same word class is more significant than
> different word classes formed from the same root.
> Identical roots are more significant than suppletive
> roots.[4]

What Clark writes about the infrequency of a repeated word and
about the degree of verbal identity would seem generally applicable. Some variations of word form may be required by the

syntax of a sentence; some may reflect the writer's desire for
variety. Other factors, however, also need to be considered.
A series of words may constitute a hook phrase even if the individual words are frequent (e.g., καὶ εἰσελθὼν/εἰσῆλθεν πάλιν εἰς
2:1, 3:1; λέγει τῷ ἀνθρώπῳ 3:3,5). Perhaps the most important
factors are how the repeated words function in their context and
where they occur in the overall pattern. P. Mourlon Beernaert
writes:

> Il s'agit d'y mettre surtout en valeur les multiples
> relations et les dépendances internes....Notre atten-
> tion se portera donc sur un ensemble d'indices relevés
> dans le texte considéré comme un tout, reconnaissant
> volontiers que des détails isolés de l'analyse, pris
> en eux-mêmes, n'ont pas grande valeur et peuvent
> souvent être refusés: cela seul a du poids qui est
> vérifié par l'ensemble du passage et confirmé par la
> convergence des indices.[5]

Thus both Mourlon Beernaert and I cite "heart" in 2:6,8 and 3:5
as a hook word supporting the parallelism of A and A'.[6] In each
case, the word is used in the central debate with Jesus' opponents. And neither of us (nor Clark) has cited οὐδέποτε, in
2:12 and 25, the first occurrence at the end of A, in the crowd's
acclamation of Jesus, and the second in the middle of B', used
as an interrogative, in Jesus' question to his opponents. The
usages are not sufficiently parallel, even though the word is
rare--these are its only occurrences in Mark. The occurrence
of word repetition is not necessarily in itself meaningful.

Summary. What is meaningful or significant is the existence
of multiple congruent parallelisms, of content, or form-critical
classification, of structure, and of word repetition. In the
words of Mourlon Beernaert, "La 'structure' littéraire qui permet
de synthétiser le plus grand nombre d'éléments textuels démontre
par la même sa richesse et sa fécondité,"[7] or in the words of
Clark, "As with the force of catchwords, so with the chiastic
criteria as a whole, *the impact is cumulative*."[8]

The identification of a symmetrical pattern, then, is in
part objective. Content parallels, parallels of form and structure and word repetitions may be demonstrated in the text. The
pattern formed by multiple congruent parallels may be described
and diagrammed. The recognition of the symmetrical structure,

however, is in part subjective as well. The interpretation of
the parallels, the significance (if any) laid upon them, the
awareness of the cumulative effect, is a matter for the discre-
tion and judgment of the literary critic. The recognition is
in part dependent upon the aural sensitivity of the audience.

Recognition of Mark 2:1-3:6
as a Symmetrical Pattern

If the concentric structure of 2:1-3:6 is as well-defined
in the text and as elegant as has been argued, should not the
structure be a commonplace of biblical exegesis? First, it will
be argued that an increasing number of modern scholars have
recognized the symmetrical pattern of 2:1-3:6. In surveying
their work, the discussion of adequate criteria for identifying
patterns will be continued through evaluation of the criteria
these scholars used to identify the structure. Second, the
question of first century recognition of the structure will be
addressed by means of an analysis of how Matthew and Luke have
edited Mark's structure.

Recognition in Contemporary Scholarship

The symmetrical pattern of Mark 2:1-3:6 is sufficiently
marked that it has come increasingly to be recognized by twentieth century scholars, even with our heritage and training in
strictly linear, logical thinking. That the last two pericopes
both concern sabbath law has probably always been self-evident.
It was stressed by J. Weiss in 1903[9] and Bacon in 1909.[10] Sundwall in 1934 pointed out that the first two controversies, like
the last two, formed a pair, this time connected by the concern
with sin.[11] Farrer in 1952 noted that the middle three controversies all dealt with eating.[12] Rudolf Grob in 1965 appears
to have been the first to call attention to the striking similarities between the first and last controversy stories: both
are healings, in both Jesus speaks while the opponents remain
silent, in both Jesus commands the man to rise, in both Jesus
stands alone facing his opponents, while in the three middle
ones the disciples are a part.[13] Grob also notes some content
connections between each two successive controversies.

Giuseppe G. Gamba in 1966 was the first scholar to recognize a symmetrical pattern in Mark 2:1-3:6.[14] He is concerned to demonstrate that the synoptic gospels are literary writings following the ancient rhetorical rules of *dispositio* or arrangement.[15] In 2:1-3:6, Gamba focuses on the content pattern: sin-fasting-sabbath, 2:1-17, 18-22, 23-3:6. He notes the continuity in content between 2:1-12 and 13-17 and between 2:23-28 and 3:1-6, and the formal parallels between 2:1-12 and 3:1-6. Each contains a miracle and a narrative conclusion (audience reaction), while the middle three pericopes end abruptly with the words of Jesus.[16]

Gamba does not observe the congruent concentric pattern of healing-eating-healing, 2:1-12, 13-28; 3:1-6, in which the disciples participate in the eating but not in the healing. Gamba ignores the element of conflict or controversy in interpreting the entire section. He sees no linear or climactic development. Thus Gamba misses some major rhetorical features of the section. Nonetheless, by viewing it from the point of view of arrangement and noting just a few of the content and structure parallels, he became aware of the symmetrical pattern.

Then, in 1973, Mourlon Beernaert[17] and I[18] presented independently of each other somewhat different proposed concentric patterns for Mark 2:1-3:6. Mourlon Beernaert's method, similar to mine, has already been cited in the discussion on criteria above: he seeks to determine pattern on the basis of the convergence of multiple indices of textual elements. His actual analysis employs content parallels and word repetition, but not formal or structural indices.

Mourlon Beernaert has stated his purpose as follows:

> ...l'effort de notre étude viserait à dégager la structure à *la fois* littéraire et théologique de l'ensemble de ce passage de Marc (2,1-3,6).[19]

> Nous sommes invités...à examiner si ces controverses ne se conditionnent pas l'une l'autre dans leur composition littéraire *et* théologique.[20]

Thus, Mourlon Beernaert emphasizes the identity of the literary and theological structure while I would argue that the literary structure is an avenue toward understanding theological meaning.

Mourlon Beernaert summarizes his concentric structure as follows (my pericope letters are given in the left margin for comparison):

A	W	2:1-9	Healing by Jesus, silence of opponents ("And entering again," "heart")
	X	2:10-12	Declaration on the Son of Man (authority)
B	Y	2:13-17	Action of Jesus, reaction to the disciples ("eat," "have need")
C	Z	2:18-22	Sayings of Jesus on the bridegroom and newness
B'	Y'	2:23-26	Action of disciples, reaction to Jesus ("eat," "have need")
	X'	2:27-28	Declaration on the Son of Man (lord)
A'	W'	3:1-6	Healing by Jesus, silence of opponents ("And he entered again," "heart")[21]

Mourlon Beernaert's insistence on the identity of the theological and literary structure[22] appears to be the reason that his structure deviates from Gamba's and mine. In studying 2:1-3:6, he seeks to discover "*ce qui est contesté* dans la personne de Jésus," and focuses on the most striking christological feature of the section, the Son of Man sayings. "La double affirmation sur l'autorité du Fils de l'Homme, assez solennelle dans le récit,...peut nous amener à une nouvelle lecture du passage."[24] Using the two sayings as his starting points, he then builds his structure around them: "Cette double déclaration nous invite à être attentifs à d'autres parallélismes littéraires, de manière à percevoir progressivement l'architecture globale du texte."[25]

Placing the two Son of Man sayings in symmetrical parallelism (X and X') results in breaking the first and fourth pericopes into two parts each, thereby obliterating the formal and structural parallels between the two healing miracles, the first and last pericopes, and between the general proverbs and christological sayings climaxing the second and fourth pericopes.

In so doing, Mourlon Beernaert has lost much of the richness the structure of the five stories helps bring out. He has obscured the healing-eating-healing pattern, the role of the disciples, and the life-death theme of the first and last pericopes. He has destroyed the chiastic relationship of the first two and last two pericopes (2:1-12,13-17 : 23-28; 3:1-6). Rather he focuses on 2:18-22, the center, hinge, or pivot, "qui donne la clef de l'ensemble,"[26] and how it helps to elucidate the entire controversy section.[27] Mourlon Beernaert tends to consider the center of a concentric structure the most important part by definition.[28] Since his structure obscures the pattern among the four outside pericopes, it gives Mourlon Beernaert no reason to modify his concentration upon the center as the key to understanding.

Thus, Mourlon Beernaert's method for identifying a structure (concentric or otherwise) suggests various reflections on adequate criteria. First, to assume the identity of theology and literary structure is to invite definition of a *literary* pattern around its *theological* content--in this case the Son of Man sayings. If literary/rhetorical patterns are to be a useful means of bringing out the meaning or theology of a passage, then the literary pattern should be determined as far as possible by literary/rhetorical means alone. The argumentation should not be more circular than it need be.

Second, formal and structural parallels should be included along with content and word repetition among the criteria for identifying symmetrical (or other) patterns. This does not mean that every pattern with a symmetrical rhythm will necessarily contain marked formal or structural parallels. It does mean that a rhetorical critic must analyze a passage for such parallels and take them into account. When they do exist, they provide an important control on the fancies of any literary/rhetorical critic as well as considerable support for (or against) a given structure.

At minimum, the overall structure, "l'architecture globale," should *not* conflict with the literary structure of the individual parts of the whole. In breaking 2:10-12 from 2:1-9, Mourlon Beernaert has separated Jesus' final statement to the opponents from the interposition which it climaxes, and associated it with the healing. Given all the rhetorical clues provided in 2:1-12,[29] it seems improbable that either the composer/redactor intended or the audience would hear a break before v. 10.

Finally, insofar as a rhetorical pattern is something which may be sensed or felt (on some level) by the audience,[30] then the

rhetorical pattern must respect the major literary divisions
contained within it--that is, the individual episode or pericope. For it is the individual pericope or story which most
immediately stands out as a unit. A listener is not likely to
be aware (consciously or unconsciously) of a complex pattern or
higher level structure which conflicts with--rather than builds
upon--the obvious aural units, as Mourlon Beernaert's three-part
divisions of 2:1-17 and 2:23-3:6 do.[31]

Recognition in the First Century

If symmetrical patterning is truly a literary structure
heard consciously or unconsciously by at least some of Mark's
audience, it is more important to be able to demonstrate that
first century people were aware of such patterns than that twentieth century biblical scholars are. One way to approach the
question of audience awareness is to look at how Matthew and
Luke have employed the material from Mark 2:1-3:6, to see if it
can be determined if they recognized the symmetrical pattern.

Matthew certainly did not retain Mark's structure. The
first three controversy pericopes are to be found in Matthew
9:1-17, and the last two not until 12:1-14. The content of the
last two, the sabbath pericopes, are modified to include halachic-
type arguments.[32] Nonetheless, there is some evidence that
Matthew may have recognized the concentric pattern--or at least
the parallelism of pericopes B and B', eating with tax collectors
and sinners and plucking grain on the sabbath. For in each pericope, just before the final christological saying, he inserts
the quotation from Hosea 6:6: "I desire mercy, and not sacri-
fice." In 9:13 (B), he introduces it with the phrase, "Go and
learn what this means." In 12:7 (B'), he introduces it with
the accusation: "And if you had known what this means...you
would not have condemned the guiltless." And in both cases,
the final christological saying is connected by means of the
conjunction, γάρ. These are the only two citations of Hosea
6:6 in Matthew. The connection between the quotation and its
context is not very clear in either instance.[33] It would seem
more probable that Matthew's recognition of the parallelism of B
and B' in Mark lies behind his double insertion of the quotation
that that the parallel insertion is the result of chance.
chance.

The evidence that Luke recognized and deliberately kept
Mark's concentric structure is virtually conclusive. He keeps
the section intact; he keeps the large majority of Mark's parallels of content, hook words, form and structure; and, most convincing, he adds several additional parallels.

The five controversy apophthegms, in Mark's order, are
found in Luke 5:17-6:11, near the beginning of Jesus' public
ministry in Luke's gospel. Like Mark, Luke has set the controversies into a frame--but a different frame from Mark's. Instead
of Mark's picture of Jesus out in the country with people streaming to him from everywhere (Mk 1:45; 3:7-8), Luke pictures Jesus
in the country by himself, praying:

Lk 5:16   αὐτὸς δὲ ἦν ὑποχωρῶν ἐν ταῖς ἐρήμοις καὶ
           προσευχόμενος.

Lk 6:12   Ἐγένετο δὲ ἐν ταῖς ἡμέραις ταύταις ἐξελθεῖν
           αὐτὸν εἰς τὸ ὄρος προσεύξασθαι, καὶ ἦν
           διανυκτερεύων ἐν τῇ προσευχῇ τοῦ θεοῦ.

The two parts of Luke's frame may be derived from Mark: Luke
5:16 from Mark 1:35, and Luke 6:12 from Mark 6:46, neither of
which Luke uses in its markan context.[34] Whatever the source,
Luke has maintained the device of a frame around the five conflicts, while changing the content of the frame.

Luke extends the parallelism of content and hook words in
the two healing controversies, A and A' (Lk 5:17-26; 6:6-11),[35]
often picking up a word or phrase from one of the two pericopes
and incorporating it into the other.

(1)   In A, Luke changes the introduction from Mark's "Jesus
was speaking the word" to Jesus "was teaching." In A', Luke adds
that Jesus taught (ἦν διδάσκων, διδάσκειν, Lk 5:17; 6:6).

(2)   In Mark, in A, the handicapped man is always referred
to as the paralytic, while in A', he is referred to as the man
(ἄνθρωπος) having or with a withered arm (Mk 2:3,4,5,9,10; 3:1,
3,5). Luke keeps Mark's use of ἄνθρωπος in A', and inserts it
into A, introducing the paralytic first as "the man who" (Lk
6:6; 5:18).

(3)   Luke also makes the description of the opponents more
parallel: in both A and A' they are described as οἱ γραμματεῖς
καὶ οἱ Φαρισαῖοι.[36] In both instances, not just in A, Jesus
knows, τοὺς διαλογισμοὺς αὐτῶν (Lk 5:21, 22; 6:7,8).

(4) In both A and A', Luke keeps the basic structure of address to the handicapped man, address to the opponents, address to the handicapped man. Although he does not repeat τῷ παραλυτικῷ/τῷ ἀνθρώπῳ in the addresses to the man in need of healing, he does introduce Jesus' address with εἶπεν in all four instances (Lk 5:20,24; 6:8,10).

(5) Unlike Matthew, who drops Mark's awkward expression, ἔγειρε εἰς τὸ μέσον from the concluding healing, Luke modifies Mark's wording in A' to make it smoother Greek and smoother narrative, and adds some of the terminology from A' into A: A' reads, "Εγειρε καὶ στῆθι εἰς τὸ μέσον· καὶ ἀναστὰς ἔστη (Lk 6:8). Luke adds εἰς τὸ μέσον to A, in 5:19, as the description of where the men lowered the paralytic.[37] In both A and A', the handicapped man is placed in the middle. And in A, after Jesus commands the paralytic, ἔγειρε καὶ ἄρας, immediately he was ἀναστὰς ἐνώπιον αὐτῶν (5:24-25). In both A and A', Luke has the command, ἔγειρε, and the response, ἀναστάς.

(6) Finally, Luke emphasizes the (antithetical) parallelism of the audience response to the two healings by the use of a hook word: in A, ἐπλήσθησαν φόβου; in A', ἐπλήσθησαν ἀνοίας (5:26; 6:11). Πίμπλημι is used thirteen times in Luke, but only in these two instances and 4:28 in describing audience reaction.[38]

On the other hand, Luke has deleted Mark's hook words καὶ εἰσῆλθεν πάλιν εἰς and καρδία. These two deletions seem more than offset by the number and clarity of the parallels Luke has added to A and A'. One or two of Luke's changes or additions might possibly be attributed to consistent stylistic preference, but the sheer number of them indicates recognition--and extension --of Mark's parallelism between the two healing controversies.

That Luke recognized not just the parallelism of A and A' but a symmetrical pattern in the whole of Mark 2:1-3:6 may be seen in two significant changes Luke makes in stories B, C, and B'. In the first place, he makes the roles of the opponents, disciples, and Jesus exactly parallel in B and B'. In each instance the opponents ask the disciples about their own behavior. (The verbs are 2nd person plural.) In each case, Jesus formally answers the opponents:

B   5:31   καὶ ἀποκριθεὶς ὁ Ἰησοῦς εἶπεν πρὸς αὐτούς
B'   6:3   καὶ ἀποκριθεὶς πρὸς αὐτοὺς εἶπεν ὁ Ἰησοῦς

The word order of πρὸς αὐτούς and ὁ Ἰησοῦς is reversed (chiastic); otherwise the two clauses are identical.

Secondly, Luke makes more explicit than Mark the theme of
eating which connects the three middle pericopes.[39]   In B, the
opponents ask the disciples, Διὰ τί μετὰ τῶν τελωνῶν καὶ ἁμαρτωλῶν
ἐσθίετε καὶ πίνετε; in C, the opponents ask Jesus why the disciples of John and the Pharisees fast, οἱ δὲ σοὶ ἐσθίουσιν καὶ
πίνουσιν. Finally in B', the disciples pluck καὶ ἤσθιον τοὺς
στάχυας (5:30,33; 6:1). The content is present in Mark--ἐσθίω,
νηστεύειν and φαγεῖν. Luke adds the aural cue by the use of
"eat" from the root ἐσθίω in all three pericopes, and "drink"
in B and C.[40]   Luke, for one, recognized Mark's concentric structure.

Two further comments may be made about Luke's narrative
technique in comparison to Mark's in the controversy section as
a whole. First, Luke considerably weakens Mark's linear or
climactic development of the increasing level of opposition to
Jesus. He does not present a sequence of opponents, questioning
first the disciples and then Jesus directly. The conclusion
does not present a plot to kill Jesus, but merely a discussion
about what to do to Jesus (6:11).[41]

On the other hand, Luke has given the passage the impression of linear continuity by smoothing out some of the geographical and chronological sequences of the narrative.[42] Luke explicitly makes Levi the giver of the banquet in B (Lk 5:29). The
discussion over fasting in C is presented as a continuation of
the conversation at Levi's banquet (5:33). The healing in the
synagogue is on a different sabbath from the incident of the
grain plucking. Thus, in Luke as well as Mark, a linear movement is maintained as well as a clearly concentric pattern.

Other Concentric Structures in the Gospel of Mark

The second question raised by the structural pattern of
Mark 2:1-3:6 was whether such an extended concentric rhythm was
an isolated occurrence in the gospel of Mark or whether the
technique occurs elsewhere, and frequently enough, so that it
may be considered one of Mark's compositional techniques. The
answer would appear to be the latter. Although scholars have
yet to study much of the gospel of Mark from a rhetorical

perspective, they have already proposed extended symmetrical or chiastic patterns in chapters 1, 3, 4, 8-9, 13, and 15.[43]

Specifically, D. Dideberg and P. Mourlon Beernaert have suggested a seven-part (A B C D C' B' A') structure for 1:21-45.[44] Clark has suggested a five-part structure for 1:21-2:12 which overlaps and parallels the five-part structure of 2:1-3:6.[45] Jan Lambrecht has proposed that 3:20-35 is a five-part concentric structure, in which the middle section, C, is itself a ring composition, a b a'.[46] Lambrecht has also suggested that 4:1-34 has a five-part concentric pattern, with the second and third parts each containing a ring composition.[47] René Lafontaine and Mourlon Beernaert have argued that 8:27-9:13 has a seven-part concentric pattern, in which the middle section, D, is a six-member chiasm (8:34-9:1).[48] Lambrecht proposes that the apocalyptic discourse (13:5b-37) is a ring composition, in which both A and A' have five-part symmetrical patterns.[49] Ernest R. Martinez has recognized a thirteen-part chiastic or concentric ordering of the account of the death of Jesus in 15:29-41.[50]

A systematic rhetorical analysis of the entire gospel of Mark for extended concentric patterns is clearly beyond the scope of a single study. Even a detailed review and evaluation of the individual studies cited in the previous paragraph would occupy many pages. Therefore, the following analysis will be limited to a consideration of three texts: Mark 1:1-8; 4:1-34, and 11-12. The first two passages have been selected to demonstrate that concentric and chiastic patterns are employed elsewhere in Mark, and to suggest some of the variations of the technique. The third selection, Mark 11-12, is the discussion of the Jerusalem public debate material. Here it will be argued that Mark has employed the technique of symmetrical rhythm to organize some of the material.

Mark 1:1-8

Mark 1:1-8 is, of course, part of a larger rhetorical unit, the prologue of the gospel, 1:1-15. The entire prologue is delimited by the use of the inclusio, εὐαγγέλιον.[51] The prologue falls into two parts, vv. 1-8, concerned with John, the forerunner; and vv. 9-15, concerned with Jesus. The second part, vv. 9-15, is marked off by its own inclusio:

v. 9   ἦλθεν Ἰησοῦς ἀπὸ Ναζαρὲτ τῆς Γαλιλαίας

v. 14 ἦλθεν ὁ Ἰησοῦς εἰς τὴν Γαλιλαίαν

Further, the conclusion of the first part, John's preaching concerning the coming of Jesus (vv. 7-8), parallels the conclusion of the second part, Jesus' preaching concerning the coming of the kingdom of God (vv. 14-15). The two parts are also closely interrelated by extensive and varied use of word repetitions (e.g., ἡ ἔρημος, βαπτίζω/βάπτισμα, πνεῦμα, κηρύσσω, μετανοέω/μετάνοια, ἄγγελος). A full rhetorical analysis of Mark 1:1-15 would be extensive indeed. The following analysis, however, will be restricted to the elements of symmetrical rhythm and chiasm in vv. 1-8.

The text of 1:1-8 may be laid out structurally as follows:

A 1 Ἀρχὴ τοῦ εὐαγγελίου Ἰησοῦ Χριστοῦ [υἱοῦ θεοῦ].

   2 Καθὼς γέγραπται ἐν τῷ Ἡσαΐᾳ τῷ προφήτῃ,

B   Ἰδοὺ ἀποστέλλω τὸν ἄγγελόν μου πρὸ προσώπου σου,
         ὃς κατασκευάσει τὴν ὁδόν σου·
   3   φωνὴ βοῶντος ἐν τῇ ἐρήμῳ,
         Ἐτοιμάσατε τὴν ὁδὸν κυρίου,
         εὐθείας ποιεῖτε τὰς τρίβους αὐτοῦ--

C 4   ἐγένετο Ἰωάννης βαπτίζων ἐν τῇ ἐρήμῳ
            καὶ κηρύσσων βάπτισμα μετανοίας εἰς ἄφεσιν ἁμαρτιῶν.
   5   καὶ ἐξεπορεύετο πρὸς αὐτὸν πᾶσα ἡ Ἰουδαία χώρα
            καὶ οἱ Ἱεροσολυμῖται πάντες, καὶ ἐβαπτίζοντο ὑπ'
            αὐτοῦ
            ἐν τῷ Ἰορδάνῃ ποταμῷ ἐξομολογούμενοι τὰς ἁμαρτίας
            αὐτῶν.

B' 6   καὶ ἦν ὁ Ἰωάννης ἐνδεδυμένος τρίχας καμήλου
         καὶ ζώνην δερματίνην περὶ τὴν ὀσφὺν αὐτοῦ,
         καὶ ἐσθίων ἀκρίδας καὶ μέλι ἄγριον.

A' 7 καὶ ἐκήρυσσεν λέγων, Ἔρχεται ὁ ἰσχυρότερός μου ὀπίσω μου,
      οὗ οὐκ εἰμὶ ἱκανὸς κύψας λῦσαι τὸν ἱμάντα τῶν ὑποδημάτων
      αὐτοῦ·
   8 ἐγὼ ἐβάπτισα ὑμᾶς ὕδατι, αὐτὸς δὲ βαπτίσει ὑμᾶς ἐν πνεύματι
      ἁγίῳ.

The symmetrical rhythm is indicated by the content. A and
A' concern Jesus, the beginning of the gospel of Jesus (v. 1),
and John's preaching concerning his coming (vv. 7-8). The middle
parts, B, C, and B' are concerned only with John the Baptist.
B and B', one an Old Testament quotation and the other containing
an Old Testament allusion, both point beyond John to his significance in salvation history. C, on the other hand, describes
John's earthly activity.

C itself has a symmetrical rhythm with a verbal chiasm in
the middle. First, John preaches *baptism* for the forgiveness
of *sins*. Then people come to him, π͞α͞σ͞α ἡ ᾿Ιουδαία χώρα καὶ
οἱ ᾿Ιεροσολυμ͞ῖ͞τ͞α͞ι π͞ά͞ν͞τ͞ε͞ς.[52] Finally, the people are *baptized*,
confessing their *sins*.

An alternate rhetorical analysis of vv. 4-8 could be as
follows:

v. 4:   A summary: John baptizes and preaches
v. 5:   John's baptizing activity
v. 6:   Description of John
vv. 7-8: John's preaching activity

Such a view seems less satisfactory than the structure proposed
earlier. First, it breaks the symmetrical unity of vv. 4-5.
Second, the preachings of v. 4 and vv. 7-8 are not related in
content, whereas v. 4 relates to v. 5b, and vv. 7-8 relate to
v. 1 and vv. 14-15. Lastly, the placing of v. 6 makes no particular sense or logic in this rhetorical arrangement, while it
does in the one proposed first.

Verse 6, B', is on the surface a description of John. It
is also an allusion to 2 Kings 1:8, where a man is described to
the king as follows: "'He wore a garment of haircloth, with a
girdle of leather about his loins'" (RSV). From this description,
the king concluded that the man was Elijah. Thus in B', Mark is
identifying John as Elijah for the reader.[53] By so doing, Mark
clarifies for the reader that God's messenger in B refers to
John (Elijah) and not to Jesus. B' completes the thought of B.
A, B : B' A' have a chiastic pattern; all four point beyond Jesus
and John to their theological significance. C in the middle
describes John's actual activity.

In summary, the same type of concentric and chiastic ordering of material is found in Mark 1:1-8 as was found in 2:1-3:6.

Within the space of a single narrative, no longer than some of
the individual controversy pericopes, the same structuring techniques have been used. Moreover, Mark 1:1-8 are the opening
verses of the gospel. Mark's audience is alerted from the very
beginning to Mark's use of symmetrical and chiastic patterns.

Mark 4:1-34

The combination of materials to be found in the parable
discourse presents two problems for the exegete: first, the
problem of Jesus' audience within the narrative, and second,
the problem of the conflict in meaning between the notion that
Jesus taught in parables to hinder general understanding (4:11-
12,33-34) and the idea that the purpose is understanding (4:21-
22).[54]

The first problem, that of internal audience, is inescapable
and insoluble. The narrative opens with Jesus in a boat on the
lake, teaching the crowd on the shore (4:1-2). Then, in v. 10,
a change of scene is depicted, and Jesus is alone with the twelve
and those with them. In vv. 33-34, the conclusion of the discourse, the narrative assumes that Jesus has been continuing all
along to address the crowd. And in vv. 35-36, Jesus is depicted
still sitting in the boat. Nowhere in the narrative is the
reader informed how Jesus could be alone with his disciples yet
remain seated in the boat addressing the multitude.

It is not clear, however, that the shift in internal audience and setting was a real problem for first century readers.
The discrepancy remains as obvious in Matthew (Mt 13:1-2,10,34,
36), and is softened but not obviated in Luke (Lk 8:4,9,19).
The same phenomenon of shifts in Jesus' audience which are not
logically accounted for has already been observed in Mark's and
Luke's versions of the healing of the paralytic (Mk 2:1-12, Lk
5:17-26).[55] If the parable discourses and the healing of the
paralytic are any indication, perhaps it was not important for
a first century popular author to account for changes in the
internal audience of a narrative.

The second problem, essentially whether the purpose of
Jesus' teaching was to hide or reveal, was clearly recognized
as a problem by Matthew and Luke. Each of them transposes some
of the material found in Mark 4:1-34 to other parts of his gospel

so that the strong juxtaposition found in the markan discourse
is avoided.[56] However, the juxtaposition--or contrast or para-
dox--may be part of Mark's intention in the parable discourse,
and he may be employing concentric ordering of material in order
to make his point. It was noted in the first chapter that Lund
found one of the characteristics of concentric structure to be
the introduction of an opposing idea in the middle of the pattern: "At the centre there is often a change in the trend of
thought, and an antithetic idea is introduced. After this the
original trend is resumed and continued until the system is concluded."[57] Such a shift was found in 2:1-3:6: it was observed
that in the first and last pericopes, when the opponents posit
capital charges against Jesus, he triumphs, accomplishing resurrection-type miracles, while in the middle pericope, when opposition
to Jesus is virtually absent, he himself alludes to his coming death.

There is abundant evidence of symmetrical rhythm to be found
in Mark 4:1-34. The introduction to the parable discourse, vv.
1-2a, is a short independent scene such as that found in 2:1-2
and 2:13.[58] It has a concentric pattern which cannot be attributed to the natural ordering of content:

a   Καὶ πάλιν ἤρξατο διδάσκειν παρὰ τὴν θάλασσαν.

b   καὶ συνάγεται πρὸς αὐτὸν ὄχλος πλεῖστος,

c   ὥστε αὐτὸν εἰς πλοῖον ἐμβάντα καθῆσθαι ἐν τῇ
                                                    θαλάσσῃ,

b'   καὶ πᾶς ὁ ὄχλος πρὸς τὴν θάλασσαν ἐπὶ τῆς γῆς ἦσαν.

a'   καὶ ἐδίδασκεν αὐτοὺς ἐν παραβολαῖς πολλά,

The order runs, Jesus teaching, the crowd, Jesus gets into a
boat, the crowd, Jesus teaching. Only then does the introduction to the parable of the sower follow, "And he said to them
in his teaching..." (4:2b).[59]

The introductory scene is an elegant rhetorical unit. Lines
a, b, b', and a' all begin with "and"; line c employs the sub-
ordinating conjunction, "so that." The verb "to teach" is used
in lines a and a' only. The word "crowd" occurs only in lines
b and b'. In b, the modifier of "crowd" follows it, and the
phrase occurs at the end of the line. In b', the modifier of
"crowd" precedes it, and the phrase occurs at the beginning of
the line. And line c, εἰς πλοῖον ἐμβάντα καθῆσθαι ἐν τῇ θαλάσσῃ
has a chiastic syntactical rhythm: prepositional phrase, verb

(participle), verb (infinitive), prepositional phrase. Both prepositional phrases serve to define Jesus' precise place--in a boat on the lake.

Mark 4:2b-20, the parable of the sower and its accompanying interpretation, also has a five-part concentric pattern.[60] The parable of the sower in vv. 3-9 is balanced at the end by the interpretation of the parable in vv. 14-20. Verses 10-13 contain the disciples' question about the parables in v. 10, and two separate and contradictory answers by Jesus in vv. 11-12 and 13. Verse 13,

καὶ λέγει αὐτοῖς, Οὐκ οἴδατε τὴν παραβολὴν ταύτην,
καὶ πῶς πάσας τὰς παραβολὰς γνώσεσθε;

is not a logical continuation of vv. 11-12. On the other hand, the phrase "You do not know this parable?" is an unambiguous reference to the parable of the sower and the disciples' question following it. Thus v. 13 rhetorically functions as an answer to the disciples' question in v. 10, implying that they should be able to understand the parables. And interposed between vv. 10 and 13 is Jesus' first answer, the sayings on the mystery of the kingdom and on parables as impenetrable riddles to those outside.

Thus 4:2b-20 may be outlined as follows:

a   vv. 2b-9   The parable of the sower

b   v. 10   The question of the disciples about its
                  meaning

c   vv. 11-12   The sayings on mystery and obduracy,
                  an interposition

b'   v. 13   The reproof to the disciples for not
                  understanding

a'   vv. 14-20   The interpretation of the parable of the
                  sower

This rhetorical structure brings out the contrast between the idea presented in the center (c), that parables are a mystery in need of explanation, and the idea in the remainder of the narrative (which reads smoothly without the interposition of c), that parables are intended to be understood.

If the foregoing rhetorical analysis of 4:1-2a and 2b-20 is accepted, then it seems reasonable to suggest that the entire

parable discourse has a loose five-part symmetrical rhythm. The
hearer of the discourse has been attuned to five-part symmetry,
first by the rhetorically elegant introduction, and then by the
repetition of the pattern in vv. 2b-20. He may well be prepared
for it in the section as a whole.

The entire discourse may be outlined as follows:

A   vv. 1-2a   Introduction

B   vv. 2b-20   Parable material

C   vv. 21-25   Sayings material

B'   vv. 26-32   Parable material

A'   vv. 33-34   Conclusion[61]

The conclusion, A', forms an inclusio with the introduction,
A: Jesus is speaking to the people in parables. The conclusion
also recapitulates the idea of the interposition in B (vv. 11-12),
that parables are a means of hindering understanding for outsiders:

> With many such parables he spoke the word to them, as
> they were able to hear it; he did not speak to them
> without a parable, but privately to his own disciples
> he explained everything. (4:33-34, RSV)

The conclusion to the entire discourse, directly following two
parables for which no explanation is given, reinforces the idea
of vv. 11-12, so that, in effect, the entire parable discourse
stands under the idea that parables are incomprehensible riddles
to outsiders.

In spite of the fact that B has a five-part symmetrical
pattern, while B' consists of two parallel units, there seem to
be sufficient rhetorical clues to consider B and B' parallel to
each other in the rhetorical pattern of the parable discourse.
In the first place, B and B' each contain two major parable
units: in B, the parable of the sower and its interpretation;
in B', the two parables on the kingdom of God. Further, B and
B' are also connected by hook words. The "kingdom of God," the
subject of the two parables in B', is introduced into B by means
of the interposition (vv. 11, 26, 30). The verb "to sow" occurs
only in the parable discourse, three times in the parable of the
sower, six times in its interpretation in B, and two times in

the second parable in B' (vv. 3bis,4,14,15bis,16,18,20,31,32).
"Earth" is used four times in B, three times in the parable and
once in its interpretation, and four times in B', twice in each
parable (vv. 5bis,8,20,26,28,31bis). Καρποφορέω is used only
twice in Mark, at the end of B, and near the beginning of B' (vv.
20,28). Likewise, πετεινόν is used only twice in Mark, but at
the beginning of B and the end of B' (vv. 4,32). Some of these
hook words (e.g., "to sow") may well be the accidental result
of the content. But they do indicate the similarity of content
between B and B'. And the balance in number of uses and the
placing of some of them suggest that they are functioning as
hook words as well.

C, the middle section, is set off from B and B' by difference in form: it contains general sayings material, not parables
strictly speaking. (The fact that Mark can call general sayings
"parables" [e.g., 3:23] does not need to imply that he is unaware
of the difference in form between proverbial material and a true
parable.) In structure, the section has a chiastic pattern:
sayings, exhortation to the audience : exhortation to the audience, sayings (vv. 21-22, 23 : 24a, 24b-25). Exhortations to
the audience at the beginning and/or ending of teaching are
found elsewhere in Mark, in the parable discourse and in the
apocalyptic discourse in Mark 13. However, nowhere else in Mark
are two exhortations found adjacent to each other, separated
only by an introductory formula, "And he said to them." The
fact that it occurs here helps to give a symmetrical rhythm to
the overall parable discourse, and to indicate to the hearer
that C is the middle or hinge section.

C, with its idea of everything being made manifest and
coming to light, counters the idea that the purpose of parables
is to hinder understanding, which through its occurrence in vv.
11-12 and 33-34, dominates the understanding of parables in the
discourse as a whole. Further, the same contrast, between parables as riddles needing interpretation and parables as a means
of open communication, occurs in part B (vv. 2b-20) and again
in the entire discourse (vv. 1-34). In B, the idea of secrecy
is found only in the center, in contrast with the rest of B. In
the discourse as a whole, the idea of open revelation is found
in the center, in contrast with the rest of the discourse.

Twice, using the same rhetorical means, the same juxtaposition or paradox is presented to the reader. The juxtaposition
is also rhetorically stressed. In each instance, the opposite
idea is presented in the middle of a larger symmetrical unit,
and set somewhat apart from it. Thus, the symmetrical rhythm
employed in 4:1-34 functions to highlight the contrast or paradox of parables as a means of revelation *and* as riddles. Both
understandings are presented to the reader at one and the same
time as true, depending perhaps on whether the reader chooses to
be among those "with Jesus" or among "those outside."

To be sure, Mark 4:1-34 has a looser structure than that
to be found in Mark 2:1-3:6. Nonetheless, there seem to be sufficient congruent parallelisms of content, form, and hook words
to posit a symmetrical pattern. Further, the prior use of the
same rhythm in 4:1-2a and again in 2b-20 has prepared the hearer
for the use of the pattern in the larger unit.

Mark 11-12

Mark 1:1-8 and 4:1-34 were selected as examples of extended
symmetrical patterns in the gospel of Mark. Mark 11-12, the
Jerusalem public ministry, was selected not specifically as an
example of concentric structure, but rather as a good text for
comparison with Mark 2:1-3:6. It contains the second major
block of public debate material in the gospel and it presents
a different problem for the rhetorical critic: that of delimit-
ing rhetorical units larger than a single pericope.[62] In Chapter Two of this study, a brief overview of the narrative from
a literary perspective was given. It was concluded that day one
(10:46-11:11) was a prologue to the Jerusalem ministry proper,
that day two and the first incidents on day three (11:12-12:12)
spelled out the conflict between Jesus and the legitimate Jewish
authorities over who truly represented God, and that the remaining events of day three (12:13-44, public debate, public teaching and private teaching) had no easily recognizable narrative
coherence.[63] It was also concluded that the material in Mark 12
could not be explained on the basis of a premarkan collection
or rhetorical structure.[64]

Here, it will be argued that Mark has set off the Jerusalem
public debates by the use of framing incidents, the interposition

technique, and overlapping rhetorical units larger than the pericope. Within the public ministry a loose symmetrical rhythm is
to be recognized in 12:1-40. The rhythm clarifies the structure
and helps to illumine the function of the public debate material
in the Jerusalem public ministry. In Mark 11-12, Mark has used
a variety of rhetorical techniques, some linear, some symmetrical, to structure his material. Before turning to the symmetrical pattern in Mark 12, some of these features, in particular
the frames and the rhetorical units in Mark 11:12-12:12, need to
be described. They delimit the Jerusalem ministry proper and
help to indicate a little of the variety of Mark's rhetoric.

Rhetorical Features

The use of Frames to Delimit the Public Ministry

Mark 11:11 and 13:1-2. Day one, the prologue to the Jerusalem ministry, ends with Jesus entering the temple for the
first time, "looking around at everything," and then departing
for Bethany with the twelve (11:11).[65] On day three, when Jesus
leaves the temple for the last time, one of his disciples observes, "Look, what wonderful stones and what wonderful build-
ings!" (13:1). Mark 13:1 could follow 11:11 directly, without
any disjuncture in the narrative. Indeed, the exclamation of
the disciple would seem more appropriate upon his first sight
of the temple complex than after the two event-filled days in
the temple precincts.

Thus 11:11 and 13:1, the first entrance and last exit from
the temple, may serve as a narrative frame for the public ministry in the temple of days two and three. It is similar to the
narrative frame of people streaming to Jesus from everywhere
surrounding the Galilean controversy section (1:45; 3:7-8).[66]
Unlike the frame around 2:1-3:6, however, this frame does not
reflect a shift in content from the material it surrounds.
Jesus' saying in 13:2 on the coming destruction of the temple
confirms the themes of the proleptic destruction of the temple,
the destruction of the wicked tenants, and the giving of the
vineyard to others found in Mark 11-12. The use of the address,
"Teacher," in 13:1 emphasizes the verse's connection with Mark
12 in which Jesus as teacher is stressed. The notion that the

days of Israel are nearing an end may also be implied in the
phrase, ὀψίας ἤδη οὔσης τῆς ὥρας, in 11:11.[67] Here the frame
emphasizes a major theme of the material it encloses, and points
ahead to the apocalyptic discourse.

Mark 12:41-44; 14:3-9. The story of the widow's mite (12:
41-44) and the story of the woman annointing Jesus at Bethany
(14:3-9) serve as a frame for the apocalyptic discourse at the
end of day three, much as the two healings of blind men frame
the way section (8:22-26; 10:46-52). The two stories have much
in common. In both, Jesus praises a woman who shows the way of
service or self-giving. These are the only two such incidents in
Mark in which an individual's act is praised. The widow's mite
in the first contrasts with the huge amount of money the nard is
worth in the second. In both, Jesus' saying is introduced by
ἀμὴω λέγω ὑμῖν (12:43; 14:9). The stories are joined by the hook
word, "poor," used twice in each story (12:42,43; 14:5,7).[68]
The parallelism of the two stories is beyond question.

They are also suitable as a frame for the apocalyptic discourse, dealing with events to come after Jesus' passion. For
both stories anticipate the events of 15:21-16:8. The widow
gives "her whole life" (12:44), while Jesus says that the woman
has annointed his body for burial (14:8). As in the two healings
of blind men, in which there is progression from the two-stage
healing in 8:22-26 to the instantaneous healing of Bartimaeus
who then followed Jesus on the way in 10:46-52, so in the two
stories about women, there is progression from the giving up of
life to burial after death.

Each story is also contrasted with its immediate setting.[69]
The story of the widow is joined to the preceding narrative of
the condemnation of the scribes, not only by the hook word,
"widow,"[70] but also by the contrast between the bad example of
the scribes who act only for show, and the good example of the
widow, who makes no showing at all with her two copper coins.[71]
The generous act of the woman at Bethany is interposed between
the chief priests seeking to arrest Jesus, and Judas coming to
them to betray Jesus (14:1-2; 10-11).

Conclusion. The double use of the framing technique in
the Jerusalem ministry marks 11:12-12:40 as the rhetorical unit
to be investigated. It also confirms the earlier conclusion
that the entrance scene is part of the prologue to the Jerusalem
ministry.[72] The intertwining of the literary connections is
also impressive. The two frames overlap, 12:41-44 pointing
ahead, while 13:1-2 refers back. Mark 13:2 itself points back
and ahead in the narrative. The stories constituting the second
frame, the widow's mite and the annointing at Bethany, not only
serve as a frame for Mark 13, but also serve to point up contrast
in their immediate context. The literary intertwining of material, while certainly not symmetrical, is as elaborate as the
intertwining in 2:1-3:6. And it serves basically the same rhetorical function, to invite the reader/hearer to interrelate
the material presented to him.

The rhetorical units in Mark 11:12-12:12

The rhetorical units in 11:12-12:12 were already discussed
in the narrative overview in Chapter Two, and need only be summarized here. First, 11:12-26 is a rhetorical sub-unit in the
Jerusalem ministry in which the public cleansing of the temple
is interposed into the frame of the cursing and withering of
the fig tree witnessed only by the disciples. Here, the frame-
interposition technique serves to set apart material from the
on-going narrative--the same function it served in 2:1-12 and
1:45-3:8. In this instance, however, it is the frame, private
teaching to the disciples (and the reader), which is set apart
from the linear narrative, not the interposition.

Secondly, 11:15-18, 27-33; 12:1-12 form a rhetorical unit
in structure, like an extended controversy of the action-objection-vindication type. In the temple cleansing, Jesus acts
objectionably. In the question on authority, the chief priests,
elders and scribes question his authority to act. Jesus parries
the question, but in the following allegorical parable of the
wicked tenants, justifies his authority as that of God's Son
(12:6). These three pericopes are also connected by the statement to the reader of the Jewish authorities' desire to destroy/
arrest Jesus, found at the close of the first and last pericopes,
and their fear of the crowd, noted in all three.

As in the case of the frames in Mark 11-13, the two rhetorical units in 11:12-12:12 overlap. The cleansing of the temple
serves as part of both of them. In the first, the frame around
it helps interpret for the reader the meaning of Jesus' acts in
the temple--the proleptic fall of the temple and the end of the
time of Israel. In the second, the temple cleansing serves as
the starting point of Jesus' confrontation with the legitimate
Jewish authorities.

Further, 12:12 may recall 3:6 to the reader's mind. In 3:6,
the Pharisees, the leaders of the synagogues, abandon the synagogue to Jesus after their confrontation with him, but with the
intention of destroying him. In 12:12, the chief priests (Sanhedrin), the leaders of the temple, leave the temple to Jesus
after their confrontation with him, but with the intention of
arresting him.

A Symmetrical Pattern in Mark 12:1-40

In the foregoing discussion of rhetorical features, it has
been argued that 11:11 and 13:1-2, and 12:41-44 and 14:3-9 are
frames around Jesus' public ministry and the apocalyptic discourse respectively. Further, it has been argued that the use
of the frame-interposition technique in 11:12-26 has served to
set apart the frame from the ongoing narrative of Jesus' ministry.
If these arguments are accepted, then the Jerusalem public ministry consists of 11:15-18,27-12:40.

It has also been argued that 11:15-18,27-33 and 12:1-12
are a rhetorical sub-unit within the public ministry. Mark 12:
13-40 remains to be investigated to see if it has any rhetorical
pattern of its own. It will be argued below, first, that the
three questions of Mark 12:13-34 are a clearly delineated ring
composition, and second, that this ring composition may be extended to a larger, but looser, symmetrical pattern encompassing
the entirety of 12:1-40. Given the numerous literary intertwin-
ings, overlappings and double uses of pericopes and verses already noted in the Jerusalem material, it should not surprise
the reader that 12:1-12 functions rhetorically in two ways.
Finally, brief consideration will be given to the question of
how the symmetrical rhythm helps the reader to understand the
role of the public debate material in the Jerusalem ministry.

12:13-34 as a rhetorical unit. It was suggested in the narrative overview in Chapter Two that the debates over taxes, resurrection and the first commandment were a rhetorical subunit. In spite of the fact that the first two have hostile opponents while the third does not, they are similar in form. In all three, the debate is initiated by people seeking Jesus' opinion on some issue. Thus all three belong to the variant of the debate form in which Jesus engaged in no objectionable acts.[73] They all belong to the type in which extended dialogue often occurs.[74] And in all three, the dialogue is expanded beyond simple question and answer.[75] In all three, the type of answer which Jesus gives is similar, a direct answer to the question posed.[76] Unlike 2:1-3:6 in which Jesus bases his answer on his own authority and/or his ability to heal, the Jesus of Mark 12: 13-34 argues on grounds that the Jews would accept. He plays the game according to his questioners' rules. In all three, Jesus is addressed as "teacher" (12:14,19,32).[77] In all three stories, Jesus appears as a successful and skilled debater, a teacher of wisdom.[78]

In content, all three do concern issues current in the Judaism of the time.[79] That political subservience to Rome symbolized by the tribute was an issue is sufficiently evident from the two Jewish wars. The intra-Jewish debate over resurrection between the Sadducees and the Pharisees is attested to by Paul's confrontation with the Sanhedrin in Acts 23 and by Josephus.[80] The question of the fundamental law was also an issue, as can be seen from the story of the proselyte who wished to be taught the law while standing on one foot.[81]

Further, the content of Jesus' answers would appeal to the same group within first century Judaism. The Pharisees may wonder at Jesus' escape from the political dilemma posed him but they are basically in agreement with his answer (12:17). Moreover, the Pharisees and scribes would agree with Jesus' response to the Sadducees in regard to resurrection: that they know neither the scriptures nor the power of God (12:24). In the question of the first commandment, Jesus and the scribe explicitly agree on the fundamental demand of God (12:32-34). Thus, in all three public debates, Jesus and the Pharisaic scribal faction of Judaism are on common ground.[82] The three debates serve the function of showing Mark's reader where Jesus agrees with Judaism.

Thus, the three public debates are similar in form, in the
type of dialogue and in content. Jesus' agreement with Judaism,
which they portray, contrasts with Jesus' criticism of the Jewish
leaders in his direct teaching which precedes and follows 12:13-
34. The similarity of the three debates and their contrast with
their immediate setting are sufficient to establish 12:13-34 as
a rhetorical sub-unit within the Jerusalem public ministry.

12:13-34 as a ring composition. The parallels (and differences) among the three pericopes go beyond the similarities mentioned above to indicate that the three are structured as a ring
composition. In structure, the first and the third have a double
interchange of dialogue between the questioner and Jesus.[83] In
the middle debate, there is only a single exchange of dialogue,
but, in effect, a double question and answer. The Sadducees,
trying to discredit the idea of resurrection, posit the conundrum
of the women who married seven brothers. Jesus first resolves
the riddle and then argues for resurrection, answering the issues in reverse or chiastic order.

The first and third debates are also related in content.
In the first, Jesus says to give to God the things of God (12:17).
In the third, Jesus spells out what the things of God are--to
love God and neighbor (12:29-31). It completes the thought of
the first, while the middle story deals with an entirely different issue, resurrection. In both the first and the third,
the questioners praise Jesus' teaching (12:14,32). The pericopes are joined by the hook phrase, ἐπ' ἀληθείας, both times
in the mouth of the questioner. The Pharisees say in the preface to their question to Jesus, "*with truth* you teach the way
of God" (12:14). In the third, the scribe responds to Jesus'
answer to his question about the first commandment, "good, *with
truth* you say" (12:32).[84] These are the only two uses of ἐπ'
ἀληθείας in Mark, and they serve, in effect, as an inclusio for
Mark 12:13-34.

Finally, the first and third stories are closely interwoven
into their setting. In the first, the Pharisees and Herodians
are sent by the Sanhedrin to see if they can entrap Jesus in
his words (12:13). They open their question by a long (and in-
sincere) introduction praising Jesus as a teacher (12:14). At

the end of the debate, they marvel at him (12:17). In the third, the scribe, having heard the earlier debates and seeing that Jesus had answered well, asks his question (12:28). At the end of it, no one any longer dares question Jesus (12:34). The middle story, in contrast, is simply framed by the other two. The Sadducees are given no narrative introduction connecting them to the preceding narrative, and there is no audience reaction at the end.

The interweaving of the first and third stories into the continuing narrative also serves to give the section a sense of linear or climactic progression. The question of the Pharisees and Herodians is hostile in intent, and Jesus is aware of their hypocrisy (12:15). The scribe, after hearing the ensuing debates, is well-intentioned toward Jesus, and the scribe and Jesus praise each other's answers (12:32,34). Unlike 2:1-3:6, in which the level of hostility increased throughout the narrative, here the level of hostility decreases. Mark 2:1-3:6 and 12:13-34, however, are alike in that the middle story does not contribute significantly to the increase or decrease of hostility. They are also similar in that both linear development and symmetrical rhythm occur in the same composition.

The extension of the symmetrical pattern to 12:1-40

There seems to be no *a priori* reason why the rhetorical symmetrical rhythm might not end with the ring composition of 12:13-34. However, that would leave two loosely attached episodes of Jesus' teaching in the Jerusalem public ministry, a unit otherwise quite clearly structured and, in rhetorical terms, extensively interconnected and interwoven. Further, the beginning of the ring composition is closely interwoven with the preceding pericope. It is the Sanhedrin, the opponents of 12: 12 who send the Pharisees and the Herodians to try to discredit Jesus (12:13). Also, the pericope following the ring composition may well be connected. It begins, Καὶ ἀποκριθεὶς ὁ ᾿Ιησοῦς ἔλεγεν (12:35). This is the *only* instance in the gospel of Mark in which ἀποκρίνομαι occurs at the beginning of a unit of narrative and the only instance in which it occurs without an obvious referent. This suggests that its use in 12:35 may also have a referent, the preceding debates.[85] Thus at both the

beginning and the end of the ring composition, there appear to
be rhetorical indications of continuity. It would seem to be
worthwhile to investigate if the ring composition may be part
of a larger symmetrical pattern.

   Mark 12:10-12, 35-37. Turning to the material directly
adjacent to the ring composition, several parallels between 12:
10-12 and 12:35-37 are readily apparent. Both are direct teachings of Jesus, not an answer to any specific question addressed
to Jesus. In both, Jesus explicitly quotes from scripture.
Both are citations from Psalms, Ps. 118:22-23 in vv. 10-11, and
Ps. 110:1 in v. 36. The two passages are similar in content as
well as in form. In both, Jesus uses the psalm to attack Jewish
messianic expectations: in the first, Jesus warns the Jewish
leaders that they will reject the one whom God will establish;
in the second, Jesus warns indirectly that no Davidic Messiah
is coming to restore the fortunes of Israel.[86]
   Moreover, both passages are followed by audience reactions.
The content of the reactions is antithetic (as in 2:1-3:6). In
12:12 the opponents seek to arrest Jesus, but fear the crowd,
so they depart. In 12:37, the great crowd listens to Jesus
gladly. While the crowd presumably witnesses all the debates
and teaching in 12:1-40, they play no role in the three public
debates in vv. 13-34. The word "crowd" is only employed in vv.
12 and 37 in Mark 12:1-40. Further, in both instances the crowd
supports Jesus.[87] There are sufficient congruent parallels of
form, content and hook words between vv. 10-12 and 35-37 to
establish their parallelism, and thereby to posit the extension
of the symmetrical pattern beyond the ring composition in 12:13-
34.

   Mark 12:1-9, 38-40. The foregoing analysis suggests that
vv. 1-9, the parable about the wicked tenants, and vv. 38-40,
the woes on the scribes, may also be parallel and part of the
symmetrical pattern. Here the parallels are not so substantial
or numerous. Nonetheless, they do exist. The form is different:
vv. 1-9 are an allegorical parable; vv. 38-40 are a warning
against the scribes. Both, however, are direct teachings of
Jesus. Further, there is similarity of content. In both, Jesus

attacks the behavior of the Jewish leaders. In vv. 1-9, he
criticizes the leaders' treatment of God's messengers. In vv.
38-40, Jesus criticizes the scribes for seeking their own world-
ly position in the market places and synagogues and ignoring
God's demands for justice to widows.[88] And each passage ends
with a prophecy of doom on the Jewish leaders: "What will the
owner of the vineyard do? He will come and destroy the tenants,
and give the vineyard to others"; "They will receive the greater
condemnation" (12:9,40, RSV).

Against the parallelism of vv. 1-9 and 38-40, it may be
argued that vv. 1-9 are substantially longer than vv. 38-40 and
that 12:1-12 constitutes a single unit marked by the inclusio,
παραβολαῖς/παραβολὴν (vv. 1,12) while vv. 35-40 are clearly two
separate units, each with its own introduction (vv. 35,38).[89]
These arguments would not seem sufficient to discredit the parallelism of the symmetrical pattern. Even in the elegant pattern
in 2:1-3:6, the healing of the paralytic is substantially longer
than the healing of the man with the withered hand. In the
parable discourse in Mark 4, the B section on the parable of
the sower (4:2b-20) is longer than B' (4:26-32).[90] Further, B
is a single rhetorical unit, while B' consists of two short
independent parables. The technique of symmetrical patterning
exhibits considerable variation, and the pattern in Mark 12:1-40
would seem to fall well within the limits of that variety.

Finally, the idea of God's ultimate judgment found in 12:9
and 40 is contrasted with the idea of God's power of resurrection
or salvation found in the middle public debate with the Sadducees.
Those who are resurrected will be "like angels in heaven," for
"He is not God of the dead, but of the living" (12:25,27, RSV).
As has been seen in 2:1-3:6 and 4:1-34, opposite ideas often
occur in the extremes and center of a symmetrical pattern.

For the symmetry indeed ends with 12:1-40. Mark 12:41-44,
the story of the widow's mite, is private teaching to the disciples and functions as part of a frame around Mark 13. Mark
11:27-33 is a controversy apophthegm attacking Jesus' behavior.
Mark 11:27-33 and 12:41-44 are not parallel.

The rhetorical pattern of Mark 12:1-40 as a whole

The symmetrical pattern. The symmetrical structure of 12:
1-40 may be outlined as follows:

A   vv. 1-9   Public teaching: The parable of the wicked
                                     tenants; threat of God's
                                     judgment

B   vv. 10-12   Public teaching: Psalm citation; audience
                                     reaction

C   vv. 13-17   Public debate: The things of God are to
                                     be given to God; audience
                                     reaction

D   vv. 18-27   Public debate: The hope in resurrection
                                     is real

C'   vv. 28-34   Public debate: The things of God are the
                                     commands to love God and
                                     neighbor; audience reaction

B'   vv. 35-37   Public teaching: Psalm citation; audience
                                     reaction

A'   vv. 38-40   Public teaching: Warning against the scribes;
                                     threat of God's judgment

First, Jesus in direct teaching attacks the behavior of the
Jewish leaders, prophesies their destruction, and their rejection of the one whom God will establish (A, B, 12:1-12). Then
in three interwoven debates, Jesus answers questions on basic
issues of Judaism, showing his agreement with the Pharisaic
scribal position on the political issue of taxation, on the
hope of resurrection, and on the fundamental demand of God (C,
D,C', 12:13-34). Then once again in direct teaching, Jesus attacks the scribes' understanding of christology, warns against
their behavior, and prophesies their condemnation (B', A', 12:
35-40).

A, B, B' and A' are all direct teachings of Jesus in which
he attacks the Jewish leaders' behavior and messianic ideas.
C, D, and C' are all public debates in which Jesus' responses
show his agreement with Jewish tenets. Thus, the symmetrical
rhythm of 12:1-40 may be viewed as an extended ring composition.
The shift in form is congruent with the shift in content. Mark
12:1-40 has a pattern of Jesus' provocation of Jewish leaders,
followed by his affirmation of basic Jewish (Pharisaic) beliefs,
followed again by provocation of the scribes. The three public

debates and Jesus' two attached teachings against the scribes
have their place in the structure of the Jerusalem public ministry as constituent elements of the symmetrical pattern of provocation, defense, provocation. As in 2:1-3:6, and 4:1-34, a symmetrical rhythm or concentric structure serves to unify diverse
and *contrasting* materials into a coherent literary whole.

   Linear or climactic development. As in 2:1-3:6, 12:1-40
has a linear or climactic progression as well as a symmetrical
pattern. In both sections, the climactic progression is not in
the content per se. In 2:1-3:6, the most serious charges against
Jesus are in the first and last controversies--blasphemy and
healing on the sabbath. In 12:1-40, Jesus' provocation and denunciation of the Jewish leaders is as strong in 12:35-40 as it
was in 12:1-11. Rather the sense of climactic progression is
given by the actions and reactions of Jesus' audience, the crowd
and the opponents.

   In contrast to the Galilean controversy section, however,
in Mark 12, the development is one of the declining evidence of
overt opposition to Jesus. The section opens with the attempt
of the representatives of the Sanhedrin to arrest Jesus (12:12).
The change from hostile to friendly questioners in the sequence
of public debates has already been described. Overt opposition
to Jesus ends entirely after the third debate, when the reader
is informed that no one dared question Jesus further (12:34).
Finally, in 12:37 the reader is told that "the great crowd heard
him gladly." The emphasis in 12:1-40 is not on the growing opposition to Jesus but on Jesus' triumph over his opponents, his
successful vindication of himself. As R.H. Lightfoot writes:

> We are struck by the supremacy and, if we may use the
> word, the buoyancy of Jesus in dealing with the situa-
> tions which successively confront him, and his complete
> success. This impression is confirmed by the references
> to the astonishment and interest of the multitude,
> which is represented as giving him support and even
> sympathy.[91]

   The double function of 12:1-12 in Mark 11-12. As noted
earlier, 12:1-12 is both part of the rhetorical unit, 11:15-18,
27-12:12, the climax of the sequence begun with Jesus' cleansing
of the temple, and part of the rhetorical unit of 12:1-40, the
beginning of the symmetrical pattern.

A somewhat similar rhetorical overlapping may be seen in
2:1-12, the story of the healing of the paralytic. It is clearly the first controversy story in the gospel and the opening or
introduction to the Galilean controversy section. Yet it also
continues and heightens the theme of Jesus' popularity with the
crowd begun in 1:21-22 (2:1-2,12).[92] The crowd, as a character,
does not fade out of the Galilean controversy section until
after the second controversy, the call of Levi. In 12:1-12, the
reiteration of the Sanhedrin's desire to destroy Jesus heightens
the opposition already stated at the end of the temple cleansing
(11:18; 12:12). It is only gradually in 12:1-40 that the opposition recedes, and the theme of Jesus' success and popularity
comes to dominate the narrative. Thus 2:1-3:6 and 12:1-40 exhibit a parallel if antithetic development of the motifs of the
opposition to and popularity of Jesus.

The healing of the paralytic, however, is rhetorically set
off from the material which precedes it by means of the contrasting frame around 2:1-3:6. Such is not the case with 12:
1-12. The lack of any rhetorical break at 12:1 is an indication
of the rhetorical and content unity of the entire Jerusalem public ministry (11:15-18,27-12:40).

Mark 12:1-40 in the Jerusalem Public Ministry

As in the case of the Galilean controversy section, so in
Mark 12:1-40 both the symmetrical pattern and the climactic
development help the reader to interpret the materials presented
in the text. Given the interconnection of the two rhetorical
units, 11:15-18,27-12:12 and 12:1-40, a full discussion of how
the structure aids in understanding the text would have to encompass the entire Jerusalem public ministry. Since the focus
of this chapter, however, is on concentric structure, the following discussion will be limited to a brief indication of how
the symmetrical pattern helps to bring out the theme of 12:1-40
and to clarify the function of the three public debates.[93]

Jesus or the Jewish leaders?

It was suggested earlier that 12:1-12 may be understood as
Jesus' reply to the question on the source of his authority,
whether it is from God or men (11:27-33).[94] Here it is suggested

that the entire section, 12:1-40, is an answer to that question
in which Jesus not only affirms that his authority is from God,
but charges in turn that the Jewish leaders' authority in fact
derives from men.[95] In 12:1-11, at the beginning of the symmetrical pattern, Jesus accuses the legitimate Jewish authorities of rejecting and mistreating God's messengers. In 12:38-40,
at the close of the pattern, Jesus accuses the scribes of seeking their own status and violating the ethical rights of others.
In both, Jesus claims God's authority when he speaks as a prophet
announcing God's judgment against the Jewish leaders (12:9,40).

Material in the central public debate section also emphasizes the theme of who--Jesus or the Jewish authorities--is
acting for God. In the first debate, the Pharisees and the
Herodians in their preface to their question say to Jesus, οὐ
γὰρ βλέπεις εἰς πρόσωπον ἀνθρώπων, ἀλλ' ἐπ' ἀληθείας τὴν ὁδὸν
τοῦ θεοῦ διδάσκεις (12:14). Their intention in making the statement is hypocritical (12:15). However, the content of the statement from Mark's point of view is correct.

In the third debate, the double command of love underscores
the idea that the Jewish leaders are not acting for God but for
"men." Rejection of God's messengers is contrary to the command
to love God with all one's heart, soul, mind and strength. De-
vouring widows' houses is a violation of the command to love
one's neighbor as oneself. The contrast between God's demand
for love of God and neighbor and the Jewish leaders' behavior
highlights the fact that the section is not only a defense that
Jesus' authority is from God, but an indictment of the Jewish
establishment for not deriving its authority from God.

The role of the three public debates, 12:13-34

It was noted in the narrative overview of Mark 11-12 in
Chapter Two that the function of the three public debates in
the Jerusalem public ministry has not been clear to exegetes.
Here it will be argued that the fact that the debates exhibit
Jesus' *agreement* with basic Jewish beliefs explains their rhetorical function in the narrative of the Jerusalem public ministry.

In the cleansing of the temple and again in 12:1-12, Jesus
has acted as an angry prophet denouncing the Jewish authorities

and prophesying their destruction. Further, by means of the
images of the beloved son and the rejected stone which God establishes as head of the corner (12:6,10-11), the narrative implies that Jesus is not only a prophet, but more than a prophet,
that he is God's Son, the Messiah.

As a prophet, Jesus may not be dismissed by the Jewish
leaders out of hand, as Jeremiah could not be killed outright
when he predicted the fall of the first temple (Jer 7,26). The
Jewish establishment must first show Jesus to be a false prophet,
not speaking for God. In the ensuing public debates, however,
Jesus demonstrates that he stands on the ground of true Judaism.
The agreement between Jesus and Jewish belief is made explicit
in the scribe's and Jesus' approval of each other's answers to
the question of God's fundamental command (12:32-34). Jesus'
opponents' attempts to discredit him have instead served to establish Jesus as an orthodox Jew, therefore perhaps a legitimate
prophet, when he hints at the destruction of the temple and the
giving of the vineyard to others. It is precisely the agreement
of Jesus with the Jewish leaders on matters of belief which
silences Jesus' opponents so that they dare not question him
further.[96]

The placing of the public debates after Jesus' attack on
the Jewish leaders is effective dramatic narrative.[97] Jesus'
triumph over the Jewish leaders by means of his *agreement* with
them on basic Jewish beliefs establishes Jesus' innocence as a
Jew.[98] The Jews are left with no legal grounds for accusing
Jesus.[99]

The Jerusalem public ministry might well have ended in 12:
34 with the linear climax of Jesus' vindication of himself as a
Jew, possibly a true prophet of God. The narrative, however,
returns to Jesus' offensive against the Jewish leaders, chal-
lenging their Davidic messianic hopes and prophesying their
eschatological doom (12:35-40). The reversion to the earlier
theme of Jesus' attack on his opponents recalls to the reader's
mind the parable of the wicked tenants and its accompanying messianic challenge. By means of the symmetrical pattern, Mark is
underlining for the reader Jesus' messianic status and its
eschatalogical consequences for the old Israel and its leaders.[100]

Conclusion

In the beginning of this chapter the question was raised whether 2:1-3:6 was an isolated example of symmetrical patterning in Mark, or whether symmetrical structures should be considered a markan literary or rhetorical technique. The evidence from the rhetorical structure of Mark 1:1-8, 4:1-34 and 12:1-40 is that concentric patterns should be considered a markan literary technique. Mark's fondness for circular rhythms includes not only the devices of interposition, "insertion," and "intercalation," but also more extended symmetrical patterns.

In Chapter One, it was noted that concentric structure could be employed in original composition or as a means of structuring traditional material. Mark appears to use symmetrical rhythms in both ways. Mark 1:1-8 and 4:1-2a would seem to be markan compositions. The larger structures, 2:1-3:6, 4:1-34, and 12:1-40, obviously contain controversies, parables, etc., found in the tradition. Even here, the extent and type of Mark's redactional activity to create the concentric pattern may vary. In 4:1-34, Mark may be working from a parable collection or source into which he has interpolated additional materials at various points, giving the whole a symmetrical pattern.[101] In 12:1-40, Mark does not appear to be building upon any premarkan collection or source.[102] Except for the probable premarkan joining of the parable of the wicked tenants and the psalm citation about the rejected stone, Mark appears to have constructed the section by joining previously independent traditions.[103] Here, Mark has used the device of a symmetrical pattern to structure disparate material.

Whatever the degree of Mark's compositional or redactional activity, Mark appears to employ symmetrical patterns to interrelate and contrast material. In Mark 1:1-8, the symmetry clarifies the role of John the Baptist as the forerunner, Elijah. In Mark 4:1-34, the pattern highlights the paradox of parables as a means of revelation and as a mystery in need of explanation. In Mark 12:1-40, the pattern contrasts Jesus' attack on the Jewish leaders with his defense of himself as a good Jew. In these instances, as in 2:1-3:6, awareness of the symmetrical rhythm helps the reader to understand the text.

Criteria for Identifying Concentric Patterns, Reconsidered

Criteria Employed in Mark 1:1-8; 4:1-34 and 12:1-40

In the earlier discussion of criteria, it was concluded that a concentric structure may be posited in the text on the basis of multiple *congruent* parallelisms of content, form-critical classification, structure, and word repetition (hook words).[104] The impact of the various criteria is cumulative. Mark 2:1-3:6 met all of the criteria: parallelisms of content, form, structure and the presence of hook words. None of the concentric patterns posited in this chapter is as elegant or elaborate as 2:1-3:6. A brief review of the criteria employed to identify these structures may help to clarify the relative importance of the various criteria and suggest additional criteria.

Mark 1:1-8. In Mark 1:1-8, the symmetrical pattern was posited almost entirely on the basis of manifest content. The question of form is not really applicable in so short a narrative. The argument based on content was supported by two additional arguments. First, the rhetorical structure of C, the middle section, is itself a ring composition, an a b a pattern in which the middle element, b, contains a verbal chiasm. Second, recognition of the symmetrical structure of vv. 1-8 helps to explain the function of v. 6 (B') in the composition: B' serves to elucidate the meaning of B (vv. 2-3).

Mark 4:1-34. The concentric pattern in the parable discourse was based primarily on the congruent parallelism of form and content. A and A' are the editorial introduction and conclusion concerning Jesus' teaching in parables. B and B' are similar in form, consisting primarily of parable material. Further, the parables are similar in content. All the parables concern the earth and vegetation, sowing or harvest. The rhetorical structure of B and B' are found to be quite different: B has a symmetrical pattern while B' consists of two parallel parables. B and B' are however, connected by hook words. C, the middle section, is different in form--sayings material not parables, and in content--everything is to be revealed.

As in the case of Mark 1:1-8, the argument in Mark 4 for the overall concentric pattern is buttressed by arguments based on the rhetorical structure of individual sections of the pattern. A, the introduction, is itself an elegant symmetrical construction alerting the reader to the possibility of a symmetrical pattern in the larger unit. B also has a symmetrical pattern. C, the mid-section, has a chiastic structure: saying, exhortation : exhortation, saying. In both Mark 1:1-8 and 4:1-34, the rhetorical structure of the middle section has helped to indicate to the reader that the center or turning point of the pattern has been reached.

Mark 12:1-40. The symmetrical structure of 12:1-40 was based on the congruent parallelism of form, content and structure. In content, A and A' are both attacks on the behavior of Jewish leaders and prophecies of their condemnation; B and B' concern the messiah; C and C' concern the demands of God, and D is about resurrection. In form, A, B, B', and A' are all direct teachings of Jesus. B and B' both feature centrally a citation from the psalms. C, D, and C' are all public debates in which Jesus answers a question about Jewish belief. The parallelism of structure goes beyond the parallelism which may be attributed to formal similarity in the placing (not the content) of audience reactions following B, C, C' and B' but not A, D or A'. Further, in the public debate material, C and C' are closely interwoven into the larger narrative while D is not. Also C and C' consist of a double interchange between the questioner and Jesus, while D has only a single interchange.

The symmetrical pattern receives some confirmation from the presence of hook words. The word "crowd" occurs only in the audience reactions at the end of B and B'. The phrase "with truth" occurs near the beginning of C and near the end of C'. Jesus is addressed as "teacher" in all three public debates, C, D, and C'.

The arguments for the detailed symmetrical pattern are supported by the fact that the pattern as a whole may be viewed as a ring composition in which Jesus' direct teachings critical of the Jewish leaders and their messianic understanding alternate with public debates in which Jesus appears as a good Jew. Finally,

this pattern of provocation : defense : provocation helps to
clarify the function of the public debates and the two teachings
against the scribes in the Jerusalem public ministry.

Conclusion. The foregoing summary suggests that parallelism of manifest content may be the most important criterion for
identifying concentric patterns. Form, whenever applicable,
also appears to be central. The congruent shift of content and
form (in which the content is not just a consequence of the form)
in a symmetrical pattern appears to be a, if not the, central
rhetorical feature of the extended concentric patterns in 2:1-
3:6; 4:1-34 and 12:1-40. Parallelism of structure not attributable to similarity of form is a strong argument for a rhetorical pattern when it exists, as in 2:1-3:6 and 12:1-40. It
does not, however, appear to be a necessary feature of a symmetrical pattern since it is not found in 4:1-34. In the texts
surveyed, every audience reaction at the close of a pericope
was paralleled by another audience reaction fitting the symmetrical pattern.[105] Editorial introductions beginning pericopes,
however, were not always paralleled.[106]

Hook words congruent with the symmetrical pattern were
noted in all the texts surveyed except for 1:1-8. In all instances, the hook words were supporting evidence for a parallelism already posited on the grounds of content and/or form
or structure.[107] And in none of the passages analyzed were hook
words a major indicator of the overall structure. These facts
suggest that, in Mark, hook words are a secondary criterion for
identifying extended rhetorical patterns, although they are reassuring confirmatory evidence. Given the multiple rhetorical
functions of word repetition--as key words, for anticipation or
retrospection, for rhetorical emphasis, in addition to use as
hook words--it is not surprising that word repetition should be
a secondary consideration in identifying extended rhetorical
patterns.

The review of criteria employed suggests two additional aids
in identifying extended rhetorical structures. First, the rhetorical structure of the individual elements of the pattern may
help to alert the reader to the larger pattern. This fact is
of fundamental methodological importance for the rhetorical or

literary critic interested in structure. It means that any attempt to determine larger rhetorical structures or the over-all structure of a work should be based upon an analysis of the structure of the smaller units making up the whole. If Mourlon Beernaert in his study of 2:1-3:6 and Lambrecht in 4:1-34 had paid attention to the structure of the individual units of their texts, the difficulties in their respective rhetorical patterns might have been avoided.[108]

The rhetorical structure of the middle section appears to be particularly important. In both 1:1-8 and 4:1-34 the symmetrical and/or chiastic structure of the middle element of the pattern helps to indicate that the center or turning point of a symmetrical pattern has been reached. In the larger ring composition of 12:1-40, teaching-debate-teaching, the debate section itself is a ring composition. In 2:1-3:6, the middle portion had a two-part rhetorical structure, while the remaining pericopes all had three-part structures.

The rhetorical structure of the initial element in a rhetorical pattern may also be a useful indicator. The elegant symmetrical pattern of 4:1-2a, the introduction to the parable discourse, may suggest to the reader that the entire discourse may be so structured. The use of the frame-interposition technique in 2:1-12 may prepare the reader for the use of the same device in 1:45-3:8 as a whole. Finally, the employment of a concentric rhythm in Mark 1:1-8, the opening of the gospel, may alert the reader to the possible use of such patterns later in the gospel.

Second, when a rhetorical pattern elucidates the meaning or function of otherwise obscure passages, then this fact is useful supporting evidence for the existence of the pattern. Examples of this would be the function of v. 6 in Mark 1:1-8, the meaning and function of 2:25-26 in 2:1-3:6, and the role of the public debates and the attached teachings against the scribes in 12:1-40. This type of argumentation, however, should be used with caution, and the critic should be wary of imposing a pattern on a text in order to explain an element which is obscure.

Mark 1:21-45(2:12): A Passage Without a Concentric Structure

A second method of approaching the question of criteria for
identifying concentric patterns is to look at a text which exhibits parallels of content, form, structure, and contains word
repetitions, but which does not appear to be symmetrically pat-
terned. Since two conflicting symmetrical patterns have been
proposed for Mark 1:21-45(2:12), indicating an abundance of
parallels, it seems a good passage to select. Also, the preceding analysis of 2:1-3:6 has indicated many rhetorical interconnections between 2:1-3:6 and 1:16-45. A consideration of
the function of 2:1-3:6 in the gospel of Mark must take into
consideration its relationship to Mark 1. The following discussion of structure in Mark 1:21-45(2:12) will help to prepare
for the discussion of the relationship of 2:1-3:6 to Mark 1.

D. Dideberg and P. Mourlon Beernaert have proposed a seven-
part symmetrical pattern for Mark 1:21-45.[109] D. Clark has proposed a five-part symmetrical pattern for Mark 1:21-2:12.[110]
The respective proposals may be outlined as follows:

Dideberg and Mourlon Beernaert			Clark
A	1:21-27	Healing of man with unclean spirit in synagogue.	A
B	1:28	Report of Jesus in all of Galilee.	
C	1:29-31	Healing of Simon's mother-in-law.	B
D	1:32-34	Entire village at door; sick and demoniacs healed.	
C'	1:35-38	Departure of Jesus alone; four companions find Jesus; Jesus' mission to preach	C
B'	1:39	The coming of Jesus into all Galilee.	
A'	1:40-45	Healing of the leper	B'
	2:1-12	Healing of the paralytic	A'

The two patterns are not compatible. According to Dideberg
and Mourlon Beernaert, 1:21-27 is parallel to 1:40-45. According
to Clark, the same verses parallel 2:1-12, while 1:29-34 parallels 1:40-45. For Dideberg and Mourlon Beernaert, the central

or pivot section is 1:32-34. For Clark, the middle portion is
1:35-39. Here it is not a question of a symmetrically structured
unit being part of a larger rhetorical unit as in Mark 1:1-8 or
4:2b-20. Nor is it a question of overlapping rhetorical patterns
as in Mark 11-12 in which 12:1-12 serves both as the climax to
the unit, 11:15-18,27-12:12, and as the beginning of the unit,
12:1-40. The two proposed patterns are in conflict with each
other. Both cannot be true, and the fact that scholars have
found enough evidence of parallelism to propose the two contradictory structures suggests the possibility that neither is the
rhetorical pattern of the text. A consideration of the weaknesses and strengths of the arguments for the respective structures and the ways in which arguments fail to be convincing should
shed light on the question of how to identify symmetrical patterns. The two proposed symmetrical patterns will be discussed
separately.

    1:21-45: Dideberg and Mourlon Beernaert. The markan text
does not support the proposed rhetorical pattern of Dideberg and
Mourlon Beernaert. First, 1:21-45 is not established as a rhetorical unit or sub-unit in the gospel. If the theme is Jesus'
arrival in Galilee, as the title of their article suggests, then
one would expect the rhetorical unit to begin at 1:14: ἦλθεν
ὁ ʼΙησοῦς εἰς τὴν Γαλιλαίαν κηρύσσων τὸ εὐαγγέλιον, a verse
relevant in content and with strong verbal parallels to 1:39,
the proposed B'. Or if vv. 14-15 are considered transitional
verses concluding the prologue and outside the rhetorical structure of the public ministry, the question must still be addressed
as to whether or not the calling of the first disciples (1:16-20),
Jesus' first act in Galilee, is or is not part of the following
rhetorical unit. The extent of a rhetorical unit needs to be
argued on rhetorical grounds.[111]

    Second, some of the parallels adduced to argue for a sym-
metrical pattern do not appear to support such a pattern. A
and A' (1:21-27,40-45) are indeed similar in form--both are
healing miracles. They also have similarities in content: in
the first, a man with an *unclean* spirit is healed; in the second
a leper is *cleansed*.[112] The parallelism of A and A' seems in
itself tenable.[113] However, looking at the entire passage,

Jesus' healing activity does not fit the proposed symmetrical
pattern. A, C and A' recount specific healings; D reports many
healings, B' reports that Jesus cast out demons throughout
Galilee, while B and C', the second and fifth elements, do not
refer to healing at all.

B and B' (1:28,39) are similar in content and word repetition. In B, the report of Jesus ἐξῆλθεν...εἰς ὅλην...τῆς
Γαλιλαίας (1:28). In B', Jesus ἦλθεν κηρύσσων...εἰς ὅλην τὴν
Γαλιλαίαν (1:39). B' is certainly likely to recall B to the
reader's mind, but it also would recall 1:14. Furthermore, the
verb "to preach," an important word for Mark,[114] occurs not only
in 1:14 and B' but also in C' and A' (1:38,45). Other word
repetitions also occur in the text. For example, εὐθύς occurs
in 1:18,20,21,23,28,29,30,42,43. It does not occur at all in
sections D, C' or B'.[115] Ἐκβάλλω occurs in D, B' and A' (1:34,
39,43). Word repetition is used in Mark for many rhetorical
purposes: as hook words indicating structure, as key words
indicative of theme but not structure, and also for rhetorical
emphasis. If it is to be argued that certain word repetitions
function as hook words, all repetitions of words must be considered and evaluated to see in what way the repetition is
functioning. Dideberg's and Mourlon Beernaert's use of "coming
into all of Galilee" as hook words does not take into consideration all the relevant data in the text.

The parallel between C and C' (1:29-31,35-38) is posited
on the grounds of the frequency of verbs of motion--which are
frequent throughout the passage being studied--and the presence
of the disciples as active characters in both. In C, they tell
Jesus of Simon's mother-in-law's illness; in C', they seek out
Jesus in desert places. The parallel is valid as far as it goes.
But there does not appear to be an overall symmetrical pattern
based on character roles. The crowd is an important character
in A and D. In A', however, the crowd is not a character in
the healing narrative, and only begins to gather at the end as
the result of the healed leper's preaching. Furthermore, C and
C', except for the presence of the disciples, are in no way
parallel in content: in one, a specific healing is recounted;
in the other, the disciples seek out Jesus to tell him everyone
is looking for him.

Another and serious problem with the proposed structure is that B and B' have been separated from their respective pericopes (A and C') so that the overall rhetorical pattern conflicts with the obvious literary divisions within the pattern, the pericope units.[116]

In 1:21-45, Dideberg and Mourlon Beernaert have not shown any consistent overall symmetrical pattern based on content (or form). The parallelism of the various sections is posited on the basis of different criteria. A and A' are parallel on the basis of content, healing--the exorcism of an unclean spirit and the cleansing of the leper.[117] The parallelism of B and B' is based on the presence of word repetition and the fact that both are general notations, not particular scenes.[118] The parallelism of C and C' is based on character roles--the presence of the disciples. It would seem, however, that a symmetrical structure, to be posited in the text, should show a (symmetrical) alternation in the text based consistently on at least one major criterion.[119] Moreover, the pattern posited does not exhibit *congruent* parallelisms based on content *and/or* form *or* structure *or* character roles *or* setting. It would seem that an extended concentric structure consisting of several pericopes should exhibit at least some congruent parallelisms based on more than one criterion.

1:21-2:12. Clark. Building upon my proposed concentric structure for 2:1-3:6,[120] Clark has proposed a "double pyramid chiasm" as follows:[121]

1:21-28	A1		
1:29-34		B1	
1:35-39			C
1:40-45		B2	
2:1-12	A2		
2:13-17		D1	
2:18-22			E
2:23-28		D2	
3:1-6	A3		

Thus Clark views 1:21-2:12 and 2:1-3:6 as two overlapping concentric patterns in which A1 and A2 form the outer ring of the first pattern, and A2 and A3 the outer ring of the second.[122] As may be seen from the use of different letters (B1,C,B2; D1,E, D2), Clark does not view the middle parts of the two concentric

patterns as interrelated. The second concentric pattern, 2:1-
3:6, is the pattern proposed in Chapter Four of this study and
need not be considered here. The parallelism of the "A" layer
(1:21-28; 2:1-12; 3:1-6) and the proposed symmetrical pattern
of 1:21-2:12 will be evaluated.

The case for the parallelism of Clark's A2 (the healing of
the paralytic) and A3 (the healing of the man with the withered
hand) has already been argued in Chapter Four. Clark's argument
for the parallelism of A1 with A2 and A3 seems viable.[123] The
settings are comparable: A1 is set at Capernaum, in a synagogue
(1:21); A2 is set at Capernaum (2:1); and A3 is set in a synagogue (3:1).[124] (Clark's argument may be buttressed by the fact
that the πάλιν's in both 2:1 and 3:1 refer back to 1:21.) All
three recount healings accomplished by word alone. All three--
and only these healings in 1:21-3:6--are followed by an audience
reaction to the miracle. There is also a partial overlap of
hook words among the three pericopes. All three include the
introductory phrase εἰσῆλθεν/εἰσελθὼν εἰς (1:21; 2:1; 3:1).[125]
A1 and A2 are linked by "authority" (1:22,27; 2:10); A1 and A3
by "sabbath" (1:21; 3:2,4).

Clark's argument for the parallelism of 1:21-28, 2:1-12 and
3:1-6 may be strengthened by additional parallelisms. In 1:21-
28 as well as in 2:1-12 and 3:1-6, there is conflict involving
dialogue: in A1, between Jesus and the demon; in A2 and A3,
between Jesus and the opponents.[126] Mark 1:21-28, like 2:1-12
and 3:1-6, is a ring composition in structure. The actual exorcism is framed at the beginning and end by similar audience reactions: amazement at Jesus' teaching with authority (1:22,27).
In the three pericopes, there is a progressive shift in the
third character role in the narrative--the character in addition
to Jesus and the person being healed. In 1:21-28, the third
character throughout is the crowd, the people in the synagogue,
who are favorably impressed by Jesus. In 2:1-12, the third
character in the outer ring at the beginning and the end is still
the friendly crowd, while in the central portion, the third
character is played by the hostile opponents. In 3:1-6, the
third character role throughout is that of the hostile opponents.[127] There is a movement from the popularity of Jesus to
the opposition to him.

Moreover, 1:21-28 (A1) and 2:1-12 (A2) have additional
parallels. The mention in A1 by the crowd that Jesus teaches
with authority unlike the *scribes* prepares the reader for the
objection by the *scribes* in A2 to Jesus' claim to have authority
to forgive sins (1:22,27; 2:6-10a). The concluding audience reaction in A1 takes no cognizance of the demon's recognition of
Jesus as "the holy one of God" just as the crowd reaction in
A2 takes no cognizance of Jesus' claim to be the Son of Man with
authority on earth (1:24,27; 2:10,12). Finally, it is possible
that ἀπολέσαι/ἀπολέσωσιν in 1:24 and 3:6 may be an additional
connection between A1 and A3.[128] Jesus indeed has come to destroy the demons; the Jewish authorities will destroy Jesus,
bringing about their own destruction in turn (12:9).[129]

There would appear to be sufficient evidence based on structure, content (setting and character roles) and hook words to
posit some connection or parallelism between A1, A2 and A3.
Furthermore, Luke apparently recognized some interrelationship
of the three pericopes for he inserts the phrase εἰς τὸ μέσον
from A3 not only into A2 but also into A1 (Lk 4:35; 5:19; 6:8).
These are the only uses of the phrase in Luke. And the three
times he uses πίμπλημι for the audience reaction in his gospel
are found in these three pericopes (4:28; 5:26; 6:11).

Clark's argument for a concentric pattern in 1:21-2:12,
however, does not seem viable. The parallelism of 1:29-34 and
40-45 (B1 and B2) seems strained and the setting apart of 1:35-
39 (C) as the middle element is debatable. Clark argues for
the parallelism of B1 and B2 as follows: in both, a specific
healing occurs (Simon's mother-in-law and the leper); in both,
"Jesus is as a result overwhelmed by the crowds" (1:33,45); and
in both, there is a demand for silence (1:34,44). In addition,
the hook words χείρ and ἐξέβαλεν are to be noted (1:31,41; 34,
43).[130]

In his arguments, Clark has paid insufficient attention to
content as distinct from form. The first part of B1 (1:29-31)
and B2 as a whole report specific healings. There, however, the
similarity of the two healings ends. In B1, the healing is a
"raising," a resurrection-type miracle; there is no dialogue;
and the disciples play a role. In B2, the healing is a cleansing;
there is considerable dialogue; and for the healing proper, there

are no characters except Jesus and the leper. The use of "hand" in both miracles may simply be a commonplace of the healing form.[131] In content, the healing of the leper (B2) is closer to the exorcism (A1), as Dideberg and Mourlon Beernaert have argued. And the cure of Simon's mother-in-law (B1) is closer to the raising of the paralytic (A2)[132] than either A1 is to A2 or B1 is to B2. The similarity of form-critical type—a healing— is not sufficient to posit parallelism.

Furthermore, as Dideberg and Mourlon Beernaert recognized, B1 consists of two independent scenes, the private specific healing and the multiple public healings (1:29-31,32-34). The presence of the crowd in the second scene is not, as Clark asserts, a consequence of the healing of Simon's mother-in-law, but of the events in the synagogue in A1. The injunction to silence to the leper in B2 (1:44) is a direct command to the leper to keep quiet (similar to the command of silence to the demon in A1). The injunction to silence in B1 is not part of the specific healing, but an aside to the reader at the close of the scene of multiple healings (1:34). The parallelism of B1 and B2 cannot be maintained.

Finally, the middle element (C, 1:35-39) is not clearly set apart from the other elements in the symmetrical pattern (as the central element was set off in the symmetric patterns described earlier: 1:4-5; 2:18-22; 4:21-25; and either 12:13-34 or 18-27). Contra Clark,[133] 1:35-39 does not differ from the other pericopes in its concentric pattern by the absence of miracles (Jesus casts out demons in 1:39) nor by a distinctive setting (Jesus is in a desert place in 1:35 and in 1:40-45). Thus, while the parallelism of A1 and A2 may be maintained, the symmetrical arrangement of the material between them, 1:29-45, cannot be maintained.

Clark's methodology appears to be at fault in that he does not distinguish clearly between content per se and form, which inevitably involves some parallelism of content—e.g., a healing form necessarily reports a healing but the type of healing and the way it is told may vary greatly. In addition, Clark's practice of his methodology is sometimes weak or erroneous. A closer reading of the text would have enabled Clark to see that the gathering of the crowd in 1:32-34 was the consequence of

1:21-28, not of the private healing in 1:29-31, and to see the
connections between C and the other pericopes in the section.

Summary. Neither Dideberg's and Mourlon Beernaert's analysis nor Clark's seems sufficient to posit a symmetrical pattern
in the text of 1:21-45(2:12). All rhetorical units in the gospel of Mark are *not* concentrically structured or organized. Yet
both of their proposals have pointed out many parallels which
exist in the text, awareness of which may enrich the reader's
experience of the text. Further, Clark's analysis (and the
critique of it) have stressed parallels between 1:21-45 and 2:1-
3:6 in addition to the retrospective references already noted
in the first reading of 2:1-3:6 in Chapter Three. In particular,
Clark's recognition of the relationship of 1:21-28, 2:1-12 and
3:1-6 appears valid.

Conclusion

The failure of both proposed symmetrical patterns in Mark
1:21-45(2:12) to be convincing reaffirms the conclusions reached
on the basis of the criteria used to establish the proposed symmetrical patterns in 1:1-8; 2:1-3:6; 4:1-34 and 12:1-40.[134]
Neither proposal shows a clear symmetrical alternation on the
basis of manifest content. Neither has a congruent shift of
form and content. Neither takes into consideration the rhetorical structure of the individual elements of the overall pattern.[135] Finally, neither helps to elucidate the meaning or
purpose of otherwise obscure passages.

In addition to the above, the respective proposals have
two weaknesses in common. First, neither argument pays adequate
attention to the criterion of form. Dideberg and Mourlon Beernaert basically ignore form as a possible indication of parallelism and as a result posit some strange parallels, e.g., the
specific healing in 1:29-31 with the biographical apophthegm in
1:35-38. Clark, on the other hand, treats the elementary similarity in form of 1:29-31 and 1:40-44 as a real similarity in
content which the respective verses do not support. The observation of Muilenburg that rhetorical criticism builds upon the
results of form criticism would appear to be vindicated.[136]

Secondly, both proposals fail to consider *all* the relevant
data, *all* the possible parallelisms in the text. While all possible interrelationships are not significant for identifying
rhetorical structure, they must be considered and accounted for
in the determination of a rhetorical pattern. The pattern of
specific and general healings, the type and manner of each healing, the alternation of specific scenes and general notations,
setting and temporal notations, character roles (disciples,
crowd), and audience reaction need to be analyzed throughout
the entire passage. Particularly in the determination that an
instance of word repetition is functioning as a hook word, all
word repetitions within a passage need to be considered. The
existence of *some* symmetrical parallelisms, when there exist
other equally significant conflicting parallelisms, is not sufficient to posit a concentric pattern in the text.

Finally, in a discussion of criteria or methodology for
identifying concentric patterns, a point made earlier should be
recalled. Rhetorical analysis is an art as well as a science.
It depends not only on the evidence of the text and the skill
of the rhetorical critic in analyzing the text but also on the
sensitivity of the critic to the text. While an adequate
methodology for identifying rhetorical patterns may be described, while explicit criteria may be established, the ap-
plication of the methodology, the weighing of the relative importance of the various arguments, remains dependent upon the
ability and sensitivity of the rhetorical critic. Rhetorical
criticism, like redaction and form criticism, is not an exact
science.

CHAPTER VI

MARK 2:1-3:6 IN THE GOSPEL OF MARK

With Chapter Five, the rhetorical analysis of selected portions of the gospel of Mark and the discussion of an adequate
methodology for determining rhetorical structure, in particular
criteria for identifying concentric patterns, have been completed. It is now necessary to return to the subject of the
Galilean controversy section, Mark 2:1-3:6, and to consider the
redactional question raised in Chapter Two: that is, is 2:1-
3:6 with its elegant concentric and linear pattern a markan construction or is it to be attributed to Mark's interpolation of
a source into his narrative? Finally, as a conclusion, there
will be a brief summary of the meaning and function of 2:1-3:6
in Mark's gospel.

Is Mark 2:1-3:6 a Markan Construction?

In Chapter Five, it was concluded that concentric structuring of material, whether by original composition, compilation
of independent traditions, or by editorial modification of a
collection or source, may be considered one of Mark's literary
techniques. However, to observe that 2:1-3:6 is concentrically
structured does not in itself prove that the concentric structure is due to Mark. Symmetrical patterning is a rhetorical
technique available to compilers of collections or sources as
well as to Mark. Also, as noted in Chapter Two, 2:1-3:6 quali-
fied for consideration as an insertion or interpolation into a
larger narrative. The controversy section is set into the frame
of 1:45 and 3:7-8, in which there is no hint of opposition and
in which 3:7 could follow immediately upon 1:45 without narrative disjunction. The section, *if* it had a premarkan existence,
could have been inserted between 1:45 and 3:7.

Given the tightly-knit linear and concentric structure of
2:1-3:6, it would seem that *either* Mark created the rhetorical
structure of 2:1-3:6 by means of redaction, compilation and/or
composition *or* Mark took over the structure from an earlier
source virtually as it now stands.[1] Here, it will be argued

that Mark created the structure of 2:1-3:6. It will be argued, first, that the interconnections of Mark 1:16-45 and 2:1-3:6 point towards markan construction of 2:1-3:6; second, that the literary techniques employed to create the structure are frequently markan devices; and third, that the theology brought out by the literary structure appears to be consonant with Mark's theology elsewhere in the gospel. Finally, there will be a brief excursus on the question of whether Mark employed the earlier collection proposed by Kuhn in 2:1-28 or whether he composed 2:1-3:6 from previously independent traditions.

Interconnections between Mark 1:16-45 and 2:1-3:6

Numerous rhetorical and content interconnections of 2:1-3:6 with 1:16-45 were noted in the first reading of 2:1-3:6 in Chapter Three and also in the discussion of Mark 1:16-45 (2:12) at the end of Chapter Five. If these interconnections are essential to the concentric structure of 2:1-3:6, then 2:1-3:6 in its present rhetorical form is unlikely to have had an independent existence prior to its connection with Mark 1:16-45.

Thus, the first question to be asked is whether the markan retrospective allusions in 2:1-3:6 can be deleted without appreciably marring the rhetorical symmetry. In order to remove the explicit references to Mark 1:16-45, it is necessary to delete πάλιν in 2:1,13 and 3:1, the introductory scenes in 2:1-2 and 2:13, and the call of Levi in 2:14.[2] The three uses of πάλιν may easily be omitted. The entire introductory scene in 2:1-2 with its references to 1:21,29,33,45 could be Mark's elaboration of an existing introduction placing Jesus in a house surrounded by a crowd. The introductory scene in 2:13 also is not necessary. With the deletion of 2:14 as well, pericope B could begin at 2:15.

The removal of 2:14, the call of Levi, however, would destroy much of the parallelism between B and B' (2:13-17,23-28).[3] If B began at 2:15, it would have a two-part rhetorical structure like C, not a three-part structure like B'. The parallelism of the two three-part structures in which eating is explicitly mentioned only in the central portion of each would be lost. Further, the close of B, "I came not to call the righteous but sinners" (2:17b), would refer only to the question about

eating with sinners in 2:16 and not back to the call of Levi at
the beginning of B. Thus the parallel with B' in which the last
part, 2:27-28, refers back to the opening in 2:23-24 would also
be lost.

It has already been argued that 2:14 is a markan construction based on 1:16-20 and not an independent tradition.[4] It has
also been argued that 2:25-26 is a secondary addition to the
controversy over sabbath behavior in B', functioning not only
in its own pericope but as an answer to the question about eating in B.[5] It would seem most probable that 2:14 and 2:25-26
were added at the same time by a redactor as part of the construction of the present concentric pattern. The additions contribute to the parallelism of structure of B and B'. In content,
both additions emphasize the role of the disciples (in 2:25-26
through the inclusion of David's followers). Furthermore, 2:25-
26 brings the subject of eating into B'. Discipleship *and* eating are essential content features of the symmetrical pattern in
2:13-28. If Mark composed 2:14, or even if Mark added 2:14 from
tradition to its present setting as most scholars argue, then
it would seem to be Mark who has constructed the symmetrical
pattern.[6] In summary, while most of the retrospective references
in 2:1-3:6 may be dropped without impairing the symmetrical pattern, 2:14 is an important if not essential element of that pattern.

The interconnection between Mark 1:16-45 and 2:1-3:6 extends beyond the specific retrospective references in 2:1-3:6
to include the motif of Jesus' increasing popularity, which begins in 1:21-28 and is continued into 2:1-15, the theme of Jesus'
authority found in 1:21-28 as well as in 2:1-28, and the parallelism of 1:21-28, 2:1-12, and 3:1-6. The motif of Jesus' growing popularity is found most explicitly in 2:1-3:6 in 2:1-2
which, as already noted, may be a markan editorial expansion.[7]
On the other hand, the theme of Jesus' authority and the parallelism of 2:1-12 and 3:1-6 are part of the rhetorical structure
of 2:1-3:6. Their connection to Mark 1, however, could be explained on the basis of markan editorial modification of the
sabbath exorcism in 1:21-28. Both 1:22 and 27 may well be markan
additions to the exorcism.[8] Without those verses, both the
theme of Jesus' authority in Mark 1 and the parallel between

1:21-28 and the two healings in 2:1-3:6 would be greatly dimin-
ished.

If, however, Mark is inserting a source between 1:45 and
3:7, and has redacted 1:21-28 in such a way as to introduce the
theme of Jesus' authority and to make it, like 2:1-12 and 3:1-6,
a ring composition, then Mark, the final redactor, has modified
his independent traditions to fit his source. It would seem
more reasonable to suppose that Mark has redacted both 1:21-28
and the material presented in 2:1-3:6 to serve his own interests.
In this case, the thematic and structural interrelationships of
1:16-3:6 would seem to be markan. Therefore, the rhetorical
structure of 2:1-3:6 is in all probability markan as well. Thus,
the rhetorical and content interconnections of Mark 1:16-45 and
2:1-3:6 suggest that Mark 2:1-3:6 is a markan construction.

Literary Techniques

Taylor has already observed that the vocabulary and style
of Mark 2:1-3:6 do not differ from that found in the rest of
the gospel. [9] Further, it has been argued in Chapter Five that
extended concentric structure may be considered a markan
literary technique. There seems no reason on literary grounds
to suppose that Mark 2:1-3:6 is not markan.

The argument on the basis of literary techniques, however,
can be carried further to constitute an argument *for* markan construction. The concentric pattern in 2:1-3:6 is characterized
by an alternation of form (healing controversy with the healing
at the end vs. non-healing controversies of the action:objection:
vindication type). A symmetrical alternation of form was also
observed in 4:1-34 and 12:1-40. As in 12:13-34, so also the
middle three pericopes of 2:1-3:6 (2:13-28) constitute in themselves a ring composition in content and structure. Further,
the parallel placement of audience reactions which are antithetic in content characterizes both 2:1-3:6 and 12:1-40. In
both instances a contrast is made between the crowd which wholeheartedly supports Jesus and the Jewish leaders who desire to
destroy him. A fondness for stressing contrast is characteristic
of markan style and literary technique. [10]

Moreover, the use of frames to block off sections of the
gospel would appear to be a markan literary device used to structure the gospel. The healings in 8:22-26 and 10:46-52 block off

the way section. Mark 8:22-26 and 9:14-29 block off the first
portion of the way section in which the teaching on discipleship
is public, not private, teaching. The two pericopes in which
Jesus points to women as good examples (12:41-44; 14:3-9) frame
the apocalyptic discourse in Mark 13. Finally, the Jerusalem
public ministry is set in a narrative frame in which 13:1-2
might follow 11:11 without narrative disjunction.[11] The last
frame is similar in type to the frame around 2:1-3:6, and 11:12-
12:44 certainly cannot be considered a source which Mark has
interpolated. The frame around 2:1-3:6 would seem to be an instance of Mark's framing technique and need not be explained as
an indication of Mark's incorporation of a source.

Finally, the frame of 1:45 and 3:7-8, showing people streaming to Jesus from everywhere, functions rhetorically to block
off 2:1-3:6, showing opposition to Jesus, from the ongoing narrative. By means of the frame-interposition technique, Mark is
enabled to continue the narrative without immediately dealing
with the death threat of 3:6. Exactly the same rhetorical technique is employed in 2:1-12, the first pericope of the larger
interposition. The conflict between Jesus and his opponents
over blasphemy in 2:6-10a is interposed into the frame of Jesus'
miracle which is enthusiastically received by the crowd in 2:1-
5,10b-12. Here also, the use of the interposition-frame technique enables the narrator to continue without dealing immediately with the conflict over blasphemy. The use of the same rather
unusual rhetorical technique for the same narrative purpose in
2:1-12 and 1:45-3:8 suggests that the same redactor was responsible for both.[12] Since both frames and interpositions (including
intercalations and insertions) are markan literary devices, the
redactor would seem to be Mark.

Theology

On theological as well as on literary grounds, there seems
to be no reason to suppose that Mark 2:1-3:6 cannot be Mark's
own redaction of tradition. The theology of 2:1-3:6 does not
appear to conflict with the theology of the rest of the gospel;
therefore there is no need to hypothesize a source to explain
the presence of 2:1-3:6 in Mark. First, Albertz' objections to
the markan origin of 2:1-3:6 will be reviewed. Second, since

the tight concentric structure of 2:1-3:6 indicates that either
Mark incorporated the concentric structure from his source or
he created that structure, the theological emphases brought out
by that structure will be considered in terms of Mark's interests.

Albertz' objections

As noted earlier, Albertz argued that 2:1-3:6 could not be
markan because the use of the title, Son of Man, in 2:10 and 28
is not Mark's use of the title and because the allusion to Jesus'
death in 2:20 and the mention of the plot against Jesus in 3:6
come too early in Mark's plan.[13]

The use of Son of Man. The two uses of the Son of Man for
Jesus' earthly authority are indeed unique in Mark's gospel.
Yet, they do not appear to conflict with Mark's later use of
the title.[14] Rather, as argued earlier, they serve the purpose
of identifying Jesus as the Son of Man for the reader and preparing the reader for the later uses of the title for the suffering, death and resurrection of Jesus.[15] Since the title is
to be used for the death and resurrection of Jesus (8:31; 9:9,
12,31; 10:33-34,45), the redactor of the gospel needs to establish the Son of Man as a title for the earthly Jesus, not just
for a heavenly figure. Mark 2:10 and 2:28 serve this purpose
well. Further, 2:10,28 continue the theme of Jesus' earthly
authority begun in 1:22,27.[16] Since the uses of the title point
both backwards and forwards in the gospel narrative, there is
no need to view 2:10,28 as contrary to Mark's christology, and
as such, evidence for a source.[17]

The early hints of Jesus' death. Scholars have long viewed
Mark 2:1-3:6 as an explanation of why Jesus was killed.[18] In
2:20, Jesus alludes to his own death, which he does not explicitly reveal to the disciples until 8:31. In 3:6, the opponents begin to plot to destroy Jesus; the activity of the opponents does not again reach the intensity of 3:6 until 11:18 when
the authorities again seek to destroy him. Is the emphasis upon
Jesus' coming death in 2:1-3:6 too early in the plan of Mark's
gospel, and thus evidence for Mark's incorporation of a source?

The hypothesis of the interpolation of a source would not seem necessary to explain the emphasis upon Jesus' death so early in the gospel of Mark. The theme of opposition to Jesus continues the theme begun in 1:16 of the varied responses to Jesus and the bringing of the kingdom. In 1:14-15, the verses closing the prologue and introducing Jesus' ministry, Jesus announces the coming of the kingdom of God and calls for the people to respond: μετανοεῖτε καὶ πιστεύετε ἐν τῷ εὐαγγελίῳ. Mark 1:16-3:6 portrays the arrival of the kingdom in Jesus' authoritative words and deeds, teaching and healing.[19] "Mark creates a new beginning by announcing the arrival and present reality of the Kingdom in Galilee....The beginning of the Kingdom spells the ending of an older order of things."[20] Mark 1:16-3:6 *also* shows the two responses to the arrival of the kingdom. Five incidents showing the popularity of Jesus (1:21-45) are followed by five scenes which portray the opposition to Jesus (2:1-3:6).[21] The numerous retrospective references in 2:1-3:6 help to interrelate the material of 2:1-3:6 with 1:16-45 and thus to contrast the two responses to Jesus. The enthusiastic response of the disciples who leave everything to follow Jesus (1:16-20; 2:14) and of the crowd who seek Jesus out (1:32-33,37,45; 2:2,13; 3:7-8) is contrasted with the total rejection of Jesus and the kingdom by the Pharisees (3:6). As L. Kech writes,

> The response of the people from the regions around Galilee [3:7-8] is thus set against that of the Pharisees (2:1-3:6). The entire section [1:16-3:12] presents Jesus as teacher, healer-exorcist, and liberator from the Law....This brings about the far-reaching response....With this general picture of Jesus' work, Mark is ready to begin the next phase of his gospel story. In this first section, he has presented the Jesus who calls men to discipleship and the responses elicited.[22]

Thus, as narrative, 2:1-3:6 is a fitting continuation of 1:16-45. In both sections, Jesus is presented as the bringer of the kingdom. In the two sections, the two possible responses to Jesus and the kingdom are portrayed: enthusiastic acceptance of Jesus and the new way or the attempt to destroy Jesus and maintain the old way. In terms of the gospel story, Mark has shown in 1:16-3:6 what happened in response to Jesus and his message; in terms of Mark's audience, Mark is calling upon his hearers to side with the disciples/crowd or to side with the opponents, to choose for or against the kingdom.[23]

Nor does the information to the reader in 3:6--that the
opponents want to destroy Jesus--seem to come too early in
Mark's plan. Mark is an "omniscient narrator."[24] He reveals
to his readers at the beginning what the internal audience of
his story only learns much later on. For example, the reader
is told in 1:1,11 that Jesus is the Christ, the Son of God; the
disciples only learn this in the middle of the narrative (8:29;
9:7); and the opponents are only told near the end (14:62).[25]
Mark 3:6 would seem to be part of the same technique of alerting
the reader to facts that are only worked out much later in the
plot. By means of 3:6, the reader knows that the Jewish leaders
want to destroy Jesus, that Jesus stands under the threat of
death. The point is made that the bringing of the kingdom aroused
the hostility of the Jewish leaders from the start.[26]

Theological emphases of Mark 2:1-3:6

In Chapter Four, it was argued that awareness (conscious
or unconscious) of the symmetrical pattern in 2:1-3:6 helps the
reader to realize the role of healing and eating as important
elements of Jesus' ministry which served to arouse the implacable
hostility of the Jewish authorities, and the theme of life vs.
death. If the symmetrical structure is to be attributed to Mark,
then one would expect these same ideas or themes to be markan
interests and to recur elsewhere in the gospel of Mark. This
would seem to be the case.

Opposition to Jesus and the role of healing and eating.
As described in Chapter Four, healing and eating both play a
prominent role in Mark's presentation of Jesus' proclamation and
bringing of the kingdom in 1:14-8:26. Both are an important
part of Mark's picture of the life of the kingdom as it is lived
in this world.[27] In 3:6, Jesus' healing (and eating) behavior
are given as the cause of the Pharisees' and Herodians' desire
to destroy Jesus. Neither healing nor eating, however, is presented as the cause of Jesus' death in Mark, as the healing of
Lazarus is in John. As is brought out in 12:1-40,[28] Mark shows
Jesus innocent of all charges except that of being (or claiming
to be) the Messiah.[29]

Is, then, the fact that healing (and eating) are used in 2:1-3:6 to demonstrate the opposition to Jesus an argument against the markan provenance of 2:1-3:6? It would seem not. In the first place, in 3:1-6, when the opponents are seeking legal grounds to accuse Jesus, Jesus does not act illegally.[30] The Pharisees have no legal way to accuse him, so they go away to plot against him. Thus, the picture in 2:1-3:6 is similar to that in Mark 11-12. In 2:1-3:6, the opponents object to Jesus' healing and eating behavior which arises out of his messianic status as bringer of the kingdom but find no legal grounds for charging him. In 11:12-12:40, the opponents object to Jesus' prophetic/messianic acts and words in the temple and the parable of the wicked tenants but are unable to find legal grounds for charging him.

Second, both healing (3:22-30) and eating (7:1-23) are the subject of controversies with the Jewish authorities later in the gospel. Healing and eating continue to be foci of conflict.

Third, the confrontation of 2:1-3:6 is recalled in the later confrontations with the authorities. When the representatives of the Sanhedrin fail to arrest Jesus in 12:12, they promptly send the Pharisees and Herodians to try to trap Jesus (12:13), recalling 3:6 to the reader's mind. Furthermore, the Sanhedrin trial recalls the healing of the paralytic in 2:1-12 with its charge of blasphemy (2:7; 14:64). The first and last confrontations of Jesus with the Jewish authorities concern the issue of blasphemy. They also contain the first and last references in the gospel to the Son of Man, and the only ones preceded by a verb addressed to the internal audience of the pericope (εἰδῆτε, ὄψεσθε 2:10; 14:62). Further, the scene before Pilate recalls 3:1-6. The words συμβούλιον and κατηγορέω are repeated (3:2,6; 15:1,3,4).[31] In 3:4, Jesus asks if it is legal to do evil (κακοποιῆσαι). In 15:14, after having heard the charge that Jesus is king of the Jews, Pilate asks the crowd what evil Jesus has done (Τί γὰρ ἐποίησεν κακόν;).[32] In both 3:1-6 and 15:1-15, Jesus appears innocent of any legal charge. Thus in the first healing controversy (2:1-12) and the Sanhedrin trial, Jesus affirms his divine authority or status. In the second healing controversy (3:1-6) and the trial before Pilate, Jesus is portrayed as legally innocent. The two healing controversies in 2:1-3:6 point ahead to the two trials in the passion narrative.

Thus, the healing controversy motif in 2:1-3:6 does not seem out of place in Mark's gospel. The Jewish authorities are shown objecting to Jesus' behavior, whether in healing, eating or temple cleansing, but are unable to find legal grounds against him. Even Pilate, having heard the title, King of the Jews, finds no grounds against him. In Mark, the Jewish authorities arrange to have Jesus put to death because of their refusal to accept his messianic status. In 2:1-3:6, the theme of unjustified opposition to Jesus is introduced, a theme which culminates with Jesus' death on the cross.

The theme of life vs. death. As argued earlier, the concentric structure of 2:1-3:6 places emphasis upon the theme of life vs. death.[33] Jesus' actions to "make alive" result in the opponents' plot to destroy him (3:6). The middle pericope of the structure, 2:18-22, suggests that the new community called by Jesus will continue to exist after Jesus' death, while the new wine brought by Jesus will destroy the old wine skins of Judaism.

The theme of life vs. death recurs in a variety of forms at crucial points in Mark's gospel. In the three passion predictions, the theme of life and death is stated for Jesus. Jesus' announcement of his coming death is coupled with the announcement of his resurrection (8:31; 9:31; 10:33-34). In 8:34-9:1, the paradoxical relationship of life and death is stated in relation to discipleship. Mark 8:34-9:1 is the only general or public invitation to discipleship in Mark's gospel and thus serves as an invitation not only for the internal audience of the narrative but also for Mark's readers. First, the reader is told that if he wishes to follow Jesus, he must deny himself and take up his cross, that is, accept the possibility of death (8:34). Then the paradox is stated:

> For whoever wants to save his life will lose it; but whoever loses his life for my sake and for the sake of the gospel will save it. For what does it profit a person, to gain the whole world and forfeit his life? For what can a person give in exchange for his life? (8:35-37)

As in the case of the Jewish authorities, the disciple's life or death is related to his reception of Jesus. Giving up of life

is for the sake of Jesus and the gospel (8:35). Mark 8:38 makes
it clear that one's ultimate fate depends upon one's present attitudes toward Jesus.[34]

Furthermore, the theme of life vs. death is developed in
11:12-12:40 in much the same way it occurs in 2:1-3:6. The intertwined fates of Jesus and the Jewish authorities/nation implicit
in 2:1-3:6 is made explicit in the Jerusalem ministry.[35] The
Jewish authorities' rejection of Jesus brings about not only
Jesus' death but their own destruction and the destruction of
the Jewish nation (11:20; 12:1-9; 13:1-2). In the psalm citation about the rejected stone becoming the head of the corner
(12:10-11) and in the statement of the reality of the resurrection (12:26-27), there is assurance of continued or new life
for Jesus and others as well.

Thus, the theme of life vs. death which is brought out by
the symmetrical pattern of 2:1-3:6 would not seem foreign to
the gospel of Mark.[36] Rather, as in the case of the role of
Jesus' healing and eating behavior giving rise to the Jewish
authorities' seeking to destroy Jesus, so also the theme of
life vs. death in 2:1-3:6 serves as an introduction for the
reader to a motif that recurs throughout the gospel. The gospel of Mark might be likened to a musical composition in which
motifs introduced early in the composition are brought forward
and developed later in the piece. The fact that the structure
of 2:1-3:6 emphasizes themes which again become prominent in the
gospel suggests that there is no need to hypothesize interpolation of a source to explain the presence of 2:1-3:6 in the gospel.
This fact would even seem to be an argument for Mark's construction of 2:1-3:6 from traditions available to him.

Summary

The tight rhetorical structure of 2:1-3:6 suggests that
Mark took over 2:1-3:6 from a source virtually as it now stands,
or Mark created the present structure himself. The three separate arguments, the interconnections of Mark 2:1-3:6 with 1:16-
45, the literary techniques of 2:1-3:6, and the theological
emphases of 2:1-3:6, all individually point towards the markan
construction of 2:1-3:6. Taken together, they would seem to
demonstrate that the rhetorical structure of Mark 2:1-3:6 is due
to Mark, not to a premarkan source.

Excursus: Did Mark Use a Shorter Controversy Collection in
             Constructing 2:1-3:6?

The redactional question raised in this study has been answered: the construction of the Galilean controversy section
is due to Mark's editorial activity and not to his interpolation
of a source.   The issue remains open, however, whether Mark employed Kuhn's proposed collection or whether he constructed the
section from traditions, most of which had previously been independent.   The issue of the existence of Kuhn's collection is
primarily one of the history of the Christian tradition and outside the scope of this study.   However, the argument for Kuhn's
collection would be strengthened if it can be shown that 2:1-3:6
is more easily explained upon the basis of Mark's use of such a
source than on the basis of his use of independent traditions.
Two questions appear relevant: first, are the uses of Son of
Man in 2:10 and 28 more easily accounted for on the hypothesis
of Mark's use of Kuhn's collection, and second, is the rhetorical complexity of 2:1-3:6 more easily explained as Mark's development of an earlier collection?

   Son of Man.   As argued in Chapter Four, the uses of Son of
Man in 2:1-3:6 function primarily to prepare the way for the
later uses of the title in Mark's gospel for the suffering, death
and resurrection of Jesus.   The identification of the title with
the earthly Jesus needs to be made before 8:31, if that verse is
to be comprehensible to the reader.   Further, it was argued that
in 2:1-3:6 Mark is not attempting to convince his audience of
any particular christology but rather shares the christological
assumptions of his audience.

   Both arguments suggest that the sayings about the Son of
Man's authority over sin and the sabbath were traditional sayings, not creations of Mark.   If the use of a title is preparing
the reader for a later and polemical use of the title, the first
use should be one with which the reader is more or less familiar,
and which he accepts.   Kuhn's hypothesis of a premarkan collection in 2:1-28 (extolling the authority of the Son of Man) provides a convenient explanation for the provenance of the sayings
and the fact that they occur so close together in the gospel.

   However, Kuhn's collection is not a necessary explanation
for the double occurrence of the title in the sense of earthly

authority in 2:1-3:6. Morna Hooker notes that the issue which
links all the different types of Son of Man sayings in Mark is
that of Jesus' authority: the term "can appropriately be used
when the authority of Jesus is claimed or accepted, and this is
why it is used in conversation with those who follow or challenge
him."[37] Perrin suggests that Mark balances the two uses of Son
of Man in 2:10 and 28 with the two uses of Son of God in 3:11
and 5:7.[38] The use of the title in 2:10,28 can be explained
either on the basis of Mark's use of the collection Kuhn posits
or on the basis of Mark's own compilation of tradition.

Rhetorical complexity. Mark 2:1-3:6 has a rhetorical richness and elegance which is greater than that in the other rhetorical structures surveyed in Mark. There is the linear development of the theme of opposition to Jesus, the pattern of
sin-fasting-sabbath, the concentric pattern of healing-eating-
healing and the chiastic relationship of 2:13-17 and 23-28.

It is perhaps easier to explain the rhetorical complexity
of 2:1-3:6 on the basis of Mark's use of a source consisting of
2:3-12 (in the order miracle, controversy, Son of Man saying),
15-17a(b?), 18-20, (21-22?), 23-24, 27-28. If Mark was employing Kuhn's proposed source, then he already had the pattern of
sin-eating-fasting-sabbath and the motif of opposition to build
upon. The issue of sin in regard to forgiveness in 2:1-12 and
in regard to associating with tax collectors in 2:15-17 already
present in the collection might suggest the doubling of the sabbath issue by the addition of 3:1-6. The addition of 3:1-6 could
be markan since it serves the markan interests of showing Jesus
innocent on legal grounds and of developing the life/death theme
of 2:1-3:6. The eating-fasting pattern of 2:15-20 may have suggested to Mark the addition of the example of David eating the
showbread in 2:25-26 to the first sabbath controversy, creating
the concentric pattern of healing-eating-healing in 2:1-3:6.
It is perhaps easier to conceive of Mark developing the rhetorical richness of 2:1-3:6 from a source such as Kuhn posits, which
provides a basis for elaboration, than to conceive of Mark
developing it from independent traditions.[39]

The Role of 2:1-3:6 in Mark's Gospel: Conclusion

The meaning of 2:1-3:6 and its role in the gospel of Mark
has been discussed in Chapter Four in terms of the significance
of the rhetorical structure for understanding the text of 2:1-
3:6 and in this chapter in the course of the argument for the
markan provenance of the present rhetorical structure of 2:1-3:6.
It may be summarized as follows: the linear development of 2:1-
3:6 portrays Jesus' triumph over his opponents on the issues of
sin, fasting, and sabbath; it stresses, moreover, the implacable
and unjustifiable hostility of the Jewish leaders to Jesus'
authoritative words and deeds in the bringing of the kingdom.
The concentric pattern emphasizes the role of healing and eating
as integral aspects of Jesus' ministry which caused his rejection
by the opponents. It emphasizes the theme of life vs. death for
Jesus and for his opponents. The structure of the text also
helps to elucidate the function of 2:25-26, David eating the
showbread, as a justification for Jesus' improper eating behavior. It clarifies the role of the disciples as one derived from
and dependent upon the person and mission of Jesus. The rhetorical analysis helps to elucidate the role of the Son of Man sayings in 2:10 and 28 as an argument for the authority of Jesus in
his earthly ministry and as a preparation for the later uses of
the title for the suffering, death and resurrection of Jesus.

In terms of the gospel as a whole, 2:1-3:6 is first of all
a continuation and completion of the theme introduced in 1:14-15:
Jesus' ministry of word and deed manifesting the coming of the
kingdom aroused two antithetical responses among the Jews. Mark
1:16-3:6 serves the function of explaining to Mark's readers his
understanding of the meaning of and the responses to Jesus' ministry of the inbreaking of the kingdom. It serves as a call to
Mark's audience to choose Jesus and the new life of the kingdom
or to choose the old way of the Jewish leaders.

Mark 2:1-3:6 also functions as an introduction to themes
and motifs developed later in the gospel. It lays the ground-
work for the later use of the Son of Man title. Along with 1:16-
20, it presents the basis of the discipleship role as one of
enthusiastic response to Jesus and his message and of dependence
upon him. It introduces the theme of the Jewish leaders' rejection of Jesus, its basis in their refusal to accept his messianic

claim (blasphemy), and the lack of legitimate legal grounds for their rejection. It also introduces the motif of life vs. death which continues to play an important role in the gospel.

Most, although not all, of these conclusions are not new. As noted in the course of this study, most of the conclusions have been advocated by scholars using methodological approaches other than that of rhetorical criticism. The rhetorical analysis of 2:1-3:6 has not led to a radically different understanding of 2:1-3:6. This is to be expected. Mark 2:1-3:6 was selected for analysis in part because it is a section of the gospel of Mark whose meaning appears relatively self-evident, which is not a focus of scholarly debate. The rhetorical approach would seem vindicated as a methodology for studying the text. It serves to confirm the conclusions reached by other methodological approaches.

The rhetorical approach, moreover, not only confirms conclusions reached on other grounds. It helps to discriminate between alternative explanations of the texts; it serves as a control for exegesis. For example, the rhetorical analysis shows that the Son of Man saying in 2:10 (and the one in 2:28) should not be interpreted as an aside by Mark to his Christian readers but as part of Jesus' claim to have earthly authority and as part of the explanation for the Jewish' leaders hostility to Jesus.[40] The understanding of the discipleship role as the positive response to Jesus is important for the proper interpretation of the later developments of that role--the disciples' misunderstanding and failure. Further, 2:1-3:6 is not simply an explication of the reasons for and the inevitability of Jesus' death; it is also an introduction of the motif of life vs. death, and the first indication of Jesus' ultimate triumph over his opponents.

What is new, however, as a result of the rhetorical analysis, is the recognition of the ability of Mark as a writer/compiler, the recognition of the extent to which Mark has interwoven the elements of his narrative into a coherent whole. He has not merely concatenated the individual traditions like beads on a string. The interconnection of the narrative is seen within 2:1-3:6. Mark 2:1-12 introduces the themes of Jesus' relation to sin, his authority as Son of Man, the paradoxical relation of

life and death, and the opposition which Jesus' actions and words
aroused. These themes are developed in 2:13-28 and climax in 3:
1-6. The concentric and chiastic pattern of 2:1-3:6 further
interrelates the material. The same interweaving of content may
be recognized in the rhetorical role of 2:1-3:6 in the gospel as
a whole. Mark 2:1-3:6 is closely connected to 1:(14)16-45 by
means of the rhetorical device of retrospection and by means of
the content motifs of the earthly authority of Jesus and the
antithetical reactions to his words and deeds. Mark 2:1-3:6 is
also related to the later development of the gospel by means of
rhetorical anticipation and by the introduction of the themes
of the opposition to Jesus and life vs. death.

The recognition of the extensive interweaving of material
in the gospel of Mark has important implications for the biblical
critic employing the text of Mark as his data for analysis. For
the *redaction* critic seeking to understand the theology and *Sitz
im Leben* of Mark or the exegete interpreting a passage in Mark's
gospel, it means that he/she must take into consideration not
only the immediate text under analysis but also its place and
function in the larger rhetorical structure in which it is embedded. For instance, the critic studying Mark's understanding
of the Son of Man must analyze not only the specific Son of Man
sayings in 2:10a and 28 along with the other Son of Man sayings
in the gospel. He must also study the rhetorical function of
2:10 in 2:1-12 and of 2:28 in 2:23-28. He must consider their
role in 2:1-3:6 and their relationship to what precedes and follows them in the markan narrative. The exegete interested in
Mark's understanding of the Son of David may not limit his study
to 10:46-52, 11:9-10 and 12:35-37, the specific references to
the Son of David. He must also seek to understand how each Son
of David reference functions in the larger context of which it
forms a part.

Furthermore, the critic interested in the *form* criticism
and tradition history of the text must take into consideration
not only the particular text which he is investigating. He must
also consider its place in its larger rhetorical context. The
details of a pericope are determined by the tradition history
of the individual pericope *and* by its redactional adaptation to
fit a larger narrative context. For example, 2:17b, "I came not

to call the righteous but sinners," may have been added to balance the pattern of a general proverb followed by a christological saying in 2:27-28 *and* to call to the reader's mind the previous "I" saying about Jesus' mission in 1:38, rather than to
complete its own pericope, 2:(13)15-17. Such extensions compli-
cate the form critic's enterprise. Yet he may welcome the com-
plication of his task, for rhetorical criticism provides him with
another avenue, another means of determining the tradition history of early Christianity and the life of Jesus. It adds to
his tools for interpreting the limited data at his disposal.

But perhaps the main value of rhetorical criticism is not
to be found in the assistance it provides to the exegete, redaction critic and form critic in their respective tasks. Perhaps
its greatest value is in providing Mark's reader--then and now--
with a greater feeling for and appreciation of Mark's gospel and
its message. There are many questions the rhetorical approach
cannot answer. The disciplines of source, form, and redaction
criticism will always be needed. However, the literary/rhetori-
cal approach can provide the reader with an insight into Mark's
gospel, how he intended it to be read and understood, which none
of the more historical approaches can. It is a valuable addition
to the tools of the biblical critic and a valuable approach for
the lay reader attempting to grasp Mark's message.

NOTES

CHAPTER I

[1]See below, pp. 19-24.

[2]George P. Ridout, "Prose Compositional Techniques in the Succession Narrative (2 Sam. 7:9-20; 1 Kings 1-2)," (Ph.D. dissertation, Graduate Theological Union, Berkeley, 1971), pp. a-b.

[3]Edwin M. Good, *Irony in the Old Testament* (Philadelphia: Westminster, 1965), p. 58.

[4]So Norman Perrin, "The Christology of Mark: A Study in Methodology," *JR* 51 (1971) 174; and Robert H. Stein, "The Proper Methodology for Ascertaining a Markan Redaction History," *NovT* 13 (1971) 184, 193-194.

[5]So, for example, John R. Donahue writes, "The second way in which redaction criticism has done does not stress the distinction between tradition and redaction, but concentrates on modes of composition, literary devices, and the discovery of patterns and structures, all of which serve as an index to Mark's thought." (*Are you the Christ? The Trial Narrative in the Gospel of Mark* [SBLDS 10; Missoula, Montana: Society of Biblical Literature, for the Seminar on Mark, 1973], p. 41).

[6]The attempt to determine the genre of Mark or the gospels is another approach to the same issue of in what light, under what rubrics, is the text to be read.

[7]With the aid of a computer, it would be possible to establish guides based on statistical probability as to how many stylistic characteristics are "sufficient" to indicate markan activity. The work would be similar to Lloyd Gaston's probability word study of individual vocabulary words (*Horae Synopticae Electronicae: Word Statistics of the Synoptic Gospels* [SBLSBS 3; Missoula, Montana: Society of Biblical Literature, 1973]). At the moment, however, such decisions are quite arbitrary and subjective.

[8]For the methodology of redaction criticism, see Perrin, *What is Redaction Criticism?* (London: SPCK, 1970); Stein, "What is Redaktion-geschichte?" *JBL* 88 (1969) 45-56; Stein, "Methodology," 181-198.

[9]For instance, after arguing on other grounds that Mk 11: 10a is redactional, Werner H. Kelber writes that, "The sheer foreignness of the Davidic acclamation is to catch the attention of the reader, and to question its validity" (*The Kingdom in Mark: A New Place and a New Time* [Philadelphia: Fortress, 1974], pp. 94, 96).

[10]See the helpful article by Roland Mushat Frye, "A
Literary Perspective for the Criticism of the Gospels," *Jesus
and Man's Hope* (eds. Donald G. Miller and Dikran Y. Hadidian;
Pittsburgh: Pittsburgh Theological Seminary, 1971), Vol. 2,
pp. 193-221, esp. p. 220, fn. 41.

[11]For Muilenburg's practice of literary criticism, see,
for example, "The Literary Character of Isaiah 34," *JBL* 59 (1940)
339-365; "Introduction and Exegesis to Isaiah, Chapters 40-66,"
IB, Vol. 5, pp. 381-773; "The Form and Structure of the Covenantal
Formulations," *VT* 9 (1959) 347-365. For the work of some of his
students, see Ridout, "Prose Techniques" and Jared J. Jackson
and Martin Kessler, eds., *Rhetorical Criticism: Essays in Honor
of James Muilenburg* (Pittsburgh Theological Monograph Series
No. 1; Pittsburgh: Pickwick, 1974).

[12]See these authors' works cited below and in the bibliography.

[13]*JBL* 88 (1969) 1-18.

[14]*Ibid.*, p. 8.

[15]*Ibid.*, pp. 8-9.

[16]*Ibid.*, p. 10.

[17]*Ibid.*, p. 7.

[18]*Ibid.*, p. 18.

[19]*La structure littéraire de l'Épître aux Hébreux* (Stud-
Neot 1; Desclée de Brouwer, 1963) and his accompanying *A Struc-
tured Translation of the Epistle to the Hebrews* (trans. James
Swetnam; Rome: Pontifical Biblical Institute, 1964). A good
brief description of the method may be found in Addison G. Wright,
"The Riddle of the Sphinx: The Structure of the Book of
Qoheleth," *CBQ* 30 (1968) 318-319.

[20]*Structure littéraire*, pp. 37-59.

[21]*Ibid.*, p. 259.

[22]"A Different Approach to the Writing of Commentaries on
the Synoptic Gospels," *A Stubborn Faith: Papers on Old Testament
and Related Subjects Presented to Honor William Andrew Irwin*
(ed. Edward C. Hobbs; Dallas: Southern Methodist University,
1956), p. 161.

[23]"The Introduction to Mark's Gospel," *NTS* 12 (1965-66)
369.

[24]"The Christology of Mark," p. 176.

[25]"The Interpretation of the Gospel of Mark," *Int* 30 (1976)
115-124.

[26]*The Synoptic Gospels* (London: Oxford University, 1960).

[27] *A Study in St Mark* (London: Dacre, 1951).

[28] *Naherwartungen: Tradition und Redaktion in Mk 13* (Düsseldorf: Patmos, 1968). For a summary of others' divisions, see pp. 50-53; for his own structure, see pp. 54-70.

[29] "Towards an Interpretation of the Gospel of Mark," *Christology and a Modern Pilgrimage* (ed. Hans Dieter Betz; Claremont, California: New Testament Colloquium, 1971), pp. 1-78; *The New Testament: An Introduction* (New York: Harcourt Brace Jovanovich, 1974), pp. 146-147.

[30] "De compositione evangelii Marci," *VD* 44 (1966) 138-141.

[31] *The Good News According to Mark* (trans. Donald H. Madvig; Richmond, Virginia: John Knox, 1970), Table of Contents and passim.

[32] *The Formation of the Gospel According to Mark* (trans. Pamela Gaughan; Philadelphia: Westminster, 1975). For a summary of others' major divisions, see pp. 74-80; for his own structure, see pp. 80-86.

[33] Perrin, "Towards an Interpretation," pp. 7-13; *The New Testament*, pp. 155-158; La Potterie, "De compositione," pp. 139-140; Stein, "Methodology," pp. 192-193.

[34] Jan Lambrecht, "La structure de Mc., XIII," *De Jésus aux Évangiles* (ed. I. de La Potterie; BETL 25:2; Gembloux: J. Duculot, 1967), pp. 141-164; Pesch, *Naherwartungen*, pp. 74-82; Anitra B. Kolenkow, "Beyond Miracles, Suffering and Eschatology," *1973 Seminar Papers* (ed. George MacRae; SBLASP 109; Missoula, Montana: Society of Biblical Literature, 1973), Vol. 2, pp. 175-176.

[35] Trans. C.H. Giblin; Collegeville, Minnesota: The Liturgical Press, 1967; first published in *NRT*, 1967.

[36] *Ibid.*, p. 5.

[37] See above, p. 11.

[38] *Structure and Theology*, p. 10. William L. Lane (*Commentary on the Gospel of Mark* [NICNT; Grand Rapids, Michigan: Eerdmans, 1974], pp. 27-28) also stresses Mark's use of contrast as a means of sharpening the issues and forcing the reader to choose sides.

[39] *Structure and Theology*, pp. 14-15.

[40] *Der Rahmen der Geschichte Jesus* (Berlin: Trowitzsch & Sohn, 1919), p. 82.

[41] Martin Albertz, *Die synoptischen Streitgespräche* (Berlin: Trowitzsch & Sohn, 1921), p. 5.

[42] Public debate, however, does occur elsewhere in Mark, in Mk 3:22-30; 7:1-13; and 10:2-9.

[43]Henry Barclay Swete, *The Gospel according to St Mark*, 3rd ed. (London: Macmillan, 1913); Marie-Joseph Lagrange, *Évangile selon Saint Marc*, 5th ed. (Paris: Lecoffre, 1929); John C. Hawkins, *Horae Synopticae: Contributions to the Study of the Synoptic Problem*, 2d ed. (Oxford: Clarendon, 1909).

[44]"Marcan Usage," *JTS* 26 (1925) 145-156.

[45](Rome: Pontifical Biblical Institute, 1937), pp. 130-132.

[46]*Ibid.*, pp. 125-126.

[47]*Duality in Mark: Contributions to the Study of the Markan Redaction* (Louvain: Leuven University, 1972), pp. 75-136.

[48]*Rahmen*, pp. 33-34, passim. Vincent Taylor agrees that lack of picturesqueness is a sign of markan composition (*The Gospel According to St. Mark*, 2nd ed. [London: Macmillan, 1966], pp. 82-83). Martin Dibelius ("The Structure and Literary Character of the Gospels," *HTR* 20 [1927] 158-160) also calls attention to a "novella" style and a less vivid "edification" style.

[49]*The Gospel According to Mark* (trans. Kevin Condon; RNT; Staten Island: The Society of St. Paul, 1968), p. 12.

[50]*Mark*, pp. 44-66.

[51]*Der Weg Jesu* (Berlin: Alfred Töpelmann, 1966), pp. 29-37. See also Nigel Turner, *Style* (Vol. 4 of James Hope Moulton, *A Grammar of New Testament Greek* [Edinburgh: T. & T. Clark, 1976], pp. 11-30.

[52]*Duality*, pp. 71-72.

[53]"Zur Erzählerkunst des Markus," *ZNW* 27 (1928) 193-198.

[54]Cf. Benjamin Wisner Bacon (*The Beginnings of the Gospel Story* [New Haven: Yale University, 1909], p. 42) who sees the point of the intertwining as the contrast between the minor crime of the family and the major crime of the scribes.

[55]*Introduction to the New Testament*, 14th rev. ed. (trans. A.J. Mattill, Jr.; Nashville & New York: Abingdon, 1966), p. 64.

[56]"Methodology," pp. 193-194.

[57]*Mysterious Revelation* (Ithaca: Cornell University, 1963), p. 121, fn. 10.

[58]*The Christ*, p. 42.

[59]*Ibid.*, pp. 58-63. He excludes Mk 5:21-43 which he believes Mark may have found in the tradition, but includes the other six listed on p. 21.

[60]*Ibid.*, p. 62.

[61]Howard Clark Kee in his recent work (*Community of the New Age: Studies in Mark's Gospel* [Philadelphia: Westminster, 1977], pp. 54-56) includes 2:1-12; 3:1-6 and 15:6-32 along with the intercalations as examples of Mark's interpolation technique. He views interpolation technique as serving different functions-- Mark's literary, practical or dogmatic aims.

[62]"Methodology," p. 184.

[63]*The Christ*, p. 241.

[64]*Ibid.*, p. 81.

[65]*Ibid.*, p. 84.

[66]*Ibid.*, p. 241.

[67]See above, fn. 33.

[68]René Lafontaine and Pierre Mourlon Beernaert, "Essai sur la structure de Marc, 8, 27-9, 13," *RSR* 57 (1969) 543-561.

[69]*Rahmen*, p. 317.

[70]Cf. G.D. Kilpatrick who argues convincingly that πάλιν is an adverb, not a connecting particle ("Some Notes on Marcan Usage," *The Bible Translator* 7 [1956] 4).

[71]*History of the Synoptic Tradition* (trans. John Marsh; Oxford: Basil Blackwell, 1963), pp. 339-341.

[72]Abo: Abo Akademi.

[73]*Ibid.*, pp. 3-6.

[74]See below, p. 144.

[75]Schmidt, *Rahmen*, p. 209; Bultmann, *History*, p. 332; Taylor, *Mark*, pp. 112-113.

[76]On the passion narrative, see Donahue, *The Christ*, and Werner H. Kelber, ed., *The Passion in Mark* (Philadelphia: Fortress, 1976).

[77]See above, p. 11.

[78]*Streitgespräche*.

[79]*From Tradition to Gospel* (trans. Bertram Lee Wolf; The Scribner Library; New York: Charles Scribner's Sons, n.d.), pp. 37-69.

[80]*History*, pp. 11-69.

[81]2nd ed. (London: Macmillan, 1964), pp. 63-87.

[82]Union Theological Seminary, New York, 1971. See also the useful discussion of a tripartite form by David Daube (*The New Testament and Rabbinic Judaism* [London: Athlone, 1956], pp. 170-175).

[83]Dibelius to his "paradigm" form.

[84]An extensive discussion of the views of the various form critics may be found in Hultgren, "Adversaries," pp. 1-71.

[85]*Ibid.*, p. 7.

[86]*Ibid.*

[87]*Ibid.*, pp. 61-64.

[88]*Ibid.*, pp. 64-66. Hultgren acknowledges Mt 22:41-46, Lk 14:1-6, and Mk 3:1-5 to be exceptions.

[89]*Ibid.*, pp. 67-70.

[90]*Ibid.*, p. 70.

[91]*Ibid.*

[92]Hultgren's statement is quite general: "These opponents question Jesus' conduct, or that of his disciples, seek to entrap him or test him, or gather against him" (*Ibid.*, p. 69).

[93]Dibelius denies that dispute is characteristic of his paradigm form (or indeed of any form). Even the element of dialogue is quite secondary (*Tradition*, pp. 68-69). Taylor views the debate leading up to Jesus' saying as part of the pronouncement story, but makes no distinction between debates which are hostile and those which are not (*Formation*, p. 63). Albertz, in spite of naming his form *Streitgespräche*, includes all synoptic stories in which Jesus is questioned by other than disciples, whether or not there is any hint of controversy—e.g., Mk 10:17-27; 12:28-34 (*Streitgespräche*, pp. 25-26, 52-54).

[94]*History*, p. 39.

[95]*Ibid.*, pp. 45, 54.

[96]"Adversaries," p. 55.

[97]*Streitgespräche*, p. 86.

[98]*Ibid.*, pp. 87-91.

[99]*Ibid.*, pp. 6, 19, 91-96.

[100]Dibelius, *Tradition*, p. 56; Bultmann, *History*, p. 62; Taylor, *Formation*, p. 63; Albertz, *Streitgespräche*, p. 6.

[101]*Streitgespräche*, pp. 93-94.

[102]C.H. Dodd, "The Dialogue Form in the Gospels," *BJRL* 37 (1954-55) 54-60.

103Mk 10:2-9, 17-27, 35-45; 11:27-33, 12:13-17; Lk 7:36-50, 10:25-37.

104*History*, pp. 12-21, 26-27. Bultmann's fourth category, "The Master is questioned (by disciples or others)," contains the school debates (*Ibid.*, pp. 21-26).

105The markan Beelzebul controversy, 3:22-30, appears to be a truncated version of the one in Q, omitting the healing altogether.

106Lk 14:1-6, a sabbath healing, contains sayings material both before and after the healing.

107The question whether one or the other healing controversy type is a later or secondary development in the Christian tradition or even due to markan redaction is outside the scope of this discussion.

108See Charles H. Lohr, "Oral Techniques in the Gospel of Matthew," *CBQ* 23 (1961) 403-435.

109*Ibid.*, pp. 424-426.

110Cf. Charles H. Talbert (*Literary Patterns, Theological Themes and the Genre of Luke-Acts* [SBLMS 20; Missoula, Montana: Scholars, 1974], p. 67) who asserts that the principle of balance or duality, his terms which include extended symmetries, "has its roots in a discernible *Zeitgeist* or cultural trait" of the Greek (and Latin) as well as Semitic milieu.

111Talbert argues that authors probably worked from a preliminary sketch (*Ibid.*, p. 79).

112*Ibid.*, p. 81. See Talbert's entire discussion (*Ibid.*, pp. 67-82).

113The basic work on classical rhetoric is Heinrich Lausberg, *Handbuch der literarischen Rhetorik*, 2 vols. (Munich: Max Hueber, 1960). For a useful brief guide to rhetorical terminology, see Richard A. Lanham, *A Handlist of Rhetorical Terms* (Berkeley: University of California, 1969).

114Lohr, "Oral Techniques," pp. 408-410.

115See Lausberg, *Handbuch*, Sects. 619, 625, 629-632.

116Inclusio (epanalepsis) is, of course, a particular type of hook word use, use at the beginning and end of some unit. It is treated separately since it indicates the limits of a rhetorical unit. The precise structural implications of other hook word types are not contained in their very definition.

117The term "hook word" is borrowed from Vanhoye, *Structure littéraire*, p. 37, (*mot-crochet*).

118See Lohr, "Oral Techniques," pp. 422-424.

[119]On these devices, see *ibid.*, pp. 411-412, 414.

[120]Ridout, "Prose Techniques," pp. 107-119.

[121]Semitic scholars generally use the term "inclusio," while classical scholars employ the term "ring composition" for the technique called inclusio in this study.

[122]Strictly speaking, an arrangement of four narrative units is an extended chiasm.

[123]Chiasm and ring composition are standard terms in classical scholarship, although neither was employed by the ancient rhetoricians. See Lausberg, *Handbuch*, Sects. 723, fn. 1, 800-803. Extended concentric structures, under varying nomenclature, have been described in many literatures.

[124]See above, pp. 21-23.

[125]Discussions of the technique and many additional references may be found in Lohr, "Oral Techniques," pp. 424-427; Talbert, "Artistry and Theology: An Analysis of the Architecture of Jn 1,19-5,47," *CBQ* 32 (1970) 341-342, 356-357, 360-365; Talbert, *Literary Patterns*, esp. pp. 67-88; Vanhoye, *Structure littéraire*, pp. 60-63.

[126]J.T. Sheppard, *The Pattern of the Iliad* (London: Methuen, 1922), passim; John L. Myres, "The Last Book of the 'Iliad,'" *JHS* 52 (1932) 274-288; Myres, "The Pattern of the Odyssey," *JHS* 72 (1952) 1-19; Cedric H. Whitman, *Homer and the Heroic Tradition* (Cambridge: Harvard University, 1963), esp. pp. 97-98, 249-284.

[127]Myres, *Herodotus: Father of History* (Oxford: Clarendon, 1953), esp. pp. 81-134; Ingrid Beck, *Die Ringkomposition bei Herodot und ihre Bedeutung für die Beweistechnik* (New York: Georg Olms, 1971), esp. pp. 34-36, 82-84.

[128]George E. Duckworth, *Structural Patterns and Proportions in Vergil's Aeneid* (Ann Arbor: University of Michigan, 1962), esp. pp. 21-24.

[129]Yehuda T. Radday, "Chiasm in Samuel," *Linguistica Biblica* 9/10 (1971) 21-31; "Chiasm in Tora," *Linguistica Biblica* 19 (1972) 12-23; "Chiasm in Joshua, Judges and Others," *Linguistica Biblica* 27/28 (1973) 6-13; "Chiasm in Kings," *Linguistica Biblica* 31 (1974) 52-67; Angelico Di Marco, "Der Chiasmus in der Bibel: 1. Teil," *Linguistica Biblica* 36 (1975) 21-97; "Der Chiasmus in der Bibel: 2. Teil," *Linguistica Biblica* 37 (1976) 49-68.

[130]Luis Alonso-Schökel, "Poésie Hébraïque," (*DBSup* 8; Paris: Letouzey Ané, 1972), esp. cols. 85-90; *Estudios de Poética Hebrea* (Barcelona: Juan Flors, 1963), esp. pp. 323-335.

[131]Phyllis Trible, "Depatriarchalizing in Biblical Interpretation," *JAAR* 41 (1973) 35-37, 42 fn. 53.

[132]Norbert Lohfink, *Das Hauptgebot: Eine Untersuchung literarischer Einleitungsfragen zu Dtn 5-11* (AnBi 20; Rome: Pontifical Biblical Institute, 1963), pp. 181-183, 194-195.

[133]Ridout, "Prose Techniques," pp. 47-74.

[134]Jack R. Lundbom, *Jeremiah: A Study in Ancient Hebrew Rhetoric* (SBLDS 18; Missoula, Montana: Scholars, 1975), pp. 61-112.

[135]Ivan Jay Ball, Jr., "A Rhetorical Study of Zephaniah," (Th.D. dissertation, Graduate Theological Union, Berkeley, 1972), passim.

[136]Paul Lamarche, *Zacharie IX-XIV. Structure littéraire et messianisme* (Paris: Lecoffre, 1961), esp. pp. 105-115.

[137]Rudolf Pesch, "Zur konzentrischen Struktur von Jona 1," *Bib* 47 (1966) 577-581.

[138]Stephen Bertman, "Symmetrical Design in the Book of Ruth," *JBL* 84 (1965) 165-168; Trible, "Two Women in a Man's World: A Reading of the Book of Ruth," *Soundings* 59 (1976) 251-279.

[139]Nils Wilhelm Lund, *Chiasmus in the New Testament* (Chapel Hill: University of North Carolina, 1942), pp. 94-136.

[140]Trible, "Wisdom Builds a Poem: The Architecture of Proverbs 1:20-33," *JBL* 94 (1975) 509-518.

[141]Trible, "Depatriarchalizing," pp. 42-43.

[142]Albert Condamin, "Symmetrical Repetitions in *Lamentations* Chapter I and II," *JTS* 7 (1906) 137-140.

[143]Arthur Jeffrey, "Daniel," *IB* (New York and Nashville: Abingdon, 1956), Vol. 6, p. 348, passim; Ad. Lenglet, "La structure littéraire de Daniel 2-7," *Bib* 53 (1972) 169-190.

[144]Barbara Thiering, "The Poetic Forms of the Hodayot," *JSS* 8 (1963) 189-209; Bonnie Pedrotti Kittel, "The Composition of the Hodayot of Qumran," (Ph.D. dissertation, Graduate Theological Union, Berkeley, 1975), pp. 34-38, 161-176.

[145]Raymond Pautrel, "Les canons du mashal rabbinique," *RSR* 26 (1936) 5-45.

[146]J.C. Fenton, "Inclusio and Chiasmus in Matthew," *Studia Evangelica* International Congress on New Testament Studies, Vol. 73 (ed. Kurt Aland, et al.; Berlin: Akademie-Verlag, 1959), pp. 174-179; Lohr, "Oral Techniques," pp. 427-434; Paul Gaechter, *Die literarische Kunst im Matthäus-Evangelium* (SBS 7; Stuttgart: Katholisches Bibelwerk, n.d.); Philippe Rolland, "From the Genesis to the End of the World: The Plan of Matthew's Gospel," *BTB* 2 (1972) 170-176; Charles Homer Giblin, "Structural and Thematic Correlations in the Matthean Burial-Resurrection Narrative (Matt. xxvii. 57-xxviii.20)," *NTS* 21 (1974-75) 406-420; Di Marco, "Der Chiasmus in der Bibel: 3. Teil," *Linguistica Biblica* 39 (1976) 38-57.

[147]See below, p. 144.

[148]M.-E. Boismard, *Le prologue de Saint Jean* (Paris: Éditions du Cerf, 1953), pp. 103-108; Xavier Léon-Dufour, "Trois chiasmes Johanniques," *NTS* 7 (1960-61) 249-255; David Deeks, "The Structure of the Fourth Gospel," *NTS* 15 (1968-69) 107-129; Vanhoye, "La composition de Jn 5,19-30," *Mélanges Bibliques en hommage au R.P. Béda Rigaux* (eds. Albert Descamps and André de Halleux; Gembloux: Duculot, 1970), pp. 259-274; Talbert, "Artistry and Theology," pp. 341-366; Di Marco, "Chiasmus: 3. Teil," pp. 69-85.

[149]Talbert, *Literary Patterns*, pp. 51-58; Di Marco, "Chiasmus: 3. Teil," pp. 62-68.

[150]Kendrick Grobel, "A Chiastic Retribution-Formula in Romans 2," *Zeit und Geschichte: Dankesgabe an Rudolf Bultmann zum 80. Geburtstag* (ed. Erich Dinkler; Tübingen: J.C.B. Mohr, 1964), pp. 255-261; Wilhelm Wuellner, "Paul's Rhetoric of Argumentation in Romans: An Alternative to the Donfried-Karris Debate over Romans," *CBQ* 38 (1976) 338; K.E. Bailey, "Recovering the Poetic Structure of I Cor i 17- ii 2. A Study in Text and Commentary," *NovT* 17 (1975) 265-296; Michael L. Barré, "Paul as 'Eschatological Person': A New Look at 2 Cor 11:29," *CBQ* 37 (1975) 502-509; John Bligh, *Galatians in Greek* (Detroit: University of Detroit, 1966), pp. 2-70.

[151]Lamarche, "Structure de l'épître aux Colossiens," *Bib* 56 (1975) 453-463.

[152]Vanhoye, *Structure littéraire*, passim.

[153]Lund, *Chiasmus*, pp. 323-411.

[154]See Lohr, "Oral Techniques," pp. 424-426, and the references cited there.

[155]Talbert, *Literary Patterns*, p. 81 (in regard to material in Homer); Birger Gerhardsson, *Memory and Manuscript* (trans. Eric J. Sharpe; Uppsala: C.W.K. Gleerup, 1961), p. 147 (in regard to Jewish haggadah).

[156]Whitman, *Homer*, especially in regard to the *Iliad*.

[157]So Radday. See the articles cited in fn. 129.

[158]So, for example, those who argue for the overall concentric or chiastic structure of Matthew. See fn. 146.

[159]See the references for Vergil (fn. 128); also Bailey, "I Cor i 17-ii 2," among others.

[160]See below, especially pp. 132-136, 168-171.

[161]Lund, *Chiasmus*, pp. 40-41. The early history of the scholarly study of chiasmus or extended concentric structure may be found in *ibid.*, pp. 25-26, 30-47.

[162]Ridout, "Prose Techniques," pp. 50-56, 63-73. Ridout has published an article on the concentric structure and other rhetorical features of the story of the rape of Tamar in Jackson and Kessler, eds., *Rhetorical Criticism*, pp. 75-84.

[163]Ernst Lohmeyer, *Das Evangelium des Markus*, 15th ed. (Göttingen: Vandenhoeck & Ruprecht, 1959). Lohmeyer overdoes it in forcing all of the gospel into triadic units, but they do occur frequently.

[164]*A Commentary on the Gospel According to St. Mark* (London: Adam & Charles Black, 1960), p. 24.

[165]See, for example, Bultmann (*History*, p. 47) writing about whether an apophthegm is unitary or non-unitary: "But I admit that I have not prescribed a recipe for dealing with all the controversy and scholastic dialogues: rather does each one require special treatment. Naturally enough, our judgment will not be made in terms of objective criteria, but will depend on taste and discrimination."

CHAPTER II

[1] This study assumes the priority of Mark.

[2] The next controversy occurs in 3:22-30.

[3] *Rahmen*, p. 104.

[4] *Streitsgespräche*, pp. 5-16.

[5] *Ibid.*, p. 2.

[6] *Ibid.*, pp. 5, 7.

[7] *Ibid.*, pp. 11-12.

[8] *Ibid.*, p. 6.

[9] Johannes Weiss (*Das älteste Evangelium* [Göttingen: Vandenhoeck & Ruprecht, 1903], p. 154) earlier also makes the point that there is no increase of hostility in the content of the questions. According to him, the first charge is the severest and the last the lightest.

[10] *Streitgespräche*, pp. 6, 14.

[11] *Ibid.*, pp. 9, 10, 14.

[12] *Ibid.*, p. 14.

[13] *Ibid.*, p. 5. Albertz also adduces a fourth--and literary or form-critical--reason: another controversy story appears shortly afterwards in the gospel (3:22-30) which is different in character and does not build on 2:1-3:6. Mark, however, might have chosen to handle the story separately from the others precisely because of its different character or content and for other reasons. Heinz-Wolfgang Kuhn (*Ältere Sammlungen im Markusevangelium* [SUNT 8; Göttingen: Vandenhoeck & Ruprecht, 1971], p. 21) suggests that its separation is due to Mark's structure. The placing of the story is not really evidence for or against a premarkan collection.

[14] *Streitgespräche*, p. 5.

[15] Prior to Albertz, Weiss (*Evangelium*, pp. 154, 161) and Bacon (*Beginnings*, pp. 22-24) have called attention to the growth of the opposition in 2:1-3:6, and neither believed it to be a premarkan collection.

[16] *Mark--Traditions in Conflict* (Philadelphia: Fortress, 1971), pp. 115, 134.

[17] *Introduction*, p. 162. So also Weeden, *Mark*, p. 67.

[18]*Introduction*, p. 148.

[19]*Formation*, pp. 177-179; *Mark*, pp. 91-92, 191.

[20]"Adversaries," pp. 103-104, 129.

[21]*Jewish Hermeneutics in the Synoptic Gospels and Acts* (Assen: Van Gorcum, n.d.), pp. 202-205. Doeve argues that the stories were transmitted in association with the use of Isaiah 57:13b-59:3, since the same subjects are treated in the same order. If true, this would be a powerful argument for a non-markan structure for the five stories. However, the parallels to Isaiah seem too forced to support the thesis.

[22]Sundwall (*Zusammensetzung*, pp. 12-13); Wilfred L. Knox (*The Sources of the Synoptic Gospels*, Vol. 1: *St Mark* [ed. H. Chadwick; Cambridge: Cambridge University, 1953], p. 8); and Trocmé (*Formation*, pp. 34-35) also have been much influenced by Albertz while disagreeing with him on significant points.

[23]*Mark*, p. 58.

[24]*Introduction to the New Testament* (trans. G. Buswell; Philadelphia: Fortress, 1968), p. 130.

[25]*Introduction*, p. 145.

[26]*Mark*, p. 101.

[27]*Ibid.*, p. 92.

[28]*Formation*, p. 35, fn. 3.

[29]See the discussion and references in Ingrid Maisch, *Die Heilung des Gelähmten* (SBS 52; Stuttgart: KBW, 1971), pp. 114-117; and Kuhn, *Sammlungen*, pp. 19-20.

[30]*Streitgespräche*, p. 5.

[31]Edward J. Mally, "The Gospel According to Mark," *The Jerome Biblical Commentary* (eds. Joseph A. Fitzmyer and Raymond E. Brown; Englewood Cliffs: Prentice-Hall, 1968), Vol. 2, p. 22; Kuhn, *Sammlungen*, p. 20; Perrin, *Introduction*, p. 148.

[32]*Gelähmten*, pp. 114-117.

[33]Maisch believes the Herodians are a markan addition (*Ibid.*, pp. 115, 116).

[34]Dibelius (*Tradition*, pp. 219, 223) views 3:6 as markan since it points ahead in the gospel to the passion narrative, preparing the reader for what is to come.

[35]Such an end, of course, would be no more abrupt than Mk 16:8.

[36]*Sources*, Vol. 1, pp. 10, 12. Knox also suggested that the source might have begun with 1:40-45 (*Ibid.*, p. 8). Anitra B. Kolenkow ("Healing Controversy as a Tie Between Miracle and

Passion Material for a Proto-Gospel," *JBL* 95 [1976] 629) also
posits a premarkan connection between 3:6 and the passion, but
not between 2:1-3:6 as a whole and the passion.

[37]So Kümmel, *Introduction*, pp. 62-63.

[38]So Bultmann, *History*, p. 321, fn. 2.

[39]Robert Henry Lightfoot, *History and Interpretation in
the Gospels* (London: Hodder & Stoughton, 1935), p. 123; Burkill,
Revelation, p. 123, fn. 15. Burton Scott Easton ("A Primitive
Tradition in Mark," *Studies in Early Christianity* [ed. Shirley
Jackson Case; New York: Century, 1928], pp. 87-92) has argued
for a collection consisting of 2:13-3:5; 12:13-27, partly on
the basis of the double use of the Pharisees and Herodians.
His collection is unconvincing since it is sometimes based on
form and sometimes on content. T.W. Manson (*Studies in the
Gospels and Epistles* [ed. Matthew Black; Manchester: Manchester
University, 1962], pp. 43-44) follows Easton, suggesting only
that the collection should begin in 2:15.

[40]*Gelähmten*, pp. 111-120. Schweizer (*Mark*, p. 60) earlier
posited a collection beginning with 2:15 or 18, but without
giving his reasons. Thomas L. Budesheim ("Jesus and the Disciples in Conflict with Judaism," *ZNW* 62 [1971] 204-205) argues
briefly for a collection consisting of 2:15-3:5, since is has
"a unified thrust revolving about the concept of conflict,"
while 2:1-12 only conforms to the conflict theme in its redacted state.

[41]*Sammlungen*, pp. 53-98. Interestingly, it was also in
1971 that Hultgren reaffirmed Albertz' hypothesis. Unfortunate-
ly, he assumes it without critical discussion, and proceeds to
a consideration of its *Sitz im Leben* ("Adversaries," pp. 103-
131).

[42]*Gelähmten*, p. 9.

[43]*Sammlungen*, p. 50.

[44]*Ibid.*, pp. 13, 45-49. Kuhn correctly faults Albertz
for his inadequate attention to *Sitz im Leben* (*Ibid.*, p. 18)
as did Bultmann before him (*History*, p. 40, fn. 2).

[45]*Gelähmten*, pp. 111-112.

[46]*Ibid.*, pp. 112-113.

[47]*Ibid.*, p. 113.

[48]*Ibid.*, pp. 115-118.

[49]So also Bultmann, *History*, pp. 14-16, 212-213; Sundwall,
Zusammensetzung, pp. 12-13, among many.

[50]*Sammlungen*, pp. 12-14.

[51]*Ibid.*, pp. 45-52, 82. Kuhn grants that the individual pericopes need not be of the same form so long as they serve the same aim, but he does not find such a situation occurring in Mark.

[52]*Ibid.*, pp. 74, 84-87.

[53]*Ibid.*, p. 83. This assumes, of course, that vv. 27-28 are the original conclusion to the plucking of grain, not vv. 25-26. Kuhn's argument is somewhat circular here.

[54]*Ibid.*, pp. 73, 76.

[55]*Ibid.*, pp. 81-85.

[56]*Ibid.*, p. 88.

[57]*Ibid.*, pp. 222-223.

[58]*Ibid.*, p. 87.

[59]See above, p. 44.

[60]Kelber, *Kingdom*, pp. 130-131; Kolenkow, "Beyond Miracles," pp. 188-189.

[61]*Sammlungen*, p. 223. Kelber, in his discussion of 2:1-3:6 (*Kingdom*, pp. 18-22) argues that Mark and his community share the belief in the Son of Man, and Mark uses this common basis to argue for his own purposes. The following rhetorical analysis would appear to support Kelber's position (see below, pp. 122-125). Mark, however, could have been using either a "Son of Man collection" or compiling isolated traditions.

[62]It is too soon to evaluate the critical response to Kuhn's theory. Kelber (*Kingdom*, p. 18) accepts Kuhn's collection. However, Kelber's analysis of 2:1-3:6 makes no use of Kuhn's theory and in places appears to contradict it (*Ibid.*, pp. 18-22). Theodore J. Weeden is critical of Kuhn's hypothesis on the grounds that it does not take account of the connection between 2:1-28 and Mk 1, and the emphasis upon the disciples found in that material ("The Conflict between Mark and his Opponents over Kingdom Theology," *1973 Seminar Papers* [ed. George MacRae; SBLASP 109; Society of Biblical Literature, 1973], Vol. 2, p. 230, fn. 9).

[63]If Kolenkow ("Healing Controversy," pp. 635-636) is correct in her argument that Mark has changed the form of 2:1-12 from the standard controversy form of behavior (miracle): objection: justification to a form with the healing at the end, Kuhn's hypothesis would be strengthened. It would make the healing of the paralytic comparable in form to the other three pericopes in his proposed collection; and it would place the climax of 2:1-12 not on the concluding healing but on the authority of the Son of Man which Kuhn sees as the thread of the collection.

[64]*Evangelium*, p. 161.

[65]In *Formation*, first published in 1933, Taylor assumes that 2:1-3:6 is premarkan. In his commentary on Mark, first published in 1952, Taylor still accepts Albertz' arguments in regard to a collection, but because of the markan vocabulary and style, suggests that Mark might have composed it prior to writing the gospel. See above, p. 45.

[66]Etienne Trocmé, *Jesus as Seen by his Contemporaries* (trans. R.A. Wilson; Philadelphia: Westminster, 1973), pp. 52-53.

[67]*Le secret messianique dans l'Évangile de Marc* (LD 47; Paris: Éditions du Cerf, 1968), pp. 160-162.

[68]In fairness to Minette de Tillesse, Kuhn's work appeared some five years after his. He could not be expected to counter it.

[69]"Healing Controversy," pp. 623-638.

[70]*Ibid.*, p. 628.

[71]*Ibid.*, p. 629. The occurrence of the words only in 3:1-6 and 15:1-4 may indicate, as Kolenkow argues, Mark's resumption of the use of a source. They may also be a markan rhetorical device to recall 3:1-6 to the reader's mind at the time of Jesus' being handed over to Pilate. The two views are not necessarily mutually exclusive.

[72]*Ibid.*, pp. 636-637.

[73]*Ibid.*, p. 628.

[74]Kolenkow, "Beyond Miracles," p. 158.

[75]Kolenkow, "Healing Controversy," p. 628, fn. 20.

[76]*Die Bedeutung der Wundererzählungen für die Christologie des Markusevangeliums* (BZNW 42; Berlin: Walter de Gruyter, 1975), pp. 33-34.

[77]*Ibid.*

[78]It is possible, of course, that some of the debate material was associated with Jerusalem in the tradition. Albertz believes the independent stories became associated through their common location in the temple (*Streitgespräche*, pp. 16, 35). Given the general freedom of the gospels in regard to the settings of traditions, traditional association would not be sufficient to explain their setting in Mark.

[79]The Beginning of day one is not in fact indicated in the markan text. The healing of Bartimaeus along with the healing of a blind man in Mk 8:22-26, form a frame for the way section. However, as Vernon K. Robbins ("The Healing of Blind Bartimaeus [10:46-52] in the Marcan Theology," *JBL* 92 [1973] 224-243) has demonstrated, the pericope also serves as a transition to the Jerusalem ministry. Since the pericope serves the double function of framing the way section and providing a transition to the Jerusalem ministry, it seems rhetorically appropriate to include it as part of day one.

[80]The nature of the triumphal scene as prologue is indicated by the fact that Mark apparently pictures it occurring
outside of Jerusalem, which is only entered in 11:11. So
Schmidt, *Rahmen*, pp. 297-298; Kelber, *Kingdom*, p. 93.

[81]See ὄχλου ἱκανοῦ, πολλοί in 10:46-52 and πολλοί, ἄλλοι
οἱ προάγοντες καὶ οἱ ἀκολουθοῦντες in 11:8,9. The crowd of course
has not been entirely absent in 8:27-10:45, but the theme of
Jesus' popularity is not emphasized there as it was in Mk 1-8
and as it will be in 11-12.

[82]On the meaning of the temple cleansing and its relation
to eschatology, see R.H. Lightfoot, *The Gospel Message of St.
Mark* (Oxford: Oxford University, 1962), pp. 60-69; Pesch,
Naherwartungen, pp. 231-235; Donahue, *The Christ*, pp. 113-115;
Kelber, *Kingdom*, pp. 98-102, 109-113, 130-144; Kolenkow, "Beyond
Miracles," pp. 172-183; Weeden, "Conflict," pp. 225-226.

[83]See Gerhard Münderlein, "Die Verfluchung des Feigenbaumes,"
NTS 10 (1963-64) 89-104.

[84]It will be argued below (pp. 73-74, 105-106) that the
technique of interposition is used in 2:6-10a and in 2:1-3:6 as
a whole to present material to the reader while setting it (or
its logical consequences) to one side in terms of narrative
development. Here the technique is used in reverse: it is the
material framing the interposition which is set apart from the
main narrative development.

[85]On the relationship of the fig tree incident and the
three day chronology, see Charles W.F. Smith, "No Time for Figs,"
JBL 79 (1960) 315-327.

[86]Donahue, *The Christ*, p. 119, fn. 2.

[87]This grouping of material is not the most common one in
biblical criticism, which usually sees a new beginning in the
first controversy on day three, the question on authority. A
full rhetorical analysis of 11:15-18 and 27-33, 12:1-12 is outside the scope of this study. My reasons for this structure are
briefly given above, the setting aside of the fig tree episode
by means of the frame and shift in audience, and the dramatic
and thematic unity of the pericopes. Several scholars do view
12:13 as a new beginning: Farrer, *Mark*, p. 118; Burkill, *Revelation*, p. 123, fn. 15; John Bowman, *The Gospel of Mark: The
New Christian Jewish Passover Haggadah* (Leiden: E.J. Brill,
1965), pp. 221, 224-226; Donahue, *The Christ*, p. 116.

[88]Ernest Best, *The Temptation and the Passion: The Markan
Soteriology* (SNTSMS 2; Cambridge: Cambridge University, 1965),
p. 85.

[89]*Streitsgespräche*, pp. 16-36, 107-108.

[90]*Ibid.*, pp. 18, 26-27, 35-36.

[91]*Ibid.*, p. 27.

[92]*Ibid.*, pp. 18-19, 113.

[93]Sundwall (*Zusammensetzung*, pp. 72-75) follows Albertz but notes that the collection is less unified than 2:1-3:6, so a premarkan source is not as certain here. Taylor, as in the case of 2:1-3:6, first accepted Albertz' hypothesis (*Formation*, p. 179) and later suggests that because of the collection's similarity of vocabulary and style to the rest of Mark, Mark himself may have compiled it prior to writing his gospel, for catechetical purposes (*Mark*, p. 101). Schmid (*Mark*, p. 213) believes Mark found the stories as a unit in the tradition. Trocmé accepts ·Albertz' collection, but thinks Mark may have added the Son of David question (*Formation*, pp. 34-36, 97; *Jesus*, pp. 52-53).

[94]*Sources*, Vol. 1, pp. 85-91.

[95]*Sammlungen*, pp. 39-43. See also Donahue, *The Christ*, pp. 115-117.

[96]Albertz notes that after the scribe of the fourth story, there were no more opponents left to question Jesus, so Jesus initiated the last (*Streitsgespräche*, p. 16). However, the single scribe is not really an opponent, and the collector could have continued with a series of individual scribes or Pharisees.

[97]*New Testament*, pp. 158-169; "The Earliest Structure of the Gospels," *NTS* 5 (1958-59) 180-184.

[98]Fred O. Francis, "The Baraita of the Four Sons," *Book of Seminar Papers* (ed. Lane C. McGaughy; SBLASP 108; Society of Biblical Literature, 1972), Vol. 1, pp. 245-266.

[99]*The Christ*, pp. 115-117.

[100]*Introduction*, pp. 158-159.

NOTES

CHAPTER III

[1]Scholars (the majority) who believe that at some point
the controversy was added to the healing differ on the exact
beginning and ending points of the addition. (See Maisch,
Gelähmten, pp. 39-48, and the literature cited there.) My division points are made not in reference to the development of the
tradition but rather to the rhetorical structure of the final
text. They will be discussed in more detail below.

[2]It should be recalled that "interposition" is a literary
device describing something foreign or different "interposed"
into a pericope or story. (See above, p. 34.) The term is
a description of the structure of the final text and implies
nothing about the tradition history or redaction of a pericope.
To my knowledge, only Minette de Tillesse (*Secret*, p. 118);
Kelber (*Kingdom*, pp. 18-19); and Kee (*Community*, p. 35) call
attention to this "interposition" as a literary procedure common in Mark.

[3]So Weiss (*Evangelium*, pp. 153-154). The return to
Capernaum is motiveless; the author is making an entirely new
beginning.

[4]Sundwall, *Zusammensetzung*, p. 12.

[5]Grammatically also, εἰσελθὼν is an anacoluthon.

[6]The same formula appears in 2:13; 4:1-2a; 6:34 and 10:1.
Variants may be found in 1:21; 3:7-8,19b-20; 5:21; 6:1-2,6b and
possibly 6:53-55(56).

[7]Schweizer ("Anmerkungen," pp. 37-38) notes Mark's stress
on Jesus' teaching activity, but not its connection with crowds
coming to Jesus.

[8]Taylor (*Mark*, p. 192) notes the vividness of the style
of the miracle portions, vv. 3-5a,11-12, as an argument for the
composite history of the pericope. Actually the vividness is
found in vv. 1-4 while the remainder of the pericope is heavily
repetitive. The change in style does not correspond to the
change in form-critical type.

[9]See above, p. 34.

[10]See William Wrede, "Zur Heilung des Gelähmten (Mc 2, 1ff.)"
ZNW (1904) 354-358; Bultmann, *History*, pp. 14-16; Taylor, *Mark*,
pp. 191-192. For arguments and literature pro and con a composite pericope, see Maisch, *Gelähmten*, pp. 21-39.

[11]So Morna D. Hooker, *The Son of Man in Mark* (London:
SPCK, 1967), pp. 87-88.

[12]Budesheim ("Jesus," pp. 193-194) writes, "In fact, the question: 'Which is easier?' virtually identifies the two."

[13]Interpreting ἵνα in the more usual final sense, "in order that," "so that." So Bauer-Arndt-Gingrich, p. 378; Blass-Debrunner-Funk, Sect. 470(3). For 2:10 as a periphrasis for the imperative, see C.J. Cadoux, "The Imperatival Use of ἵνα in the New Testament," *JTS* 42 (1941) 173; Lane, *Mark*, p. 97.

[14]Οὗτος may carry a connotation of contempt (Bauer-Arndt-Gingrich, p. 600). So here, Taylor, *Mark*, p. 195; D. E. Nineham, *The Gospel of St. Mark* (Pelican Gospel Commentary; Baltimore: Penguin, 1963), p. 90; Lane, *Mark*, p. 96.

[15]The typical conclusion to a miracle (Bultmann, *History*, p. 225).

[16]Maisch (*Gelähmten*, p. 56) recognizes the concentric structure of the healing narrative--as she reconstructs it prior to the "interpolation" of the apophthegmatic material.

[17]In 1:45 it is the leper who spreads the word; in 2:2, Jesus speaks the word. Ὥστε μηκέτι introduces, in the first instance, Jesus entering a town, and in the second, space around the door. Εἰσελθεῖν refers in both cases to Jesus entering a city/Capernaum; in 1:45 Jesus cannot do so openly, and in 2:1 he does so.

[18]The use of λέγοντας in v. 12 referring to the people is the transition to their direct speech, and appears irrelevant to the use of the word in regard to Jesus.

[19]James M. Robinson (*The Problem of History in Mark* [SBT 21; London: SCM, 1962], pp. 44-45) suggests that the model for the markan debates is to be found in the exorcisms. Certainly, in this healing controversy, the stress is on Jesus' word, just as Jesus exorcises demons by word. Geza Vermes (*Jesus the Jew* [London: Collins, 1973], p. 24) points out that healings, unlike exorcisms, are usually accomplished with the aid of some physical means--often touch. (See Mk 1:31,41; 3:10; 5:23,28-30,41; 6:5,13,56; 7:33; 8:23-25; 9:27.) The fact that this healing is by word alone confirms that the emphasis in this pericope is on the power of Jesus' word.

[20]Ἐλάλει τὸν λόγον. Λόγος, it may be recalled, is a hook word to 1:45. It may be for this reason that Mark has used "to speak the word" here instead of the more usual "he was teaching" or "he began to teach" found in pericope introductions. See 2:13; 4:1-2a; 6:32-34; 10:1. Aside from 2:2, the expression "to speak the word" is found in 4:33 and 8:32, neither of which is in a pericope introduction.

[21]Matthew omits it (9:3).

[22]For the purposes of the story, it does not matter whether or not Jesus is technically blaspheming under Jewish law (here or in 14:62). What matters is whether the audience perceives Jesus speaking blasphemy or good news.

[23]The repetition also contains variations, possibly for stylistic effect. The scribes debate "in their hearts" or "among themselves." The paralytic is to rise, take up his pallet--and walk, or go home, or go out in front of them all.

[24]Donahue (*The Christ*, pp. 81-82, 241) interprets the repetition as examples of what he calls "the markan insertion technique." (See above, pp. 22-23.) Looking at his "insertions" from a rhetorical perspective, it may be said that repetitious material, when it frames new material, may serve to highlight the new material. This is clearly good narrative technique. How much it may demonstrate Mark's additions to the text or his theological concerns would remain to be determined.

[25]Similarly, when the crowd witnesses exorcisms, they do not respond (or apparently acknowledge hearing) the titles the demons bestow on Jesus, but respond only to the act of exorcism (1:23-27; 5:1-20). Passages such as 1:34 and 3:11-12 suggest that the crowd could hear the demons quite as easily as they could hear Jesus' sayings in 2:8b-10.

[26]The emphasis in a ring composition is not necessarily on the center. See above, pp. 36-37.

[27]So Taylor, *Formation*, p. 66.

[28]So, for example, Bultmann, *History*, pp. 14-15; Lohmeyer, *Markus*, p. 50; Taylor, *Mark*, p. 192; Hultgren, "Adversaries," p. 201. For scholars who do not see it as a mixed form, see Daube, *New Testament*, pp. 170-175; Richard T. Mead, "The Healing of the Paralytic--A Unit?" *JBL* 80 (1961) 351-354, following Daube (and Dibelius). Dibelius views the form as a "pure" paradigm, but he does believe that the preacher added the middle verses (*Tradition*, pp. 43, 66-67).

[29]The fact that the paralytic is not an active character in the debate confirms the earlier conclusion that both addresses of Jesus to the paralytic are part of the healing ring and not of the apophthegm.

[30]So Blass-Debrunner-Funk, Sect. 470(3); the sentence is elided, with "I will say this" to be supplied. Farrer writes, "What is there to complain of here? The effect is magnificent, and could not be bettered" (*Mark*, p. 76).

[31]Mt 9:6 softens the construction with τότε. Lk 5:24 is similar to Mark.

[32]*Markus*, p. 50, fn. 2.

[33]Since the opposition to Jesus is just beginning to be brought forward in the narrative, it is possible of course that Mark intends the "all" to include the scribes in amazement. So Lane, *Mark*, p. 99. It seems to me more probable that Mark is careless at this point. Or is the "all" designed to strike the reader and call attention to the contrast in attitude between the scribes who charge blasphemy and everybody who glorifies God? See Budesheim, "Jesus," p. 190.

[34]Perhaps the most famous example in Mark of the ability of characters--in this case the crowd--to disappear and appear without benefit of orderly exits and entrances may be found in 4:1-36. In the narrative of the healing of the paralytic, the four who carried him are apparently abandoned still standing on the roof after lowering Jesus through it.

[35]But see Jn 5:14.

[36]Bultmann treats the pericope both under apophthegms and under miracles (*History*, pp. 14-16, 212-213).

[37]*Ibid.*, pp. 14-16. Bultmann is arguing for a two-stage development of the pericope by the community. My interest is not in the history of development, but in the form of the existing text, whenever and by whomever it came into existence.

[38]*Tradition*, p. 43.

[39]Dibelius (*Ibid.*, pp. 66-67) never specifically calls the declaration of forgiveness a healing formula. Rather he consistently places them in parallel, and writes, "That Jesus should, by the healing, confirm the forgiveness of sins, corresponds to Jewish views of the connection between sin and illness" (*Ibid.*, p. 66).

[40]*Ibid.*, p. 66.

[41]*Ibid.*, p. 67.

[42]Major independent studies of Mk 2:1-12 which come to the same opinion as Bultmann include Taylor, *Mark*, pp. 191-192, 197; Minette de Tillesse, *Secret*, pp. 116-117; Hultgren, "Adversaries," pp. 200-202; Maisch, *Gelähmten*, p. 48. Johnson (*Mark*, p. 55) asserts that Dibelius was correct. For views similar to Dibelius, see Kolenkow, "Healing Controversy," p. 630; Vermes, *Jesus*, p. 180.

[43]The historical probability of Dibelius' position has also been advanced by the find at Qumran of the Prayer of Nabonidus in which forgiveness of sins functions as a healing formula. So Kolenkow, "Beyond Miracles," p. 159. Kenzo Tagawa (*Miracles et Évangile* [Paris: Universitaires de France, 1966], pp. 40-41) argues, unconvincingly I believe, that forgiveness as a healing formula was a special instance for Nabonidus, a pagan, and not a general healing formula.

[44]The rhetorical analysis is of course based on the final text, but then a form-critical analysis must also begin with that text. It would seem that most critics have some preconviction that forgiveness and healing have no integral association. The one argument adduced, that suggests that the miracle may have once existed without any mention of forgiveness, is that the story reads as a complete miracle narrative when vv. 5b-10 are omitted. Equally, it would read as a complete miracle when vv. 6-11 are omitted. This fact may also be explained as the consequence of the circular rhetorical structure used (as distinct from the action-objection-vindication controversy form). However, if the

miracle did exist independently, then whenever the controversy
was added, the association of forgiveness with healing appears
to have been assumed and thus used as a lead-in to the controversy over Jesus' authority to forgive.

[45]The fact that forgiveness can be a healing formula does
not need to imply that all sickness is due to sin, only that
some sickness is due to sin. See Tagawa, *Miracles*, pp. 39-42.

[46]The response of the crowd that they have never seen anything like this also suggests that the forgiveness should be
associated with the healing and not with the debate. For in the
larger markan narrative, this crowd in Capernaum presumably includes those who witnessed the synagogue exorcism and who brought
their sick and possessed to Jesus at sundown (1:27-28, 32-34).
If the sequence and context of the whole narrative is to be taken
seriously, this crowd at 2:12 is seeing something which goes beyond what they saw earlier. The inclusion of the forgiveness
formula suggests that they witness a healing of sickness caused
by God (the consequence of sin) in contrast to the exorcisms in
which the sickness is caused by evil powers. See Best, *Temptation*, pp. 35-36, passim.

[47]Hooker (*Son of Man*, p. 89) presents a somewhat similar
view of the miracle.

[48]The literature on the Son of Man "problem" and 2:10 is
immense. For recent literature which views 2:10 as premarkan,
see Heinz Eduard Tödt, *The Son of Man in the Synoptic Tradition*
(trans. Dorothea M. Barton; Philadelphia: Westminster, 1965),
pp. 125-130; Hooker, *Son of Man*, pp. 81-93; Maisch, *Gelähmten*,
pp. 90-101. For views of 2:10 and 28 as part of Mark's theology,
see Perrin, "The Creative Use of the Son of Man Traditions by
Mark," *A Modern Pilgrimage in New Testament Christology*
(Philadelphia: Fortress, 1974), pp. 84-93; "The Christology of
Mark," pp. 173-187; John H. Elliott, "Man and the Son of Man in
the Gospel according to Mark," *Humane Gesellschaft: Beiträge
zu ihrer sozialen Gestaltung* (eds. Trutz Rendtorff and Arthur
Rich; Zurich: Zwingli, 1970), pp. 50-54. For a recent attempt
to interpret Son of Man not as a title but as meaning "man,"
see Lewis S. Hay, "The Son of Man in Mark 2:10 and 2:28," *JBL*
89 (1970) 69-75.

[49]*The Gospel According to Saint Mark* (Cambridge: Cambridge
University, 1959), p. 100.

[50]*Formation*, p. 173.

[51]"Mark," pp. 26-27.

[52]*Mark*, pp. 26-27, 97-98. Lane follows G.H. Boobyer,
"Mark II, 10a, and the Interpretation of the Healing of the
Paralytic," *HTR* 47 (1954) 115-120. See also Christian P. Ceroke,
"Is Mark 2:10 a saying of Jesus?" *CBQ* 22 (1960) 381-383.

[53]"The High Priest's Question and Jesus' Answer (Mark 14:
61-62)," Kelber, Ed., *Passion*, p. 92; "The Christology of Mark,"
p. 183. fn. 24.

[54]Hooker (*Son of Man*, p. 83) notes on the other hand that
this interpretation also raises the difficulty of a reference
to Jesus as Son of Man not spoken by Jesus.

[55]See above, p. 19.

[56]See above, pp. 69-70.

[57]Perrin ("The High Priest's Question," p. 90) writes,
somewhat similarly: "Verses 2:10 and 2:28, the references to
Jesus as Son of Man with *exousia* to forgive sins and to abro-
gate the Sabbath law, serve the function of equating the authority of Jesus with that of the Son of Man." Perrin's statement
assumes, undoubtedly correctly, that Mark's audience has some
preconceived ideas about the figure, "the Son of Man."

[58]Schmidt (*Rahmen*, p. 82) classifies 2:13 as a *Sammel-
bericht*.

[59]So, with some differences, Albertz, *Streitgespräche*, p.
6; Bultmann, *History*, pp. 18, 28, 92, 341; Taylor, *Formation*,
p. 65; Taylor, *Mark*, pp. 201, 203; Hultgren, "Adversaries,"
pp. 208, 214-217; Budesheim, "Jesus," p. 203; B.M.F. Van Iersel,
"La Vocation de Lévi (Mc., II, 13-17 par.). Traditions et
rédactions," *De Jésus aux Évangiles* (ed. I. de la Potterie;
BETL 25:2; Gembloux: J. Duculot, 1967), pp. 212-232; Charles
E. Carlston, *The Parables of the Triple Tradition* (Philadelphia:
Fortress, 1975), p. 111. Cf. Knox, *Sources*, Vol. 1, p. 13;
Rudolf Pesch, "Das Zöllnergastmahl (Mk 2,15-17)," *Mélanges
Bibliques en hommage su R.P. Béda Rigaux* (eds. Albert Descamps
and André de Halleux; Gembloux: Duculot, 1970), pp. 63-87;
Pesch, "Levi-Matthäus (Mc 2:14/Mt 9:9, 10:3). Ein Beitrag zur
Lösung eines alten Problems," *ZNW* (1968) 43-45.

[60]*Parables*, p. 113.

[61]See above, pp. 67-68.

[62]David Blatherwick ("The Markan Silhouette?" *NTS* 17 [1970-
71] 187) and Pierre Geoltrain ("La violation du Sabbat: Une
lecture de Marc, 3:1-6," *Foi et Vie* 69 [1970] 72) both interpret
2:13 as the first major break since 1:16. In both cases it appears due to undue reliance on the setting--Jesus beside the
lake--in isolation from other factors.

[63]The opening words of 2:13, καὶ ἐξῆλθεν πάλιν, echo in
sound the opening words of 2:1, καὶ εἰσελθὼν πάλιν, and possibly
also in content: Jesus went out (of Capernaum) beside the sea.
This repetition may reinforce the reader's sense of continuity.
Ἐξέρχομαι is of course a common markan editorial word (Gaston,
Horae, p. 58). Mark may well have used the word simply to connect pieces of his tradition without any thought of it serving
as part of a hook phrase to the beginning of 2:1. However, the
reader may hear the similarity in sound and continuity in meaning, and consciously or unconsciously, connect the two openings.

[64]The vocabulary of 2:14 also recalls 1:16-20. Καὶ παράγων,
εἶδεν, ἠκολούθησεν(αν) αὐτῷ in v. 14 are all to be found in 1:16-
20.

[65]Van Iersel ("Vocation," p. 216) lists six characteristics of call narratives of which he finds number five, abandonment of one's means of livelihood, lacking in the call of Levi. He may well be right not to interpret ἀναστάς as that motif.

[66]The last question is actually a text-critical one. However, the evidence is sufficiently inconclusive that commentators tend to decide the issue on exegetical grounds. The United Bible Society *Greek New Testament* reads ἠκολούθουν with the scribes of the Pharisees with a certainty of "C," "considerable degree of doubt whether the text or the apparatus contains the superior reading."

[67]For example, Anthony R. Ceresko ("The Chiastic Word Pattern in Hebrew," *CBQ* 38 [1976] 303-311) argues for the use of the a:b::b:a word patterns as an aid in translation when a Hebrew text is obscure.

[68]The other option is to conclude that the passage does not make sense--to decide, with Knox (*Sources*, Vol. 1, p. 13) "here we have a hopeless obscurity." Knox may, of course, be correct.

[69]Most commentators opt for Levi's house. See the references cited by Carlston (*Parables*, p. 111, fn. 7). See also Pesch ("Zöllnergastmahl," pp. 64-65, 71) for Levi's house.

[70]Weiss, *Evangelium*, p. 159.

[71]My interpretation draws on that of Van Iersel ("Vocation," p. 225). Verse 15ab might be considered an example of the markan tendency for "progressive double-step expression" (see Neirynck, *Duality*, pp. 71-72). The two-step expression (if markan in this instance) may be due to editorial modification or amplification of tradition, or to direct composition.

[72]The question what specific group, if any, the term "sinners" designated is not one that can be elucidated by the rhetorical approach. That would be a matter for historical investigation, and the referent might vary as a tradition traveled. See Donahue ("Tax Collectors and Sinners," *CBQ* 33 [1971] 39-61) and the literature cited there.

[73]So Nierynck, *Duality*, p. 112; Van Iersel, "Vocation," p. 220.

[74]So virtually all the versions and commentators. Cf. Swete, *Mark*, p. 41; N. Turner, *Style*, p. 18.

[75]Scholarly opinion is thoroughly divided. For arguments for "many" referring to tax collectors and sinners, see Swete, *Mark*, p. 41; C.H. Bird, "Some γαρ clauses in St. Mark's Gospel," *JTS* 4 (1953) 182-183; Nigel Turner, *Grammatical Insights into the New Testament* (Edinburgh: T. & T. Clark, 1965), p. 65; Schweizer, *Mark*, p. 64. For arguments for "many" referring to disciples, see C.H. Turner, "Marcan Usage," *JTS* 26 (1925) 147; Taylor, *Mark*, p. 205; Trocmé, *Formation*, pp. 115-116.

[76]See especially Van Iersel, "Vocation," pp. 225, 232.
Paul Lamarche ("The Call to Conversion and Faith: The Vocation
of Levi (Mk, 2, 13-17)," *Lumen Vitae* 25 [1970] 301, 303) argues
that vv. 15-16 extend the call from one to many, and v. 17 extends it to all.

[77]See those cited in fn. 75 for "many" referring to disciples, and in addition, Nineham, *Mark*, p. 100; Pesch, "Zöllnergastmahl," p. 72.

[78]The characters appear (and disappear) in the narrative
as needed. See the discussion of the scribes in 2:1-12 above,
pp. 75-76.

[79]Rhetorical analysis cannot elucidate the historical problem of who was meant by the scribes of the Pharisees. Rhetorically, the phrase recalls the scribes, the opponents of the first
story, and points ahead to the Pharisees, the opponents of the
later stories in this section. So J. Wellhausen, *Das Evangelium
Marci* (Berlin: Georg Reimer, 1903), p. 19.

[80]Ἰδόντες, if taken literally, can raise questions of
how the Pharisees saw Jesus in the house. Its function, however, does not appear to be accurate description, but rather
narrative connection. The same might be said about ἀκούσας in
v. 17.

[81]Kolenkow (personal communication) has suggested that
v. 17 might have been attached to 2:1-12. Cf. Carlston, *Parables*,
p. 115.

[82]So Dibelius, *Tradition*, p. 64, fn. 1; Van Iersel, "Vocation," pp. 219, 226; Carlston, *Parables*, p. 115, fn. 29 (re
Mark's theology).

[83]Καλέω is also used in 3:31 and 11:17. In neither instance does it refer to discipleship or eating. Καλέω can imply
an invitation to a meal, but it does not do so in Mark, unless
2:17b is such an instance. So Lohmeyer (*Markus*, p. 56) and
Mally ("Mark," p. 27) who view 17b as an invitation to the messianic banquet. If in fact the passage does imply the messianic
banquet, the basis would seem to be found rather in v. 15ab, the
actual meal. So Lane, *Mark*, p. 106.

[84]Isaac Kikawada drew my attention to this pattern.

[85]Lamarche, "Call," p. 309.

[86]Pesch ("Zöllnergastmahl," p. 87), and Van Iersel ("Vocation," pp. 225-226), see vv. 14, 15c, and 17b connected with the
call to discipleship in Mark's redaction.

[87]Besides those who recognize a circular pattern in 2:1-
3:6, many have noticed the continuation of theme between 2:1-12
and 13-17. So Sundwall, *Zusammensetzung*, p. 15; Lohmeyer, *Markus*,
p. 49; Minette de Tillesse, *Secret*, p. 122; Lane, *Mark*, pp. 106-
107.

[88]Pierre Mourlon Beernaert, "Jésus controversé: Structure et théologie de Marc 2,1-3,6," *NRT* 95 (1973) 143. Sundwall (*Zusammensetzung*, p. 15) also notes the use of sin and sinners as catchwords connecting the two pericopes.

[89]Lane (*Mark*, p. 106) writes "the basis of table-fellowship was *messianic forgiveness*."

[90]Cf. Perrin, *Rediscovering the Teaching of Jesus* (New York: Harper & Row, 1967), pp. 102-103. Perrin thinks that, historically speaking, it was Jesus' reinclusion of sinners in the community in table-fellowship which led to Jesus' actual death. He sees the minor role of table fellowship in the gospel tradition as "an indication of how far removed from historical reminiscence of the ministry of Jesus that tradition is, in its present form."

[91]The word is Bowman's (*Mark*, p. 115).

[92]There has been considerable debate in the literature on how "the righteous" should be understood. For differing opinions, see Lamarche, "Call," pp. 311-312; Taylor, *Mark*, p. 207; Bowman, *Mark*, p. 115; Lane, *Mark*, pp. 104-105; Carlston, *Parables*, pp. 113-114. Most of the differences evaporate if one distinguishes the understanding of internal story level audience from that of Mark's audience.

[93]Budesheim, "Jesus," pp. 202-203.

[94]See above, fn. 59. To my knowledge, the only scholar to argue that v. 14 is redactional is Pesch ("Levi-Matthäus," pp. 43-45). Pesch, arguing from a redactional and tradition history perspective has reached the same conclusion that I reach on the basis of a rhetorical analysis. The criterion of multiple methodologies suggests we may be correct.

[95]Dibelius' (*Tradition*, p. 64, fn. 1) suggestion that vv. 14 and 17 were the original paradigm is a more plausible hypothesis for a premarkan tradition, if any. Verse 14 would then be an "ideal" scene made to fit the sayings in v. 17.

[96]Sundwall, *Zusammensetzung*, p. 15.

[97]Johnson, *Mark*, p. 60. Pesch ("Zöllnergastmahl," p. 71) argues that Mark transferred the phrase, "Levi, son of Alphaeus" from its traditional setting in v. 15.

[98]That is, in tradition history terms, those defending their own behavior in being or associating with sinners/Gentiles would hardly miss the point that their opponents viewed them as sinners, not as good Jews/disciples. But cf. Daube, "Responsibilities of Master and Disciples in the Gospels," *NTS* 19 (1972-73) 1-15.

[99]*History*, p. 49. So also Hultgren, "Adversaries," p. 215.

[100]Many form critics view the "original" apophthegm as vv. 18-19a, with 19b-20 and 21-22 as separate additions. See Bultmann, *History*, p. 19; Hultgren, "Adversaries," pp. 155-159, and

the literature cited there. Dibelius (*Tradition*, pp. 65-66) and
Taylor (*Mark*, pp. 208, 211-212), on the other hand, argue that
the controversy apophthegm consisted of vv. 18-20.

[101]C.H. Turner, "Marcan Usage," *JTS* 25 (1924) 379.

[102]Matthew and Luke omit the repetition in both a and a'
(Mt 9:14-15; Lk 5:33-35).

[103]Of the 38 times Mark uses a modifier with disciples, only
here and in 4:34 does the modifier precede "disciples," and is
the dative used. Luke keeps the dative but drops the noun,
writing, οἱ δὲ σοὶ... (Lk 5:33). Matthew employs the more usual
construction, οἱ δὲ μαθηταί σου (Mt 9:14).

[104]A similar shift in word order may be found in Mk 3:31-35
(mother... brothers, four times, then brothers...mother) and in
9:42-47 (καλόν ἐστιν αὐτῷ/σε three times, followed by καλόν σέ
ἐστιν). Perhaps the four mentions of Jesus' silence in the trial
narratives should also be included here: οὐκ ἀποκρίνῃ οὐδέν
(14:60), οὐκ ἀπεκρίνατο οὐδέν (14:61), οὐκ ἀποκρίνῃ οὐδέν (15:4),
and finally οὐκέτι οὐδὲν ἀπεκρίθη (15:5).

[105]It is possible that the desire to stress the contrast
between groups of disciples is responsible for the lack of specific opponents in the story. For then the opposition between Jesus
and the opponents would add a second dimension to the story and
dilute what is now the primary contrast.

[106]A final shift in word order appears to indicate climax,
but not necessarily contrast. See the examples given above,
fn. 104. Whether or not contrast is also present depends on
the content.

[107]Albertz (*Streitgespräche*, pp. 8-9) has called attention
to the fact that the sayings in vv. 19-20 each fall into four
half lines, with intricate chiastic, antithetical, and linear
relationships. He believes this is due to the rhythm of the
semitic *Vorlage*.

[108]The rhetorical analysis has not helped to clarify whether
"that day" refers specifically to the day of crucifixion or in
general to the time after Jesus' death. For scholars' opinions,
see Kuhn, *Sammlungen*, pp. 63-72; Weeden, *Mark*, pp. 133-135;
Carlston, *Parables*, p. 120.

[109]T.A. Burkill (*New Light on the Earliest Gospel: Seven
Markan Studies* [Ithaca: Cornell University, 1972] p. 46) notes
that the same idea of the Christ absent from the community is
also to be found in Mk 14:7 in regard to alms giving.

[110]The pronouncement story parallel in the Gospel of Thomas
(logion 104) also treats the material of vv. 18-20 as a unity,
delimited by a chiastic inclusio: pray and fast:fast and pray.

[111]*The Gospel of Mark: Its Composition and Date* (New Haven:
Yale University, 1925), p. 157. So also Johnson, *Mark*, p. 66;
Lane, *Mark*, p. 113.

[112]So Taylor (*Mark*, p. 214), following C.H. Turner ("Marcan Usage," *JTS* 26 [1925] 147) who describes lines b and c as a typical markan parenthesis. This is the preferred reading (with a rating of C) of the United Bible Society's *Greek New Testament*.

[113]Bultmann, *History*, p. 19.

[114]This view is held by Lane, *Mark*, p. 113; J.B. Muddiman, "Jesus and Fasting (Marc 2,18-22)," *Jésus aux origines de la christologie* (ed. J. Dupont; BETL 40; Gembloux: J. Duculot, 1975), p. 275.

[115]So Mourlon Beernaert, "Jésus controversé," pp. 144-145.

[116]Introduced by καὶ λέγει αὐτοῖς and καὶ ἔλεγεν αὐτοῖς respectively (vv. 25,27). The phenomenon of two formally distinct answers addressed to the same audience is only found here and in Mk 7:1-13 in the apophthegmatic material in Mark.

[117]The question has been addressed mainly in terms of which answer, vv. 25-26, or (some or all of) vv. 27-28, was the original ending of the controversy apophthegm. The general opinion has been that vv. 25-26 constitute the original answer. (So Albertz, *Streitgespräche*, p. 10; Bultmann, *History*, pp. 16-17; Taylor, *Mark*, p. 218, etc.) Erich Klostermann (*Das Markusevangelium*, 4th ed. [HNT; Tübingen: J.C.B. Mohr, 1950] p. 29) in his 1926 edition was apparently the first to suggest that vv. 25-26 were the later addition. Since then, Haenchen (*Weg*, pp. 120-121); Kuhn (*Sammlungen*, pp. 74-77); Hultgren ("The Formation of the Sabbath Pericope in Mark 2:23-28," *JBL* 91 [1972] 38-43) among others have argued for this position. For an excellent and exhaustive survey of scholarly opinion, see Neirynck, "Jesus and the Sabbath. Some Observations on Mark II:27," *Jésus aux origines de la christologie* (ed. J. Dupont; BETL 40; Gembloux: J. Duculot, 1975), pp. 227-270.

[118]In 1864, H.A.W. Meyer (*Kritisch-exegetisches Handbuch über die Evangelien des Markus und Lukas* [Göttingen: 1864], p. 37; cited in Neirynck, "Sabbath," p. 259) argued that Jesus first answered the issue of illegality, and then the issue of the sabbath, thus implicitly recognizing the rhetorical links of the pericope. Meyer, however, argued that the making of a path was in itself illegal, and the Sabbath only an aggravating circumstance. The fact that gleaning was permissible (Lev 19:9; Deut 23:25), and the emphasis on the sabbath within the pericope would appear to make Meyer's position untenable.

[119]Grammatically, one would expect ἤρξαντο to be construed with the infinitive phrase, ὁδὸν ποιεῖν, not with the participle τίλλοντες as the RSV and many commentators read the text. Ἄρχομαι plus an infinitive is more normal Greek; further the other twenty-five uses of ἄρχομαι in Mark are all followed by infinitives. There seems no reason to make an exception for 2:23. Scholars who read ἤρξαντο with ὁδὸν ποιεῖν include Hawkins (*Horae*, p. 122); Bacon (*Beginnings*, pp. 30-31).

[120]Albert Henrichs writes, "For Mark, the plucking of the grain is not a means of providing food but of clearing the way for Jesus" (personal communication).

[121]Daube, "Responsibilities," p. 5.

[122]The rabbinic tradition sometimes supposes that the David incident occurred on a sabbath. See Strack-Billerbeck, Vol. 1, pp. 618-619. The connection with the sabbath, however, is not made either in 1 Samuel or in the synoptic tradition.

[123]Both Matthew (Mt 12:1) and Luke (Lk 6:1) modify the exposition so that the disciples eat the grain. In Mark, the disciples do not.

[124]Most scholars, following Matthew and Luke, make the connection between question and answer on the basis of eating. So, for example, Lohmeyer, *Markus*, p. 64; Taylor, *Mark*, p. 215. In order to make such a connection, it is necessary to force the meaning of v. 23b. For example, Taylor writes, "From the sequel, however, it appears that the disciples' offense is not that of working or of exceeding limits of a Sabbath day's journey, but of gathering and eating food on the Sabbath. Mark, therefore, must mean that the disciples 'began as they went, to pluck'" (*Mark*, p. 215). On the translation of v. 23b, see above, p. 96.

[125]In the story in 1 Sam 21:1-6, David does not have any companions. For a suggested tradition history development of this addition, see Daube, "Responsibilities," pp. 5-7.

[126]See below, pp. 113-114.

[127]Scholars have spent much time and energy trying to determine the tradition history of these two sayings, without reaching any consensus. See Neirynck, "Sabbath," pp. 237-254.

[128]See Elliott, "Man and the Son of Man," pp. 53-54.

[129]Lane, *Mark*, p. 118. Many have argued that the use of καὶ ἔλεγεν αὐτοῖς in v. 27 is a markan seam showing that Mark has added vv. 27-28 to the original apophthegm (Bultmann, *History*, pp. 16,323; Marxsen, *Introduction*, p. 122; Neirynck, "Sabbath," p. 264). Kuhn (*Sammlungen*, p. 74), on the other hand, considers the phrase as Mark's transition from his interpolation of vv. 25-26 to the original conclusion of the apophthegm in v. 27. It would seem that either (or neither) explanation may be correct. One can deduce from the phrase that there is a break in the narrative; one cannot deduce the historical development of the pericope.

[130]So Lohmeyer, *Markus*, p. 65; Robinson, *History*, p. 47; Haenchen, *Weg*, p. 120, fn. 3; Lane, *Mark*, p. 119. Cf. Nineham (*Mark*, pp. 105-106) who sees v. 27 making explicit the principle which underlies vv. 25-26--special need overrides the law. The saying in v. 27, however, does not appear to speak to the question of need vs. law.

[131]Lane, *Mark*, p. 119, fn. 98.

[132]Kuhn, *Sammlungen*, pp. 73, 76, 87. Kuhn's argument is that the Son of Man sayings frame the premarkan collection he finds in 2:1-28. Within the markan context as well, the second use of "Son of Man" would remind the reader of the first.

[133]The dependence of v. 28 on v. 10 suggests that the Son of Man saying in v. 28 was not added to v. 27 until the controversy over plucking grain was joined to the earlier controversies which included the Son of Man saying in 2:10. This would be an additional argument against a premarkan collection of 2:15-3:5(6).

[134]*Mark*, p. 115. See also Neirynck, "Sabbath," p. 270, fn. 157.

[135]Sundwall (*Zusammensetzung*, p. 19) considers σάββατον and ἄνθρωπος hook words, but not ἔξεστιν. I would consider ἔξεστιν a hook word since it is used twice in connection with the sabbath (2:24; 3:4) and because its use in 3:4 is rather arbitrary-- it is never lawful to do harm or kill. Since ἄνθρωπος is generic or part of a title in 2:27-28 and refers to a specific sick man in 3:1-5, it would not seem to be a hook word.

[136]Lane, *Mark*, p. 121; Geoltrain, "Violation," p. 76.

[137]So Bowman, *Mark*, p. 118; Budesheim, "Jesus," p. 204. In the narrative setting of 2:23-3:6, 3:6 confirms that "they" refers to the Pharisees. Cf. Turner ("Marcan Usage," *JTS* 25 [1924] 379), who considers παρετήρουν an impersonal plural functioning as a passive similar to ἔρχονται and λέγουσιν in 2:18. Given the structure of the sentence, κατηγορήσωσιν would then also be an impersonal plural. This seems improbable and Turner does not so consider it.

[138]Very few commentators have noticed the similarity in form between 2:1-12 and 3:1-6, perhaps because they share Bultmann's belief that 2:1-12 is a mixed miracle-apophthegm form and 3:1-6 is an "organically complete apophthegm" (*History*, pp. 12, 14-15). The similarity has been recognized by Rudolf Grob (*Einführung in das Markus Evangelium* [Zürich: Zwingli, 1965], pp. 38-39); Budesheim ("Jesus," p. 191); Kelber (*Kingdom*, p. 21); Kolenkow ("Healing Controversy," pp. 635-636); and Kee (*Community*, pp. 36-37).

[139]So Haenchen, *Weg*, p. 123; Budesheim, "Jesus," p. 204. Budesheim notes, "Just this expectance [of healing], devoid of the idea of hostility, has been called 'faith' in 2:5."

[140]Friedrich Büschel, "κατηγορέω," *TDNT*, Vol. 3, p. 637.

[141]For rabbinic regulations on sabbath healing, see Eduard Lohse, "Jesu Worte über den Sabbat," *Judentum Urchristentum Kirche: Festschrift für Joachim Jeremias* (ed. Walther Eltester; BNZW 26; Berlin: Alfred Töpelmann, 1960), pp. 79-89.

[142]Johnson, *Mark*, p. 71.

[143]This may be an indication of the interdependence of the narrative of 2:1-3:6. The reader already knows that Jesus can read the minds of his opponents.

[144]In his structuralist interpretation, Dan O. Via, Jr. (*Kerygma and Comedy in the New Testament: A Structuralist Approach to Hermeneutic* [Philadelphia: Fortress, 1975], p. 132)

defines the conflict as follows: "The tacit view of the Pharisees
is that one must choose one of the members from the opposition
to-do-on-the-sabbath/not-to-do-on-the-sabbath, while the view
that Jesus is trying to establish is that one must choose between
the two alternatives to-do-good/to-do-evil." As far as he goes,
Via is correct. He--or the structuralist method--however, ignores the fact that for the Pharisees keeping the sabbath is
doing good and vice versa, and that Jesus' counter-question is
presented in the narrative as a justification for violation of
the sabbath, not as an alternate principle (ἔξεστιν τοῖς σάββασιν,
3:4).

[145]Siegfried Schulz ("Markus und das Alte Testament," *ZTK*
58 [1961] 194), views Mk 3:4 as Mark's criterion for deciding
what remains valid in the Old Testament and what is abrogated.

[146]Vermes, *Jesus*, p. 25; Kolenkow, "Healing Controversy,"
pp. 636-637.

[147]Geoltrain, "Violation," p. 84.

[148]The question of who the Herodians were historically is
beyond the scope of rhetorical analysis. In the gospel narrative,
all that one can say with certainty is that Herod is associated
with the death of John the Baptist, and Herod/the Herodians are
associated with the Pharisees as opponents of Jesus (6:14-29;
3:6; 8:15; 12:13). See W.J. Bennett, Jr., "The Herodians of
Mark's Gospel," *NovT* 17 (1975) 9-14.

[149]Trocme (*Formation*, p. 185, fn. 1) writes, "The attitude of
Jesus in 3:1-5 amounts to a provocation of the leaders of Jewry."

[150]*Streitsgespräche*, p. 12.

[151]See Lane, *Mark*, p. 125. Budesheim ("Jesus," p. 209) appears correct in insisting that although the passage points to
Jesus' death, it is not yet an explicit theology of the cross.

[152]See above, pp. 73-74.

NOTES

CHAPTER IV

[1]"Pharisees" might be considered a hook word connecting the middle pericope with second, fourth, and fifth. However, it is better understood as a key word. It is part of the sequence of opponents in 2:1-3:6 and part of the rhetorical structure of 2:18-20. It does not appear to function as a hook word indicating structure in 2:1-3:6.

[2]Mt 9:1-8; Lk 5:17-26; 6:6-11. In Matthew's version of the healing of the withered hand, the healing occurs only at the end (Mt 12:9-14).

[3]The verbal similarity might be considered the result of Mark's use of his typical introductory formulas. Unlike the frequent appearance of ἔρχομαι and ἐξέρχομαι, however, εἰσέρχομαι does not appear elsewhere in Mark as the first verb in a pericope introduction. According to Gaston's statistical study (Horae, p. 72), εἰσέρχομαι is not used significantly more often in markan editorial verses than in verses in which Mark is generally considered dependent upon tradition.

[4]Used twice in the first story.

[5]Farrer (Mark, pp. 47-48) and Mourlon Beernaert ("Jésus controversé," p. 139) stress the parallelism between the healing of feet or legs in the first story, and the healing of the arm in the second. Mark, however, does not mention legs or even lameness in regard to the paralytic.

[6]Edward C. Hobbs, "The Gospel of Mark and the Exodus," (Ph.D. dissertation, University of Chicago, 1952), passim.

[7]Mark, p. 47. So also Jean Radermakers, La bonne nouvelle de Jésus selon saint Marc (Brussels: Institut d'Études Théologiques, 1974), Vol. 2, p. 92.

[8]Mark, p. 121. See also Lightfoot, Gospel Message, p. 29.

[9]Bultmann, History, p. 225.

[10]Tagawa (Miracles, p. 12) views 3:6 as taking the place of the miracle acclamation. For him, it demonstrates that controversy not miracle is the center of interest.

[11]Bultmann, History, pp. 152, 155-156.

[12]If vv. 25-26 are interpreted as justifying Jesus' behavior in vv. 15-16, then the fact that it is holy bread in vv. 25-26 may be support for those who argue for allusions to the messianic banquet in vv. 15-17.

[13]Giuseppe G. Gamba, "Considerazioni in margine alla poetica di Mc. 2,1-12," *Salesianum* 28 (1966) 331.

[14]See Talbert, *Literary Patterns*, p. 79.

[15]*Gelähmten*, p. 9.

[16]*Ibid.*, pp. 127-128.

[17]"Jesus," pp. 190, 192 (at least in its present redaction).

[18]"Adversaries," p. 200.

[19]See above, pp. 51-52.

[20]Geoltrain, "Violation," p. 84; Via, *Kerygma*, p. 149.

[21]The opposite pattern, stressing the triumph of Jesus, may be seen in the public debates in Mk 12. See below, p. 163.

[22]Contra Minette de Tillesse, *Secret*, p. 124; Geoltrain, "Violation," p. 74; Via, *Kerygma*, p. 133; Mourlon Beernaert, "Jésus controversé," p. 141.

[23]The association of eating with healing in 2:1-3:6 suggests that Jesus' table fellowship with sinners as the historical cause of Jesus' offense to the Jews may not be so far removed from the present gospel tradition as Perrin suggested. See above, Chapter III, fn. 90.

[24]On the connection of healing controversy and death, see Kolenkow, "Healing Controversy," pp. 623-638.

[25]See above, Chapter iii, fn. 141.

[26]See above, pp. 103-104.

[27]Via (*Kerygma*, p. 117) may well be right in asserting that "the opposition death/resurrection is the fundamental kernel out of which the narrative as a whole develops." It would not appear, however, that "the kingdom is the possibility of gaining life *through* death," is a point made in 2:1-3:6 (*Ibid.*, p. 133 [italics mine]).

[28]See above, pp. 36-37.

[29]See above, pp. 72-73.

[30]Of course, the sayings may well derive from the tradition. My argument is that the redactor has not incorporated them blindly.

[31]For discussion and examples, see Talbert, *Literary Patterns*, pp. 77-79.

[32]*Kingdom*, p. 22.

[33]"High Priest's Question," p. 90.

[34]See especially Weeden, *Mark*; Kolenkow, "Beyond Miracles,"
pp. 161-170. See also Joanna Dewey, *Disciples of the Way: Mark
on Discipleship* (Women's Division, Board of Global Ministries,
The United Methodist Church, 1976).

[35]A notable exception is Budesheim, "Jesus," pp. 190-209.
Hultgren ("Adversaries," p. 131) also notes the prominence of
the disciples in the controversies.

[36]See above, pp. 84-85. Budesheim ("Jesus," p. 203) is
correct in his observation that vv. 13-14 effect "an inclusion
of the disciples at a critical point in the narration of the
Jesus-tradition where they otherwise would have been only most
unobtrusively present." He is also correct in his further observation that "by following the narration of the conflict
stories with the summary of Jesus' activities with the disciples
(3:7-12, esp. v. 7!) an emphasis on them is produced without
violating the continuity of the narration" (*Ibid*.). Budesheim's
study of the various stages of redaction in 1:16-3:19 ("Jesus,"
pp. 190-209), like the foregoing rhetorical analysis, confirms
the importance of the disciples' role in 2:1-3:6. The results
of the two different methodological approaches serve to confirm
each other.

[37]Weeden, perhaps the foremost advocate of the role of the
disciples as the means to understand Mark's theology and community, virtually ignores the role of the disciples in 2:1-3:6 in
his book, *Mark*. However, later ("Conflict," pp. 206-207) he
does consider their role, adopting Budesheim's position.

[38]Hultgren ("Adversaries," p. 131) views the disciples'
behavior in 2:1-3:6 not as their sharing in the freedom of the
kingdom but as the statement (of the collector) that the disciples are approved by God, "regardless of their inability to
measure up to Pharisaic standards of religious observance." The
emphasis in 2:13-28 seems rather to be on the disciples as
sharers of the way of Jesus.

[39]Kolenkow ("Healing Controversy," p. 636, fn. 45) has
argued that 2:28 is an inappropriate conclusion to a controversy
about the disciples' behavior. On the contrary, 2:28 appears
to be a continuation of the theme of the disciples' dependence
upon the initiative and authority of Jesus.

[40]Budesheim ("Jesus," pp. 205, 207, 208) has argued that
the consequence of the inclusion of the disciples in Jesus' controversy activity is "the exaltation of the disciple-Gestalt
along with the Jesus-figure;" that in the premarkan redaction
of the tradition, there is "a parallelization of the Jesus-figure
and the disciple-Gestalt" and an "exaltation of the disciple in
the tradition to the honor of θεῖοι ἄνδρες." At least as far
as 2:13-28 is concerned, this view does not appear to be sub-
stantiated. The text emphasizes not the "exaltation" of the
disciples but their subordination to Jesus, their dependence
upon his initiative and authority. While Budesheim has acutely
observed the prominence of the disciples in the narrative, he
has paid insufficient attention to the content which describes
the disciples' relationship to Jesus.

[41]Several scholars have noted that 2:1-3:6 is not only a demonstration of Jesus' way over against that of the Jewish opponents (and the conflict Jesus' way aroused) but is also an implied criticism of Jewish Christians who adhere too closely to the old way (Trocmé, *Formation*, pp. 108-109; Schweizer, *Mark*, p. 64; Kelber, *Kingdom*, pp. 18-22; Kuhn [for his collection], *Sammlungen*, pp. 83-85, 96). The disciples, however, do not appear to be implicated in this criticism, for they follow the way of Jesus. Even in 2:18-22, in which the fasting after Jesus' death may well reflect historically a return to Jewish praxis, the text does not imply any criticism of the disciples who react appropriately to the presence/absence or death of Jesus. Insofar as 2:1-3:6 may be a markan polemic against his Jewish Christian opponents, it is the opponents not the disciples who represent the Jewish Christians.

[42]Another reason for the exclusion of the disciples from healing is the fact that 2:1-12 (A) deals with forgiveness of sins. Unlike healing in general, forgiveness remains the prerogative of Jesus alone. Even after Jesus' death, forgiveness is mediated "in the name of Jesus" or "through" him (Acts 2:38; 5:31; 10:43; 13:38; 26:18; Col 1:14).

[43]For the position that Jesus is arguing against suffering as a means to end-time glory for the disciples, see Kolenkow, "Beyond Miracles," pp. 160-165. See also Dewey, *Disciples*, pp. 81-94.

[44]Later in the gospel, acceptance or rejection of Jesus is presented as an ultimate life or death matter for the individual (8:34-9:1). However, unlike 2:1-3:6, it is not a matter of confrontation of the powers of life and death, but a matter of choice for the individual--whether to become a disciple or not.

[1]See above, pp. 35-36.

[2]David J. Clark ("Criteria for Identifying Chiasm," *Linguistica Biblica* 35 [1975] 63-66) classifies and attempts to give some "linguistic precision" to the criteria I employed in my article, "Structure," (1973). I have found his discussion helpful in clarifying my own criteria--sometimes in agreement, sometimes in disagreement with Clark.

[3]The phrase is from Clark ("Criteria," p. 65). The examples and methodological conclusions are mine.

[4]"Criteria," p. 65.

[5]"Jésus controversé," p. 132.

[6]*Ibid.*, p. 139; See above, p. 111.

[7]*Ibid.*, p. 132.

[8]"Criteria," p. 66.

[9]*Evangelium*, p. 160.

[10]*Beginnings*, p. 23.

[11]*Zusammensetzung*, p. 15. Lohmeyer (*Markus*, p. 49) views Mk 2:1-17 as three units dealing with sin.

[12]*Mark*, pp. 71-72.

[13]*Einführung*, pp. 38-39.

[14]"Considerazioni," pp. 326-331. Gamba calls his structure chiastic, although technically the term does not apply to it; he views four border scenes related to each other and all leading to the center (*Ibid.*, p. 330).

[15]*Ibid.*, pp. 324, 349. Indeed his structural outline of Mk 2:1-3:6 is a short prologue to his schematic outline or arrangement of Mk 2:1-12 into two and three-part clause divisions.

[16]Gamba (*Ibid.*, p. 329) also cites as part of the concentric structure the reversal of the role of Jesus and the disciples in 2:13-17 and 23-28. In the first, the disciples are questioned about Jesus; in the second, Jesus is questioned about the disciples. I would argue that this shift fits into the linear climactic development of the heightening of opposition. However, the reversal may be part of the parallel structure, or it may be the accidental consequence of bringing the disciples into the foreground in 2:13-28.

[17]"Jésus controversé," pp. 129-149.

[18]"Structure," pp. 394-401. My structure is essentially that presented above in Chapter IV, pp. 109—116.

[19]Mourlon Beernaert, "Jésus controversé," p. 130.

[20]*Ibid.*, p. 131.

[21]The following is virtually a translation of Mourlon Beernaert's summary ("Jésus controversé," p. 141). I have added additional hook words which he cites on pp. 138-140, and I have relettered his structure W, X, Y,... in order to avoid confusion with mine.

[22]A similar insistence on the oneness of the theological and literary structure may be found in other studies on markan structure by Mourlon Beernaert and his associates. See D. Dideberg and Mourlon Beernaert, "Jésus vint en Galilée," *NRT* 98 (1976) 306; Radermakers, "L'évangile de Marc. Structure et théologie," *L'évangile selon Marc. Tradition et rédaction* (ed. M. Sabbe; BETL 34; Gembloux: J. Duculot, 1976), p. 221, passim; Mourlon Beernaert, "Structure littéraire et lecture théologique de Marc 14,17-52," *ibid.*, p.266.

[23]"Jésus controversé," p. 129.

[24]*Ibid.*, p. 138.

[25]*Ibid.*, p. 139. The fact that even beginning with the two Son of Man sayings, Mourlon Beernaert still arrives at a concentric pattern is attributable to the large number of congruent parallels in 2:1-3:6.

[26]*Ibid.*, pp. 132-133.

[27]*Ibid.*, pp. 142-145.

[28]*Ibid.*, p. 141.

[29]See above, pp. 68-70.

[30]On the question of audience recognition, see Talbert, *Literary Patterns*, pp. 79-81.

[31]Mourlon Beernaert in his analysis does respect the natural aural subdivisions of 2:1-3:6, treating it either as five stories showing dramatic conflict or as a three-part pattern of sin and sabbath surrounding the central section. He ignores his seven-part structure in his interpretation.

[32]Daube, *New Testament*, pp. 67-71.

[33]Carlston, *Parables*, p. 11; Robert Banks, *Jesus and the Law in the Synoptic Tradition* (SNTSMS 28; Cambridge: Cambridge University, 1975), pp. 109, 117-118.

[34]Luke omits "praying" in his parallel to Mk 1:35 (Lk 4: 42), and omits Mk 6:46 altogether.

[35]Since Luke retains Mark's concentric structure, it seems permissible to refer to Luke's pericopes by the same letters used to refer to Mark's. A = Lk 5:17-26; B = 5:27-32; C = 5:33-39; B' = 6:1-5; and A' = 6:6-11.

[36]The combination and order "scribes and Pharisees" does not appear to be a set formula in Luke. He uses it in these two instances and 11:53; he uses "Pharisees and scribes" twice in 5:30 and 15:2; he uses "Pharisees and lawyers" twice, 5:17 and 7:30; and "lawyers and Pharisees" once, 14:3.

[37]Luke uses εἰς τὸ μέσον elsewhere only in 4:35, in the sabbath exorcism which has many connections to A and A'.

[38]Three of the nine uses in Acts also describe audience reaction (Acts 3:10; 5:17; 13:45).

[39]Luke also maintains the content parallels of sin in A and B, and sabbath in B' and A', although the hook words are not as exact parallels as in Mark.

[40]Luke also deletes two of Mark's parallels between B and B'. He omits "the sabbath was made for man, not man for the sabbath" in B', thus removing the structural parallelism of general proverb followed by christological saying climaxing B and B'. He drops the hook word, "have need," from B'. These seem minor compared to the parallelism of character roles in B and B', and the emphasis on eating.

[41]Since Luke has already described an attempt to throw Jesus headlong off the brow of a hill (4:29), it would not seem that Luke tones down the conclusion to the controversy section in order to moderate Mark's account of opposition to Jesus so early in his ministry. The omission of the death plot in Luke's conclusion does, however, weaken the life/death theme found in Mark.

[42]Thus Dibelius ("Structure," p. 154) writes, "Luke was the first to work them into a real unity."

[43]In addition to the passages enumerated below, Radermakers (*Bonne nouvelle*, passim) outlines many other markan sections in a concentric pattern. Some of his structures seem forced, with inadequate attention to form and to the natural episodic divisions of the narrative.

[44]"Jésus vint," pp. 306-323.

[45]"Criteria," pp. 66-71.

[46]*Marcus Interpretator: Stijl en Boodschap in Mc. 3,20-4,34* (Brugge-Utrecht: Desclée de Brouwer, 1969), pp. 74-85, 132-133.

[47]*Ibid.*, pp. 111-124, 133-134.

[48]"Structure de Marc, 8,27-9,13," pp. 543-561.

[49]"La structure de Mc., XIII," pp. 141-164. The article is a slight modification and abbreviation of the third chapter of his dissertation, *Die Redaktion der Markus-Apokalypse* (AnBi 28; Rome: Pontifical Biblical Institute, 1967).

[50]*The Gospel Accounts of the Death of Jesus* (Rome: Pontificia Universitas Gregoriana, 1970), pp. 39-42.

[51]For the argument that the prologue consists of vv. 1-15, with εὐαγγέλιον as an inclusio, see Keck, "Introduction," pp. 352-370. See also Lamarche, "Commencement de l'évangile de Jésus, Christ, Fils de Dieu (Mc 1,1)" *NRT* 92 (1970) 1035.

[52]Noted by Zerwick, *Markus-Stil*, p. 125.

[53]See Mk 9:11-13, where the disciples are told what the reader knows from the beginning.

[54]In addition, there are many problems in the exegesis of individual materials in the parable discourse. Such problems, however, fall outside the scope of the discussion of concentric structure in Mark.

[55]See above, pp. 75-76.

[56]Matthew excludes the sayings implying open teaching from his parable discourse in Mt 13. Luke ends his parallel to the markan discourse with the sayings implying revelation (Lk 8:16-18) and places his kingdom parables elsewhere (Lk 13). Thus, Luke's discourse has a movement from hidden to open. Luke, like Mark, combines parables and general sayings material, while Matthew restricts his discourse to parable material.

[57]Lund, *Chiasmus*, p. 41.

[58]See above, pp. 67-68, 80. Πάλιν in 4:1 refers back to 2:13.

[59]Lambrecht (*Marcus*, p. 121) views the entirety of vv. 1-2 as the introduction, and fails to note the concentric pattern of vv. 1-2a.

[60]Lambrecht (*Ibid.*) sees a three-part ring composition: vv. 3-9, 10-12, 13-20. He does not appear to notice that vv. 11-12 and v. 13 present two separate answers to the question in v. 10.

[61]Lambrecht's overall concentric pattern is the same, except that he makes the division between A and B between vv. 2 and 3 (*Ibid.*).

[62]See above, pp. 16-17.

[63]See above, pp. 55-60.

[64]See above, pp. 60-63.

[65] The usual explanation of the first temple visit, that Jesus was inspecting the temple prior to the temple cleansing (Taylor, *Mark*, p. 458; Schweizer, *Mark*, p. 229; Lane, *Mark*, p. 398; cf. Kelber, *Kingdom*, p. 98), would seem to reflect a continuing biographical interest foreign to the gospel of Mark. The postponement of the temple cleansing to the second day does serve a rhetorical purpose in Mark. It enables Mark to introduce a second and private approach to Jerusalem, during which Jesus curses the fig tree in the hearing of his disciples. For this, Mark needs a second approach to Jerusalem, not a previous visit to the temple in which Jesus looks around at everything.

[66] See above, pp. 105-106.

[67] Kelber, *Kingdom*, p. 98.

[68] Used elsewhere in Mark only in 10:21.

[69] While the parallelism between 12:41-44 and 14:3-9 does not appear to be mentioned in the literature, the contrast of the annointing at Bethany with its immediate context is often mentioned, and the contrast of the widow's behavior with that of the scribes is sometimes noted (Perrin, *Introduction*, p. 159; Lane, *Mark*, pp. 442, 491-492).

[70] Mk 12:40,42,43--the only uses in Mark.

[71] Given the literary relationship of 12:41-44 to 14:3-9 *and* to 12:38-40, Donahue's contention of loose catchword construction cannot be sustained (*The Christ*, p. 116). As in the instance of hook words between 1:45 and 2:1-2, the hook word "widow" is indicative of both a break and a continuity in the narrative.

[72] See above, pp. 56-57.

[73] See above, pp. 28-29.

[74] I.e., the dialogue form posited by Dodd, "Dialogue," pp. 54-60. Of these passages Dodd classifies only 12:13-17 as a dialogue. See above, pp. 27-28.

[75] Albertz (*Streitsgespräche*, pp. 19-22) rightly stresses the richness of the dialogue in the Jerusalem debate material.

[76] What Kuhn has called a "Jewish-type argument" (*Sammlungen*, p. 88).

[77] It is not clear, however, whether "teacher" should be considered a hook word indicative of structure or a key word indicating a theme of Jesus' public ministry in Jerusalem. Jesus is again addressed as "teacher" by the disciples in 13:1, part of the frame around the Jerusalem ministry. Furthermore, the verb, "to teach," introduces Jesus' sayings in the temple and about the Son of David (11:17; 12:35). It also occurs in the introductory statement by the questioners in 12:14. Finally, the noun, "teaching," is used in 11:18 and 12:38. Thus "teacher" in 12:14,19 and 32 may be part of the use of various forms of "teach" as key words in the Jerusalem ministry.

[78]Albertz, *Streitgespräche*, p. 18; Trocmé, *Jesus*, p. 53; Donahue, *The Christ*, pp. 117-118.

[79]Albertz, *Streitgespräche*, p. 26.

[80]*Jewish Antiquities*, xviii, 12-17.

[81]B. Sabbat 31a, as cited in Taylor, *Mark*, p. 486. See also Testaments of the Twelve Patriarchs, Issachar 5:2, 7:6; Dan 5:3.

[82]So Johnson, *Mark*, p. 202. Knox (*Sources*, Vol. 1, p. 91) notes that Jesus' answer to the Sadducees should lessen the Pharisees' hostility to him.

[83]In 12:13-17, Jesus speaks twice between the first and second speeches of the questioners.

[84]There are many other uses of hook words within each of the three debates (e.g., πλανάω in 12:24,27; καλῶς, ἰδὼν ὅτι... ἀπεκρίθη in 12:28,32,34) but they fall outside the scope of a discussion of larger structural units.

[85]Of the thirty uses of ἀποκρίνομαι in Mark, all but five occur in the context of dialogue, and may be translated into English (easily, if sometimes redundantly) as "answer" or "reply." In the four uses in which "say" rather than "answer" or "reply" would be the more normal translation, whatever the speaker is responding to is clear from the text: in 9:5,6, Peter is "replying to" the sight of Jesus talking with Elijah and Moses; in 11:14, Jesus is reacting to the fig tree's lack of figs; in 14:48, Jesus is responding to the fact that the group came out to arrest him away from the temple carrying swords and clubs. This brief survey of the evidence suggests that the last "odd" use, ἀποκρίνομαι in 12:35, may not be dismissed as a redundant participle but should be understood in the sense of Jesus' replying to the foregoing debates.

[86]For the use of the title, "Son of David," in Mark (10: 47-48; 11:10; 12:35-37) as part of Mark's polemic against royal messianism and Jewish nationalistic eschatological hopes, see John Dominic Crossan, "Redaction and Citation in Mark 11:9-10,17 and 14:27," *Book of Seminar Papers* (ed. Lane C. McGaughy; SBLASP 108; Society of Biblical Literature, 1972), Vol. 1, p. 28; Kelber, *Kingdom*, pp. 94-97. Johnson (*Mark*, p. 205) writes, "Mark is quite uninterested in it [Jesus' Davidic descent]; he regards it as irrelevant to Jesus' true nature...and he would ignore or deny it rather than confuse Jesus with the conventional Messiah." See also Lane, *Mark*, pp. 437-438.

[87]The parallelism of the two audience reactions may account for the apparently strange fact that the crowd reacts gladly to criticism of the idea of the Davidic Messiah.

[88]In order to enhance the parallelism, the scribes (rather than the Pharisees as in Matthew and Luke) may be the group condemned in 12:38-40. For the opponents in 12:1-12 are the chief priests, elders and scribes, the members of the Sanhedrin. Thus

the scribes are condemned in both instances. Both groups condemned are representatives of official Judaism, not of particular
religious factions.

[89]In all probability, 12:1-9 and 10-11 came to Mark already
joined in the tradition. In the Gospel of Thomas also, the texts
are adjacent (logia 65,66).

[90]The opening section need not always be the longer one.
In the three parallel passion predictions, it is the middle one
which is the shortest, and the last which is longest.

[91]*History and Interpretation*, p. 123.

[92]Johnson (*Mark*, pp. 24,55) considers 2:1-12 a transition
scene.

[93]Thus questions of Mark's anti-temple or anti-Jerusalem
polemic and his reorientation of Jewish or Jewish-Christian
eschatological hopes fall outside the scope of the discussion.
On these issues, see Kelber, *Kingdom*, pp. 92-128; Kolenkow,
"Beyond Miracles," pp. 172-183; Donahue, *The Christ*, pp. 113-135.

[94]See above, pp. 58-59.

[95]On Mark's general attitude toward civil and religious
authority, see Kolenkow, "Beyond Miracles," pp. 184-185. Lane
(*Mark*, pp. 412, 441) notes that the leading idea of 11:27-12:27
is that "the leaders of the Jewish people have rejected the will
of God," and that 12:38-40 reinforces the conflict between Jesus
and the Jewish authorities.

[96]Commentators, beginning with Matthew (Mt 22:46) and Luke
(Lk 20:40) have felt that the audience reaction, "And after that
no one dared to ask him any question" (Mk 12:34), belongs after
an incident in which Jesus and his opponents have disagreed, not
when they have agreed. Günther Bornkamm, virtually alone among
scholars, sees that it is the agreement of Jesus and the scribe
which silences opposition. He writes that the phrase, if not
displaced, "nur besagen kann: hier ist eine letzte Wahrheit
ausgesprochen, über die hinaus es nichts mehr zu fragen und zu
sagen gibt." ("Das Doppelgebot der Liebe," *Neutestamentliche
Studien für Rudolf Bultmann zu seinem siebzigsten geburtstag*,
2d ed. [Berlin: Alfred Töpelmann, 1957], p. 90).

[97]This sequence of developments is not dissimilar from
that of many radicals in the 1960's, such as the Berrigan brothers
or William Sloane Coffin. In symbolic acts of civil disobedience
and preaching, they attacked the establishment, calling attention
to themselves. And their defense was that they were the ones who
truly were acting in accord with the United States Consitution
and the Bill of Rights.

[98]The debates showing Jesus' agreement with Pharisaic
Judaism also serve the function of reassuring the Jewish-Chris-
tians in Mark's audience that Jesus is a legitimate Jew and suc-
cessor to Judaism. While the way of Jesus (and the disciples)
breaks with the Pharisaic way in matters of tablefellowship,

sabbath observance, and food regulations (2:1-3:6; 7), the way
of Jesus stands in continuity with the old way in the belief in
resurrection and in the understanding of the fundamental demand
of God.

[99]Scholars such as Lightfoot (*History and Interpretation*,
p. 124) and Burkill (*Revelation*, p. 203) have recognized the
emphasis in Mk 12 on the unjustifiable nature of the opponents'
hostility to Jesus, though they have not connected it with the
fact that the public debates show Jesus' agreement with some
Jewish beliefs.

[100]Lightfoot (*History and Interpretation*, pp. 123-124)
writes about Mark 11-12, "a connexion seems to be implied between the doom which hangs over the Jewish nation, and the impending death of the Messiah himself. Each is involved in the
ruin of the other. By rejecting the Messiah and encompassing
his end, his own nation brings condemnation on itself and he
goes down with it." In 12:1-40, the argument moves beyond the
immediate consequences for Jesus and Jerusalem, to God's ultimate
condemnation of the Jewish leaders and God's power of resurrection.

[101]For example, Kuhn (*Sammlungen*, pp. 99-146, esp. pp. 122-
146) argues, on the whole convincingly, that Mk 4:3-10, (λέγει
αὐτοῖς from v. 13), 14-20, 26-33 is a premarkan parable collection. If Kuhn is correct, then Mark has inserted vv. 11-13 into
vv. 3-20 (B) in such a way that vv. 3-20 have a five-part symmetrical pattern. And he has expanded the introduction and conclusion and inserted vv. 21-25 in such a way that the entire
parable discourse also has a five-part symmetrical pattern.
Both interpolations are necessary to their respective symmetrical structures and together they present the paradox involved
in understanding parables. If Kuhn is correct in his recon-
struction of the premarkan parable collection, then the markan
insertions are a strong argument for extended concentric patterns as a *markan* literary technique for structuring material.
(Kuhn's literary argument, however, that καὶ ἔλεγεν αὐτοῖς [vv.
2,11,21,24] is a markan introductory formula while καὶ ἔλεγεν
[vv. 9,26,30] derives from the tradition seems weak [*Ibid.*, pp.
130-131]. Mark easily could have inserted αὐτοῖς after ἔλεγεν
in his source if his preference for an indirect object were
that strong. Ἔλεγεν without an indirect object is employed in
12:35,38 which appear to be markan connectives.)

[102]See above, pp. 60-61.

[103]Knox (*Sources*, Vol. 1, p. 88) suggests that 11:27-33 and
12:13-27 might have been gathered together prior to Mark. However, he considers even this doubtful.

[104]See above, pp. 131-136.

[105]Audience reactions occurred at the end of A and A' in
2:1-3:6 and at the end of B, C, C', and B' in 12:1-40. In 2:1-
3:6, the audience reactions might be attributed to the form--
healings are frequently followed by an audience response. In
12:1-40, however, the presence of audience reaction cannot be
attributed to the form, since neither direct teachings nor pronouncement stories are usually followed by an audience response.

[106]In 4:1-34, the introductions in vv. 26 and 30 are not precisely paralleled; and in 12:1-40, the introduction in v. 38 has no parallel at all.

[107]This fact suggests that hook words not closely related to content are more significant than those which are--e.g., "heart" in 2:6,8; 3:5 is more significant than "crowd" in 12:12, 37.

[108]See above, pp. 137-140, and Chapter V, fns. 59, 60.

[109]"Jésus vint," pp. 314-317.

[110]"Criteria," pp. 66-71.

[111]The only argument presented for the rhetorical unity of 1:21-45 is that 1:21 and 1:45 are an inclusio based on the parallels of Καφαρναύμ/πόλιν, εἰσελθών/εἰσελθεῖν, ἦν/ἦν ("Jésus vint," p. 316). The inclusio appears unconvincing.

[112]Farrer (Mark, p. 65) also notes the parallel between unclean man and unclean spirit.

[113]In addition, silence is imposed in both A and A' and in the center, D. The imposition to silence in A is the actual exorcism formula (as in 4:39) and not a command to secrecy as in D and A' (1:25,34,44). In spite of this difference, the commands to silence would be a strong argument for the pattern *if* the symmetrical pattern as a whole with vv. 32-34 as a central unparalleled unit were tenable.

[114]Schweizer, "Anmerkungen," pp. 36-37; Gaston, *Horae*, pp. 20, 58.

[115]Dideberg and Mourlon Beernaert do note the frequency of "immediately" but only as an indication of the "dynamic movement" of the text ("Jésus vint," p. 312.) They do not consider its possible relationship to structure, or address themselves to the question of why it does not occur at all in 1:32-39.

[116]A similar problem was noted in Mourlon Beernaert's analysis of 2:1-3:6. See above, pp. 138-140.

[117]Dideberg and Mourlon Beernaert do not employ the criterion of form-critical similarity. Several of the similarities they posit between A and A' are in fact characteristics of the healing form ("Jésus vint," p. 315). They also argue for a similarity in structure, each a healing with three principal parts (*Ibid.*). In discussing Clark's pattern, it will be argued that the parallelisms of structure are greater between 1:21-28 and 2:1-12.

[118]"Jésus vint," p. 316. If the distinction between general notations and particular scenes is to be observed, 1:45b should be separated from its pericope as another general notation, not treated as part of A'.

[119]It has been noted several times previously that symmetrical patterns often contain asymmetrical elements (e.g., the Son

[106]In 4:1-34, the introductions in vv. 26 and 30 are not precisely paralleled; and in 12:1-40, the introduction in v. 38 has
no parallel at all.

[107]This fact suggests that hook words not closely related to
content are more significant than those which are--e.g., "heart"
in 2:6,8; 3:5 is more significant than "crowd" in 12:12, 37.

[108]See above, pp. 137-140, and Chapter V, fns. 59, 60.

[109]"Jesus vint," pp. 314-317.

[110]"Criteria," pp. 66-71.

[111]The only argument presented for the rhetorical unity of
1:21-45 is that 1:21 and 1:45 are an inclusio based on the parallels of Καφαρναούμ/πόλιν, εἰσελθὼν/εἰσελθεῖν, ἦν/ἦν ("Jesus vint,"
p. 316). The inclusio appears unconvincing.

[112]Farrer (Mark, p. 65) also notes the parallel between unclean man and unclean spirit.

[113]In addition, silence is imposed in both A and A' and in
the center, D. The imposition to silence in A is the actual
exorcism formula (as in 4:39) and not a command to secrecy as
in D and A' (1:25,34,44). In spite of this difference, the commands to silence would be a strong argument for the pattern *if*
the symmetrical pattern as a whole with vv. 32-34 as a central
unparalleled unit were tenable.

[114]Schweizer, "Anmerkungen," pp. 36-37; Gaston, Horae, pp.
20, 58.

[115]Dideberg and Mourlon Beernaert do note the frequency of
"immediately" but only as an indication of the "dynamic movement" of the text ("Jesus vint," p. 312.) They do not consider
its possible relationship to structure, or address themselves
to the question of why it does not occur at all in 1:32-39.

[116]A similar problem was noted in Mourlon Beernaert's
analysis of 2:1-3:6. See above, pp. 138-140.

[117]Dideberg and Mourlon Beernaert do not employ the criterion of form-critical similarity. Several of the similarities they posit between A and A' are in fact characteristics of
the healing form ("Jesus vint," p. 315). They also argue for
a similarity in structure, each a healing with three principle
parts (Ibid.). In discussing Clark's pattern, it will be argued
that the parallelisms of structure are greater between 1:21-28
and 2:1-12.

[118]"Jesus vint," p. 316. If the distinction between general
notations and particular scenes is to be observed, 1:45b should
be separated from its pericope as another general notation, not
treated as part of A'.

[119]It has been noted several times previously that symmetrical patterns often contain asymmetrical elements (e.g., the Son

of Man in 2:1-3:6). However, for an element to stand out as
asymmetrical, the overall symmetry must first be demonstrated.

[120]Dewey, "Structure;" Clark, "Criteria," p. 66.

[121]"Criteria," pp. 66-71. The sections have been relettered
to facilitate the discussion. Also, what Clark labels "chiasm"
is more appropriately labelled "concentric" or "symmetrical
structure" and is so referred to in the discussion.

[122]In addition, Clark has posited an "X" layer standing
outside of the pyramidal structure which he labels a "ladder
parallelism." It consists of X1, 1:16-20; X2, 2:13-14; and X3,
3:7-12 (Ibid., pp. 68-69). Clark argues, correctly, that concentric symmetry is only one type of a general literary phenomenon which may be called "recursion," and that "different types
of recursion may interpenetrate each other" (Ibid., p. 69, itali-
cized). Clark's conclusions about recursion appear valid, as
may be seen in the rhetorical structure of Mk 11-12 (see above,
pp. 153-155). His proposed "X" layer, however, does not seem
rhetorically sound. The major difficulty is that X1 and X2 are
more closely related in content to 3:13-19, the choosing of the
twelve, than to X3, 3:7-12, which appears to be a continuation
of 1:45 (see above, pp. 105-106).

[123]"Criteria," pp. 69-70. Koch (Wunderzählungen, pp. 42-
55) argues for a close connection theologically between these
three pericopes on the grounds of markan redactional additions
and ordering of materials. The fact that Clark on literary
grounds and Koch on redactional grounds both group the same
three miracles suggests that they may be correct (i.e., the
criterion of multiple methodologies).

[124]Pesch (Naherwartungen, p. 57) notes that Jesus' public
work in the first section of the gospel begins and ends in a
synagogue.

[125]Εἰσελθὼν in 1:21 is textually uncertain.

[126]Robinson (History, pp. 44-45) appears correct in his
observation of the similarity of form between the exorcisms and
the controversy apophthegms: "The demon advances upon Jesus
with a hostile challenge, only to be silenced by an authoritative word of Jesus."

[127]Pesch (Naherwartungen, p. 57) notes that the antithetical
audience reactions in 1:21-28 and 3:1-6 emphasize the contrast
between the two scenes. Clark, on the other hand, sees the
movement as one from puzzlement or mystification in 1:21-28 to
polarization for or against Jesus in 2:1-12 and 3:1-6 ("Criteria,"
p. 69). While Clark is correct in emphasizing the necessity of
choice for or against Jesus, the audience reaction in 1:21-28
would seem to be wholeheartedly favorable, both from its explicit
content, and from the facts that as a consequence of Jesus' activity, word of Jesus spread throughout all of Galilee, and at
the end of the sabbath, the whole town gathers around Jesus (1:
28,33).

[128]In Mk 1:21-3:8, Ἀπόλλυμι is also used in the middle voice, in the sense of "be lost" in 2:22.

[129]Thus I would agree with Best (*Temptation*, pp. 18-30) that the temptation represents Jesus' victory over Satan against Robinson's (*History*, pp. 28-32) argument that the temptation is the introductory confrontation. See also Howard Clark Kee, "The Terminology of Mark's Exorcism Stories," *NTS* 14 (1967-68) 242-246.

[130]"Criteria," p. 70. Clark's argument that the healings are described similarly (ἀφῆκεν αὐτὴν ὁ πυτερός, ἀπῆλθεν ἀπ' αὐτοῦ ἡ λέπρα, 1:31,42) appears to be due to the miracle form. See 3:5: ἀπεκατεστάθη ἡ χεὶρ αὐτοῦ.

[131]Mark uses the exact phrase κρατήσας τῆς χειρός in 1:31, 5:41 and 9:27. Furthermore, touching or laying on of hands by the healer is a typical method of healing (1:41; 5:23; 6:2,5; 7:35; 8:23,25).

[132]Both take place in a house in Capernaum, probably Simon's house, and both are resurrection-type miracles employing the verb, ἐγείρω. This parallelism is stressed by Farrer, *Mark*, pp. 65-66, and Radermakers, *Bonne nouvelle*, Vol. 2, p. 92.

[133]"Criteria," p. 70.

[134]See above, pp.132-136 and 168-171.

[135]The material presents many rhetorical clues. For example, 1:32-34 and 1:39 as well as 1:21-28 are ring compositions. Mark 1:35-38 and 1:40-45 are marked by inclusios.

[136]"Form Criticism," p. 18.

CHAPTER VI

[1]Much as Luke adapted the structure from Mark. See above, pp. 141-143. Mark's source, if any, would be basically that hypothesized by Albertz.

[2]In order for 2:1-3:6 to be a self-contained independent source, it would also be necessary to delete the prospective references in 3:6 to 12:13 and to Jesus' passion, particularly 15:1-4. These prospective references could be explained as Mark's editorial modification of the source's conclusion.

[3]Luke, in his editing of Mk 2:13-17, has dropped the preceding retrospective references but has kept the call of Levi (Lk 5:27-32).

[4]See above, pp. 86-87.

[5]See above, pp. 113-114.

[6]In Budesheim's hypothesis of a premarkan *Geschichtsverlauf Jesus* including 1:16-3:19, both 1:16-20 and 2:14 are viewed as premarkan ("Jesus," pp. 203, 205). In this case, the structure of 2:1-3:6 could also be premarkan. However, the fact that neither 1:16-20 nor 2:13-28 portray an exaltation of the disciples as θεῖοι ἄνδρες suggests there is no need to posit a premarkan source for 1:16-3:19. See above, Chapter IV, fn. 40.

[7]Luke has dropped this motif.

[8]Bultmann, *History*, p. 209.

[9]*Mark*, p. 101.

[10]See above, pp. 14, 151-152.

[11]On the use of frames in the Jerusalem ministry, see above, pp. 153-155.

[12]One could, of course, argue that the use of the technique in 2:1-12 in the source suggested to Mark the use of the same technique for the section as a whole. However, the unusual nature of the technique, which we know to be markan from the intercalations and the fact that the theme of Jesus' popularity with the crowd appears to be a markan motif in 1:16-3:12, suggests that Mark is responsible for the use of the technique in 2:1-12.

[13]*Streitgespräche*, p. 5. Kuhn (*Sammlungen*, p. 87) also views 2:10,20 and 28 as the result of Mark's use of a collection.

[14]For scholars who view the use of Son of Man in 2:10,28 as consonant with Mark's theology, see above, Chapter III, fn. 48.

[15] See above, pp. 122-125.

[16] For some scholars who see the emphasis on Jesus' authority as a major theme of 1:16-3:6, see Schweizer, *Mark*, pp. 7, 75; Pesch, *Naherwartungen*, pp. 57-58; "Zöllnergastmahl," p. 86; Koch, *Wundererzählungen*, pp. 33, 42-55; Perrin, *Pilgrimage*, p. 117.

[17] This does not mean that Mark necessarily created the sayings in 2:10 and 2:28, but simply that Mark was sufficiently in agreement with the sayings to employ them or to incorporate traditions which employed them. A related issue is the lack of any secrecy motif in 2:1-3:6. I would agree with Weeden (*Mark*, p. 65, fn. 20; p. 67) that the title Son of Man per se is exempt from the secrecy motif.

[18] In addition to Albertz, *Streitgespräche*, pp. 6, 107, see also Weiss, *Evangelium*, p. 154; Knox, *Sources*, Vol. 1, p. 8; Taylor, *Mark*, p. 91; Schmid, *Mark*, p. 58; Kuhn, *Sammlungen*, pp. 222-223; Hultgren, "Adversaries," pp. 279-280.

[19] The emphasis in 1:16-3:6 seems to be equally on Jesus' teaching and miracles. So Budesheim, "Jesus," p. 201; Kee, "Exorcism," p. 242. Contra Koch (*Wundererzählungen*, pp. 52-55), the miracles are not subordinated to the teaching.

[20] Kelber, *Kingdom*, p. 23. See also Robinson, *History*, p. 47; Lane, *Mark*, p. 91.

[21] Henry Beach Carré, "The Literary Structure of the Gospel of Mark," *Studies in Early Christianity* (ed. Shirley Jackson Case; New York: Century, 1928), pp. 105-106, 113-115.

[22] "Mark 3:7-12 and Mark's Christology," *JBL* 84 (1965) 344-345.

[23] So Schweizer, *Mark*, p. 75; Geoltrain, "Violation," p. 72.

[24] See Robert Scholes and Robert Kellogg, *The Nature of Narrative* (New York: Oxford University, 1968), pp. 51-52.

[25] An ancient audience, accustomed to an omniscient narrator and to familiarity with the general plot, might well interpret the disciples' lack of recognition of Jesus as the Christ until 8:29 as normal narrative technique and not in itself an indication of the disciples' lack of understanding. The indications of the disciples' lack of or misunderstanding are usually quite explicit (e.g., 4:13,35-41; 8:14-21, 32-33).

[26] For scholars who view 3:6 as part of Mark's theological interest, see above, Chapter II, fns. 29, 31.

[27] Thus I would agree with Kolenkow ("Beyond Miracles," pp. 157-160, 186-189) against Weeden (*Mark*, pp. 55-69, 160-164) that Mark is not arguing against miracle-based power in itself. Healings would appear to fade into the background after 8:26 because Mark is no longer discussing the life of the kingdom, but in 8:27-10:45, the way of the cross, discipleship and service, and in 11-13, the proper understanding of eschatology over against Jewish nationalistic eschatological hopes.

[28]See above, pp. 165-166.

[29]Ropes, *Synoptic Gospels*, p. 11.

[30]Kolenkow, "Healing Controversy," pp. 636-637.

[31]Kolenkow (*Ibid.*, p. 629) suggests that the use of these two words in 15:1-4 is due to Mark's resumption of the use of a source. Here it is argued that the words serve the rhetorical function in Mark of recalling 3:1-6 to the reader's mind. Given the various parallels between 2:1-12 and 14:55-64 and between 3:1-6 and 15:1-15, it would seem that if Mark used the source proposed by Kolenkow, he has used the source very freely, creating his own rhetorical structure.

[32]It is the only use of κακοποιέω in Mark. Κακός is used elsewhere only in 7:21.

[33]See above, pp. 121-122.

[34]On 8:34-9:1, see Dewey, *Disciples*, pp. 74-81.

[35]See above, p. 166.

[36]Via, in his structuralist analysis of Mark, argues that "the opposition death/resurrection is the fundamental kernel out of which the narrative as a whole develops" (*Kerygma*, p. 117) and for Mark, "life comes through death" (*Ibid.*, p. 128). I would agree with Via on the centrality of the death/life theme in Mark, but I would see the theme as more complex and varied than simply life through death.

[37]*Son of Man*, p. 179.

[38]*Pilgrimage*, p. 117. Perrin argues that Mark was the first to take the step of linking the authority of Jesus' earthly ministry with the Son of Man (*Ibid.*). The rhetorical analyses have shown that the authority of Jesus during his earthly ministry is indeed a markan interest in 1:16-3:6 (see especially 1:21-28; 2:1-12,23-28). If Mark was the first to make the link, then it would appear that Mark has adapted sayings about the heavenly Son of Man's authority over Christian praxis. See Minette de Tillese (*Secret*, pp. 367-368) who argues that 2:10,28 are an anticipation or retrojection of the glory of Easter. That Mark has made the transition between the heavenly authority of the Son of Man over Christian praxis to the earthly authority of Jesus could be used as an argument for Kuhn's collection. In that case Mark would have employed a source arguing for the Son of Man's authority over the church, and modified it to argue for Jesus' authority in his earthly life. Against this argument, it may be stated that the proposed collection already refers to Jesus' earthly life in his mission to sinners (2:17b, see 1:38) and in the bridegroom image (2:19-20). It is difficult to distinguish the christology of Kuhn's source from Mark's christology.

[39]The argument may not be regarded as conclusive, for, as has already been seen in Mk 11-12, Mark is capable of elaborate rhetorical structures of his own compilation.

[40]See above, pp. 77-79, 98, 122-125.

BIBLIOGRAPHY

Achtemeier, Paul J. *Mark*. Proclamation Commentaries. Philadelphia: Fortress, 1975.

Albertz, Martin. *Die synoptischen Streitgespräche*. Berlin:
Trowitzsch & Sohn, 1921.

Alonso-Schökel, Luis. *Estudios de Poética Hebrea*. Barcelona:
Juan Flors, 1963.

_____. "Poésie Hébraïque," *Dictionaire de la Bible: Supplé-
ment*. Paris: Letouzey et Ané, 1972. Vol. 8, cols. 49-90.

Ambrozic, Aloysius M. *The Hidden Kingdom: A Redaction-Critical
Study of the References to the Kingdom of God in Mark's
Gospel*. CBQMS 2. Washington: Catholic Biblical Associa-
tion, 1972.

Auerbach, Erich. *Mimesis: The Representation of Reality in
Western Literature*. Translated by Willard Trask. New York:
Doubleday Anchor, 1957.

Bacon, Benjamin Wisner. *The Beginnings of the Gospel Story*.
New Haven: Yale University, 1909.

_____. *The Gospel of Mark: Its Composition and Date*. New
Haven: Yale University, 1925.

Bailey, K.E. "Recovering the Poetic Structure of I Cor i 17-ii
2. A Study in Text and Commentary," *NovT* 17 (1975) 265-
296.

Ball, Ivan Jay, Jr. "A Rhetorical Study of Zephaniah." Th.D.
dissertation, Graduate Theological Union (Berkeley), 1972.

Banks, Robert. *Jesus and the Law in the Synoptic Tradition*.
SNTSMS 28. Cambridge: Cambridge University, 1975.

Barré, Michael L. "Paul as 'Eschatologic Person': A New Look
at 2 Cor 11:29," *CBQ* 37 (1975) 500-526.

Bauer, Walter. *A Greek-English Lexicon of the New Testament
and Other Early Christian Literature*. Translated and
adapted by William F. Arndt and F. Wilbur Gingrich from
4th Ger. ed., 1952. Chicago: University of Chicago, 1957.

Beardslee, William A. *Literary Criticism of the New Testament*.
Philadelphia: Fortress, 1970.

Beck, Ingrid. *Die Ringkomposition bei Herodot und ihre Bedeutung
für die Beweistechnik*. New York: Georg Olms, 1971.

Bennett, W.J., Jr. "The Herodians of Mark's Gospel," *NovT* 17
(1975) 9-14.

Bertman, Stephen. "Symmetrical Design in the Book of Ruth," *JBL* 84 (1965) 165-168.

Best, Ernest. *The Temptation and the Passion: The Markan Soteriology*. SNTSMS 2. Cambridge: Cambridge University, 1965.

Bird, C.H. "Some γαρ clauses in St. Mark's Gospel," *JTS* 4 (1953) 171-187.

Blass, F., and Debrunner, A. *A Greek Grammar of the New Testament and Other Early Christian Literature*. Translated and revised by Robert W. Funk from 9-10th Ger. ed. Chicago: University of Chicago, 1961.

Blatherwick, David. "The Markan Silhouette?" *NTS* 17 (1970-71) 184-192.

Bligh, John. *Galatians in Greek*. Detroit: University of Detroit, 1966.

Boismard, M.-E. *Le prologue de Saint Jean*. Paris: Éditions du Cerf, 1953.

Boobyer, G.H. "Mark II,10a and the Interpretation of the Healing of the Paralytic," *HTR* 47 (1954) 115-120.

Booth, Wayne C. *The Rhetoric of Fiction*. Chicago: University of Chicago, 1961.

Bornkamm, Günther. "Das Doppelgebot der Liebe," *Neutestamentliche Studien für Rudolf Bultmann zu seinem siebzigsten Geburtstag*. 2d ed. Edited by Walther Eltester. Berlin: Töpelmann, 1957. Pp. 85-93.

Bowman, John. *The Gospel of Mark: The New Christian Jewish Passover Haggadah*. Leiden: E.J. Brill, 1965.

Budesheim, Thomas L. "Jesus and the Disciples in Conflict with Judaism," *ZNW* 62 (1971) 190-209.

Bultmann, Rudolf. *The History of the Synoptic Tradition*. Translated by John Marsh. New York: Harper & Row, 1963.

Burkill, T.A. *Mysterious Revelation*. Ithaca: Cornell University, 1963.

_____. *New Light on the Earliest Gospel: Seven Markan Studies*. Ithaca: Cornell University, 1972.

Buschel, Friedrich. "κατηγορέω," *TDNT*. Vol. 3, p. 637.

Cadoux, C.J. "The Imperatival Use of ἵνα in the New Testament," *JTS* 42 (1941) 165-173.

Carlston, Charles E. *The Parables of the Triple Tradition*. Philadelphia: Fortress, 1975.

Carré, Henry Beach. "The Literary Structure of the Gospel of Mark," *Studies in Early Christianity*. Edited by Shirley Jackson Case. New York: Century, 1928. Pp. 105-126.

Ceresko, Anthony R. "The Chiastic Word Pattern in Hebrew," *CBQ* 38 (1976) 303-311.

Ceroke, Christian P. "Is Mark 2:10 a Saying of Jesus?" *CBQ* 22 (1960) 369-390.

Clark, David J. "Criteria for Identifying Chiasm," *Linguistica Biblica* 35 (1975) 63-72.

Condamin, Albert. "Symmetrical Repetitions in Lamentations Chapters I and II," *JTS* 7 (1906) 137-140.

Cranfield, C.E.B. *The Gospel According to Saint Mark.* Cambridge: Cambridge University, 1959.

Crossan, John Dominic. "Redaction and Citation in Mark 11:9-10,17 and 14:27," *Book of Seminar Papers.* Edited by Lane C. McGaughy. SBLASP 108. Society of Biblical Literature, 1972. Vol. 1, pp. 17-61.

Daube, David. *The New Testament and Rabbinic Judaism.* London: Athlone, 1956.

_____. "The Earliest Structure of the Gospels," *NTS* 5 (1958-59) 174-187.

_____. "Responsibilities of Master and Disciples in the Gospels," *NTS* 19 (1972-73) 1-15.

Deeks, David. "The Structure of the Fourth Gospel," *NTS* 15 (1968-69) 107-129.

Delorme, J. "Aspects doctrinaux du second Évangile. Études récentes de la rédaction de Marc," *De Jésus aux Évangiles.* Edited by I. de La Potterie. BETL 25:2. Gembloux: J. Duculot, 1967. Pp. 74-99.

Dewey, Joanna. "The Literary Structure of the Controversy Stories in Mark 2:1-3:6," *JBL* 92 (1973) 394-401.

_____. *Disciples of the Way: Mark on Discipleship.* Women's Division, Board of Global Ministries, United Methodist Church, 1976.

Dibelius, Martin. "The Structure and Literary Character of the Gospels," *HTR* 20 (1927) 151-170.

_____. *From Tradition to Gospel.* Translated by Bertram Lee Woolf. The Scribner Library. New York: Charles Scribner's Sons, n.d.

Dideberg, D., and Mourlon Beernaert, P. "Jésus vint en Galilée," *NRT* 98 (1976) 306-323.

Di Marco, Angelico. "Der Chiasmus in der Bibel: 1. Teil," *Linguistica Biblica* 36 (1975) 21-97.

_____. "Der Chiasmus in der Bibel: 2. Teil," *Linguistica Biblica* 37 (1976) 49-68.

256

_____. "Der Chiasmus in der Bibel: 3. Teil," _Linguistica
Biblica_ 39 (1976) 37-85.

Dobschütz, Ernst von. "Zur Erzählerkunst des Markus," _ZNW_ 27
(1928) 193-198.

Dodd, C.H. "The Dialogue Form in the Gospels," _BJRL_ 37 (1954-
55) 54-67.

Doeve, Jan Willem. _Jewish Hermeneutics in the Synoptic Gospels
and Acts_. Assen: Van Gorcum, n.d.

Donahue, John R. "Tax Collectors and Sinners," _CBQ_ 33 (1971)
39-61.

_____. _Are You the Christ? The Trial Narrative in the Gospel
of Mark_. SBLDS 10. Missoula, Montana: Society of Biblical
Literature for the Seminar on Mark. 1973.

Doudna, John Charles. _The Greek of the Gospel of Mark_. SBLMS
12. Philadelphia: Society of Biblical Literature, 1961.

Duckworth, George E. _Structural Patterns and Proportions in
Vergil's Aeneid_. Ann Arbor: University of Michigan, 1962.

Easton, Burton Scott. "A Primitive Tradition in Mark," _Studies
in Early Christianity_. Edited by Shirley Jackson Case.
New York: Century, 1928. Pp. 85-101.

Elliott, John H. "Man and the Son of Man in the Gospel According to Mark," _Humane Gesellschaft: Beiträge zu ihrer
sozialen Gestaltung_. Edited by Trutz Rendtorff and Arthur
Rich. Zurich: Zwingli, 1970. Pp. 47-59.

Farrer, Austin. _A Study in St Mark_. London: Dacre, 1951.

Faw, Chalmer E. "The Outline of Mark," _JBR_ 25 (1957) 19-23.

Fenton, John C. "Destruction and Salvation in the Gospel According to St. Mark," _JTS_ 3 (1952) 56-58.

_____. "Inclusio and Chiasmus in Matthew," _Studia Evangelica_.
International Congress on New Testament Studies. Edited
by Kurt Aland, et al. Berlin: Akademie-Verlag, 1959.
Vol. 73, pp. 174-179.

Francis, Fred O. "The Baraita of the Four Sons," _Book of Seminar Papers_. Edited by Lane C. McGaughy. SBLASP 108.
Society of Biblical Literature, 1972. Vol. 1, pp. 245-283.

Frye, Northrop. _Anatomy of Criticism_. Princeton: Princeton
University, 1971.

Frye, Roland Mushat. "A Literary Perspective for the Criticism
of the Gospels," _Jesus and Man's Hope_. Edited by Donald
G. Miller and Dikran Y. Hadidian. Pittsburgh: Pittsburgh
Theological Seminary (A Perspective Book), 1971. Vol. 2,
pp. 193-221.

Gaechter, Paul. *Die literarische Kunst im Matthäus-Evangelium.*
SBS 7. Stuttgart: Katholisches Bibelwerk, n.d.

Gamba, Giuseppe G. "Considerazioni in margine alla poetica di
Mc. 2,1-12," *Salesianum* 28 (1966) 324-349.

Gaston, Lloyd. *Horae Synopticae Electronicae: Word Statistics
of the Synoptic Gospels.* SBLSBS 3. Missoula, Montana:
Society of Biblical Literature, 1973.

Geoltrain, Pierre. "La violation du Sabbat: Une lecture de
Marc 3,1-6," *Foi et Vie* 69 (1970) 70-90.

Gerhardsson, Birger. *Memory and Manuscript: Oral Tradition
and written Transmission in Rabbinic Judaism and Early
Christianity.* Translated by Eric J. Sharpe. Uppsala:
C.W.K. Gleerup, 1961.

Giblin, Charles Homer. "Structural and Thematic Correlations
in the Matthean Burial-Resurrection Narrative (Matt. xxvii.
57-xxviii.20)," *NTS* 21 (1974-75) 406-420.

Good, Edwin M. *Irony in the Old Testament.* Philadelphia:
Westminster, 1965.

Grob, Rudolf. *Einführung in das Markus-Evangelium.* Zürich:
Zwingli, 1965.

Grobel, Kendrick. "A Chiastic Retribution-Formula in Romans
2," *Zeit und Geschichte: Dankesgabe an Rudolf Bultmann
zum 80. Geburtstag.* Edited by Erich Dinkler. Tübingen:
J.C.B. Mohr, 1964. Pp. 255-261.

Gros Louis, Kenneth R.R., ed. *Literary Interpretations of
Biblical Narratives.* With James S. Ackerman and Thayer
S. Warshaw. Nashville: Abingdon, 1974.

Grundmann, Walter. *Das Evangelium nach Markus.* Berlin: Evange-
lische Verlagsanstalt, n.d.

Haenchen, Ernst. *Der Weg Jesu.* Berlin: Alfred Töpelmann, 1966.

Hawkins, John C. *Horae Synopticae: Contributions to the Study
of the Synoptic Problem.* 2d ed. Oxford: Clarendon, 1909.

Hay, Lewis S. "The Son of Man in Mark 2:10 and 2:28," *JBL* 89
(1970) 69-75.

Hirsch, Eric D., Jr. *Validity in Interpretation.* New Haven:
Yale University, 1967.

Hobbs, Edward C. "The Gospel of Mark and the Exodus." Ph.D.
dissertation, University of Chicago, 1952.

_____. "A Different Approach to the Writing of Commentaries
on the Synoptic Gospels," *A Stubborn Faith: Papers on Old
Testament and Related Subjects Presented to Honor William
Andrew Irwin.* Edited by Edward C. Hobbs. Dallas: Southern
Methodist University, 1956. Pp. 155-163.

Hooker, Morna D. *The Son of Man in Mark*. London: SPCK, 1967.

Hultgren, Arland J. "Jesus and his Adversaries: A Study of the Form and Function of the Conflict Stories in the Synoptic Tradition." Th.D. dissertation, Union Theological Seminary (New York), 1971.

_____. "The Formation of the Sabbath Pericope in Mark 2:23-28," *JBL* 91 (1972) 38-43.

Jackson, Jared J., and Kessler, Martin, eds. *Rhetorical Criticism: Essays in Honor of James Muilenburg*. Pittsburgh Theological Monograph Series No. 1. Pittsburgh: Pickwick, 1974.

Jeffrey, Arthur. "Daniel," *Interpreter's Bible*. New York and Nashville: Abingdon, 1956. Vol. 6, pp. 341-549.

Johnson, Sherman E. *A Commentary on the Gospel According to St. Mark*. London: Adam & Charles Black, 1960.

Keck, Leander E. "Mark 3:7-12 and Mark's Christology," *JBL* 84 (1965) 341-358.

_____. "The Introduction to Mark's Gospel," *NTS* 12 (1965-66) 352-370.

Kee, Howard Clark. "The Terminology of Mark's Exorcism Stories," *NTS* 14 (1967-68) 232-246.

_____. *Community of the New Age: Studies in Mark's Gospel*. Philadelphia: Westminster, 1977.

Kelber, Werner H. *The Kingdom in Mark: A New Place and a New Time*. Philadelphia: Fortress, 1974.

_____, ed. *The Passion in Mark*. Philadelphia: Fortress, 1976.

Kilpatrick, G.D. "Some Notes on Marcan Usage," *The Bible Translator* 7 (1956) 2-9, 51-56, 146.

Kittel, Bonnie Pedrotti. "The Composition of the Hodayot of Qumran." Ph.D. dissertation, Graduate Theological Union (Berkeley), 1975.

Klostermann, Erich. *Das Markusevangelium*. 4th ed. HNT. Tübingen: J.C.B. Mohr, 1950.

Knigge, Heinz-Dieter. "The Meaning of Mark," *Int* 22 (1968) 53-70.

Knox, Wilfred L. *The Sources of the Synoptic Gospels*. Vol. I: *St. Mark* Edited by H. Chadwick. Cambridge: Cambridge University, 1953.

Koch, Dietrich-Alex. *Die Bedeutung der Wundererzählungen für die Christologie des Markusevangeliums*. BZNW 42. Berlin: Walter de Gruyter, 1975.

König, Eduard. *Stilistik, Rhetorik, Poetik in Bezug auf die biblische Literatur*. Leipzig: Dietericht'sche Verlagsbuchhandlung Theodor Weicher, 1900.

Kolenkow, Anitra Bingham. "Beyond Miracles, Suffering and Eschatology," *1973 Seminar Papers*. Edited by George MacRae. SBLASP 109. Society of Biblical Literature, 1973. Vol. 2, pp. 155-202.

_____. "Healing Controversy as a Tie between Miracle and Passion Material for a Proto-Gospel," *JBL* 95 (1976) 623-638.

Kümmel, Werner Georg. *Introduction to the New Testament*. 14th rev. ed. Founded by Paul Feine and Johannes Behm; translated by A.J. Mattill, Jr. Nashville and New York: Abingdon, 1966.

Kuhn, Heinz-Wolfgang. *Ältere Sammlungen im Markusevangelium*. SUNT 8. Göttingen: Vandenhoeck & Ruprecht, 1971.

Lafontaine, René, and Mourlon Beernaert, Pierre. "Essai sur la structure de Marc, 8,27-9,13," *RSR* 57 (1969) 543-561.

Lagrange, Marie-Joseph. *Évangile selon Saint Marc*. 5th ed. Paris: Lecoffre, 1929.

Lamarche, Paul. *Zacharie IX-XIV: Structure littéraire et messianisme*. Paris: Lecoffre, 1961.

_____. "Commencement de l'évangile de Jésus, Christ, Fils de Dieu (Mc 1,1)," *NRT* 92 (1970) 1024-1036.

_____. "The Call to Conversion and Faith: The Vocation of Levi (Mk 2,13-17)," *Lumen Vitae* 25 (1970) 301-312.

_____. "Structure de l'épître aux Colossiens," *Bib* 56 (1975) 453-463.

Lambrecht, Jan. *Die Redaktion der Markus-Apokalypse*. AnBi 28. Rome: Pontifical Biblical Institute, 1967.

_____. "La structure de Mc., XIII," *De Jésus aux Évangiles*. Edited by I. de La Potterie. BETL 25:2. Gembloux: J. Duculot, 1967. Pp. 141-164.

_____. *Marcus Interpretator: Stijl en Boodschap in Mc.3,20-4,34*. Brugge-Utrecht: Desclée de Brouwer, 1969.

Lane, William L. *Commentary on the Gospel of Mark*. NICNT. Grand Rapids, Michigan: Eerdmans, 1974.

Lanham, Richard A. *A Handlist of Rhetorical Terms*. Berkeley: University of California, 1969.

La Potterie, I. de. "De compositione evangelii Marci," *VD* 44 (1966) 135-141.

Lausberg, Heinrich. *Handbuch der literarischen Rhetorik*. 2 vols. Munich: Max Hueber, 1960.

Lenglet, Ad. "La structure littéraire de Daniel 2-7," *Bib* 53 (1972) 169-190.

Léon-Dufour, Xavier. "Trois chiasmes Johanniques," *NTS* 7 (1960-61) 249-255.

Lightfoot, Robert Henry. *History and Interpretation in the Gospels*. London: Hodder and Stoughton, 1935.

_____. *The Gospel Message of St. Mark*. Oxford: Oxford University, 1962.

Lohfink, Norbert. *Das Hauptgebot: Eine Untersuchung literarischer Einleitungsfragen zu Dtn 5-11*. AnBi 20. Rome: Pontifical Biblical Institute, 1963.

Lohmeyer, Ernst. *Das Evangelium des Markus*. 15th ed. Göttingen: Vandenhoeck & Ruprecht, 1959.

Lohr, Charles H. "Oral Techniques in the Gospel of Matthew," *CBQ* 23 (1961) 403-435.

Lohse, Eduard. "Jesu Worte über den Sabbat," *Judentum Urchristentum Kirche: Festschrift für Joachim Jeremias*. Edited by Walther Eltester. BNZW 26. Berlin: Alfred Töpelmann, 1960. Pp. 79-89.

Lund, Nils Wilhelm. *Chiasmus in the New Testament: A Study in Formgeschichte*. Chapel Hill: University of North Carolina, 1942.

Lundbom, Jack R. *Jeremiah: A Study in Ancient Hebrew Rhetoric*. SBLDS 18. Missoula, Montana: Scholars, 1975.

Maisch, Ingrid. *Die Heilung des Gelähmten*. SBS 52. Stuttgart: KBW, 1971.

Mally, Edward J. "The Gospel According to Mark," *The Jerome Biblical Commentary*. Edited by Joseph A. Fitzmyer and Raymond E. Brown. Englewood Cliffs, New Jersey: Prentice-Hall, 1968. Vol. 2, pp. 21-61.

Manson, T.W. *Studies in the Gospels and Epistles*. Edited by Matthew Black. Manchester: Manchester University, 1962.

Martinez, Ernest R. *The Gospel Accounts of the Death of Jesus*. Rome: Pontificia Universitas Gregoriana, 1970.

Marxsen, Willi. *Introduction to the New Testament*. Translated by G. Buswell. Philadelphia: Fortress, 1968.

_____. *Mark the Evangelist: Studies on the Redaction History of the Gospel*. Translated by Roy A. Harrisville, et al. Nashville: Abingdon, 1969.

Mead, Richard T. "The Healing of the Paralytic--A Unit?" *JBL* 80 (1961) 348-354.

261

Minear, Paul S. "Audience Criticism and Markan Ecclesiology,"
*Neues Testament und Geschichte, O. Cullmann zum 70. Geburt-
stag.* Edited by H. Baltensweiler and B. Reicke. Zürich:
Theologischer Verlag, 1972. Pp. 79-89.

Minette de Tillesse, G. *Le secret messianique dans l'Évangile
de Marc.* LD 47. Paris: Editions du Cerf, 1968.

Mourlon Beernaert, Pierre. "Jésus controversé: Structure et
théologie de Marc 2,1-3,6," *NRT* 95 (1973) 129-149.

_____. "Structure littéraire et lecture théologique de Marc
14,17-52," *L'évangile selon Marc: Tradition et rédaction.*
Edited by M. Sabbe. BETL 34. Gembloux: J. Duculot, 1974.
Pp. 241-267.

Muddiman, J.B. "Jesus and Fasting (Marc 2,18-22)," *Jésus aux
origines de la christologie.* Edited by J. Dupont. BETL
40. Gembloux: J. Duculot, 1975. Pp. 271-281.

Münderlein, Gerhard. "Die Verfluchung des Feigenbaumes," *NTS*
10 (1963-64) 89-104.

Muilenburg, James. "The Literary Character of Isaiah 34," *JBL*
59 (1940) 339-365.

_____. "A Study in Hebrew Rhetoric: Repetition and Style,"
Congress Volume. VTSup 1. Leiden: E.J. Brill, 1953.
Pp. 97-111.

_____. "Introduction and Exegesis to Isaiah, Chapters 40-66,"
Interpreter's Bible. New York and Nashville: Abingdon,
1956. Vol. 5, pp. 381-773.

_____. "The Form and Structure of the Covenantal Formula-
tions," *VT* 9 (1959) 347-365.

_____. "Form Criticism and Beyond," *JBL* 88 (1969) 1-18.

Myres, John L. "The Last Book of the 'Iliad'," *JHS* 52 (1932)
264-296.

_____. "The Pattern of the Odyssey," *JHS* 72 (1952) 1-19.

_____. *Herodotus: Father of History.* Oxford: Clarendon,
1953.

Neirynck, Frans. *Duality in Mark: Contributions to the Study
of the Markan Redaction.* Louvain: Leuven University, 1972.

_____. "Jesus and the Sabbath. Some Observations on Mark II,
27," *Jésus aux origines de la christologie.* Edited by J.
Dupont. BETL 40. Gambloux: J. Duculot, 1975. Pp. 227-
270.

Nineham, D.E. *The Gospel of St. Mark.* Pelican Gospel Commentaries. Baltimore: Penguin, 1963.

Norden, Eduard. *Die antike Kunstprosa.* 2 vols. 5th ed.
Stuttgart: B.G. Teubner, 1958.

Olrik, Axel. "Epic Laws of Folk Narrative," *The Study of Folk-lore*. Edited by Alan Dundes. Englewood Cliffs, New Jersey: Prentice-Hall, 1965. Pp. 129-141.

Osten-Sacken, Peter von der. "Streitgespräch und Parabel als Formen Markinischer Christologie," *Jesus Christus in Historie und Theologie*. Edited by Georg Strecher. Tübingen: J.C.B. Mohr, 1975. Pp. 375-394.

Pautrel, Raymond. "Les canons du mashal rabbinique," *RSR* 26 (1936) 5-45.

Perrin, Norman. *Rediscovering the Teaching of Jesus*. New York: Harper & Row, 1967.

_____. *What is Redaction Criticism?* London: SPCK, 1970.

_____. "The Christology of Mark: A Study in Methodology," *JR* 51 (1971) 173-187.

_____. "Towards an Interpretation of the Gospel of Mark," *Christology and a Modern Pilgrimage*. Edited by Hans Dieter Betz. Claremont, California: New Testament Colloquium, 1971. Pp. 1-78.

_____. *A Modern Pilgrimage in New Testament Christology*. Philadelphia: Fortress, 1974.

_____. *The New Testament: An Introduction*. New York: Harcourt Brace Jovanovich, 1974.

_____. "The High Priest's Question and Jesus' Answer (Mark 14:61-62)," *The Passion in Mark*. Edited by Werner H. Kelber. Philadelphia: Fortress, 1976. Pp. 80-95.

_____. "The Interpretation of the Gospel of Mark," *Int* 30 (1976) 115-124.

Pesch, Rudolf. "Zur konzentrischen Struktur von Jona 1," *Bib* 47 (1966) 577-581.

_____. "Levi-Matthäus (Mc 2:14/Mt 9:9,10:3). Ein Beitrag zur Lösung eines alten Problems," *ZNW* 59 (1968) 40-56.

_____. *Naherwartungen: Tradition und Redaktion in Mk 13*. Düsseldorf: Patmos, 1968.

_____. "Das Zöllnergastmahl (Mk 2,15-17)," *Mélanges Bibliques en hommage au R.P. Béda Rigaux*. Edited by Albert Descamps and André de Halleux. Gembloux: J. Duculot, 1970. Pp. 63-87.

Pritchard, John Paul. *A Literary Approach to the New Testament*. Norman: University of Oklahoma, 1972.

Radday, Yehuda T. "Chiasm in Samuel," *Linguistica Biblica* 9/10 (1971) 21-31.

_____. "Chiasm in Tora," *Linguistica Biblica* 19 (1972) 12-23.

_____. "Chiasm in Joshua, Judges and Others," *Linguistica Biblica* 27/28 (1973) 6-13.

_____. "Chiasm in Kings," *Linguistica Biblica* 31 (1974) 52-67.

Radermakers, Jean. "L'évangile de Marc: Structure et théologie," *L'évangile selon Marc. Tradition et rédaction.* Edited by M. Sabbe. BETL 34. Gembloux: J. Duculot, 1974. Pp. 221-239.

_____. *La bonne nouvelle de Jésus selon saint Marc.* 2 vols. Brussels: Institut d'Études Théologiques, 1974.

Ridout, George P. "Prose Compositional Techniques in the Succession Narrative (2 Sam. 7,9-20; 1 Kings 1-2)." Ph.D. dissertation, Graduate Theological Union (Berkeley), 1971.

_____. "The Rape of Tamar," *Rhetorical Criticism: Essays in Honor of James Muilenburg.* Edited by Jared J. Jackson and Martin Kessler. Pittsburgh Theological Monograph Series 1. Pittsburgh: Pickwick, 1974. Pp. 75-84.

Riesenfeld, Harald. *Jesus transfiguré: L'arrière-plan du récit évangelique de la Transfiguration de Notre-Seigneur.* Lund: Hakan Ohlssons, 1947.

Robbins, Vernon K. "The Healing of Blind Bartimaeus (10:46-52) in the Marcan Theology," *JBL* 92 (1973) 224-243.

Robinson, James M. *The Problem of History in Mark.* SBT 21. London: SCM, 1962.

Rohde, Joachim. *Rediscovering the Teaching of the Evangelists.* Translated by Dorothea M. Barton. Philadelphia: Westminster, 1968.

Rolland, Philippe. "From the Genesis to the End of the World: The Plan of Matthew's Gospel," *BTB* 2 (1972) 155-176.

Ropes, James Hardy. *The Synoptic Gospels.* London: Oxford University, 1960.

Schmid, Josef. *The Gospel According to Mark.* Translated by Kevin Condon. RNT. Staten Island: Alba House, 1968.

Schmidt, Karl Ludwig. *Der Rahmen der Geschichte Jesus.* Berlin: Trowitzsch & Sohn, 1919.

Scholes, Robert and Kellogg, Robert. *The Nature of Narrative.* New York: Oxford University, 1968.

Schulz, Siegfried. "Markus und das Alte Testament," *ZTK* 58 (1961) 184-197.

Schweizer, Eduard. "Anmerkungen zur Theologie des Markus," *Neotestamentica et patristica. Eine Freundesgabe, Herrn Professor Dr. Oscar Cullmann zu seinen 60. Geburtstag überreicht.* NovTSup 6. Leiden: E.J. Brill, 1962. Pp. 36-46.

_____. *The Good News According to Mark*. Translated by Donald H. Madvig. Richmond, Virginia: John Knox, 1970.

Sheppard, J.T. *The Pattern of the Iliad*. London: Methuen, 1922.

Simon, Ulrich. "The Problem of Biblical Narrative," *Theology* 72 (1969) 243-253.

Smith, Charles W.F. "No Time for Figs," *JBL* 79 (1960) 315-327.

Stein, Robert H. "What is Redaktionsgeschichte?" *JBL* 88 (1969) 45-56.

_____. "The Proper Methodology for Ascertaining a Markan Redaction History," *NovT* 13 (1971) 181-198.

Strack, Hermann L., and Billerbeck, Paul. *Das Evangelium nach Matthäus erläutert aus Talmud und Midrasch*. Vol. 1. Munich: C.H. Beck'sche, 1961.

Suhl, Alfred. *Die Funktion der Alttestamentlichen Zitate und Anspielungen im Markusevangelium*. Guttersloh: Gerd Mohn, 1965.

Sundwall, Johannes. *Die Zusammensetzung des Markusevangeliums*. Abo: Abo Akademi, 1934.

Swete, Henry Barclay. *The Gospel According to St Mark*. 3rd ed. London: Macmillan, 1913.

Tagawa, Kenzo. *Miracles et Évangile: La pensée personnelle de L'Évangéliste Marc*. Paris: Universitaires de France, 1966.

Talbert, Charles H. "Artistry and Theology: An Analysis of the Architecture of Jn 1,19-5,47," *CBQ* 32 (1970) 341-366.

_____. *Literary Patterns, Theological Themes, and the Genre of Luke-Acts*. SBLMS 20. Missoula, Montana: Scholars, 1974.

Taylor, Vincent. *The Formation of the Gospel Tradition*. 2d ed. London: Macmillan, 1964.

_____. *The Gospel According to St. Mark*. 2d ed. London: Macmillan, 1966.

Thiering, Barbara. "The Poetic Forms of the Hodayot," *JSS* 8 (1963) 189-209.

Tödt, Heinz Eduard. *The Son of Man in the Synoptic Tradition*. Translated by Dorothea M. Barton. Philadelphia: Westminster, 1965.

Trible, Phyllis. "Depatriarchalizing in Biblical Interpretation," *JAAR* 41 (1973) 30-48.

_____. "Wisdom Builds a Poem: The Architecture of Proverbs 1:20-33," *JBL* 94 (1975) 509-518.

_____. "Two Women in a Man's World: A Reading of the Book of Ruth," *Soundings* 59 (1976) 251-279.

Trocmé, Etienne. *Jesus as Seen by his Contemporaries*. Translated by R.A. Wilson. Philadelphia: Westminster, 1973.

_____. *The Formation of the Gospel According to Mark*. Translated by Pamela Gaughan. Philadelphia: Westminster, 1975.

Turner, C.H. "Marcan Usage: Notes, Critical and Exegetical, on the Second Gospel," *JTS* 25 (1924) 377-386; 26 (1925) 12-20, 145-156, 225-240, 337-346; 27 (1926) 58-62; 28 (1927) 9-30, 349-362; 29 (1928) 275-289, 346-361.

Turner, Nigel. *Grammatical Insights into the New Testament*. Edinburgh: T. & T. Clark, 1965.

_____. *Vol. 4: Style*. James Hope Moulton, *A Grammar of New Testament Greek*. Edinburgh: T. & T. Clark, 1976.

Vanhoye, Albert. *La structure littéraire de l'Épître aux Hébreux*. StudNeot 1. Paris: Desclée de Brouwer, 1963.

_____. *A Structured Translation of the Epistle to the Hebrews*. Translated by James Swetnam. Rome: Pontifical Biblical Institute, 1964.

_____. *Structure and Theology of the Accounts of the Passion in the Synoptic Gospels*. Translated by C.H. Giblin. Collegeville, Minnesota: Liturgical Press, 1967.

_____. "La composition de Jn 5,19-30," *Mélanges Bibliques en hommage au R.P. Béda Rigaux*. Edited by Albert Descamps and André de Halleux. Gembloux: J. Duculot, 1970. Pp. 259-274.

Van Iersel, B.M.F. "La vocation de Lévi (Mc., II,13-17 par.). Tradition et rédactions," *De Jésus aux Évangiles*. Edited by I. de La Potterie. BETL 25:2. Gembloux: J. Duculot, 1967. Pp. 212-232.

Vermes, Geza. *Jesus the Jew: A Historian's reading of the Gospels*. London: Collins, 1973.

Via, Dan O., Jr. *Kerygma and Comedy in the New Testament: A Structuralist Approach to Hermeneutic*. Philadelphia: Fortress, 1975.

Weber, Joseph C., Jr. "Jesus' Opponents in the Gospel of Mark," *JBR* 34 (1966) 214-222.

Weeden, Theodore J. *Mark--Traditions in Conflict*. Philadelphia: Fortress, 1971.

_____. "The Conflict between Mark and his Opponents over Kingdom Theology," *1973 Seminar Papers*. Edited by George MacRae. SBLASP 109. Society of Biblical Literature, 1973. Vol. 2, pp. 203-241.

Weiss, Johannes. *Das älteste Evangelium*. Göttingen: Vandenhoeck & Ruprecht, 1903.

Wellek, René and Warren, Austin. *Theory of Literature*. 3d ed. Harvest Books. New York: Harcourt Brace and World, n.d.

Wellhausen, J. *Das Evangelium Marci*. Berlin: Georg Reimer, 1903.

Whitman, Cedric H. *Homer and the Heroic Tradition*. Cambridge: Harvard University, 1963.

Wilder, Amos N. *The New Voice: Religion, Literature, Hermeneutics*. New York: Herder and Herder, 1969.

_____. *Early Christian Rhetoric: The Language of the Gospel*. 2d ed. Cambridge: Harvard University, 1971.

Wrede, William. "Zur Heilung des Gelähmten (Mc 2,1ff.)," *ZNW* 5 (1904) 354-358.

Wright, Addison G. "The Riddle of the Sphinx: The Structure of the Book of Qoheleth," *CBQ* 30 (1968) 313-334.

Wuellner, Wilhelm. "Paul's Rhetoric of Argumentation in Romans: An Alternative to the Donfried-Karris Debate over Romans," *CBQ* 38 (1976) 330-351.

Zerwick, Max. *Untersuchungen zum Markus-Stil*. Rome: Pontifical Biblical Institute, 1937.

AUTHORS

INDEX OF REFERENCES